# Upward
# Mobility

## Also
### from Catalyst

*What to Do with the Rest of Your Life: The Catalyst Career Guide for Women in the '80s*

*Marketing Yourself: The Catalyst Women's Guide to Successful Resumes and Interviews*

*Making the Most of Your First Job*

*Career Options Series for Undergraduate Women*

*Education Opportunity Series*

*Career Opportunity Series*

*Self-Guidance Series*

*Resume Preparation Manual: A Step-by-Step Guide for Women*

*How to Go to Work When Your Husband Is Against It, Your Children Aren't Old Enough, and There's Nothing You Can Do Anyhow,* by Felice N. Schwartz, Margaret H. Schifter, and Susan S. Gillotti

# Upward Mobility

## by the
## staff of
## Catalyst

 Holt, Rinehart and Winston
New York

Published in January 1982 by Holt, Rinehart and Winston, 383 Madison Avenue, New New York, New York 10017.

Published simultaneously in Canada by Holt, Rinehart and Winston of Canada, Limited.

**Library of Congress Cataloging in Publication Data**
Main entry under title:

Upward mobility.
  Bibliography: p.
  Includes index.
  Produced by the staff of Catalyst.
    1. Vocational guidance for women—United States. 2. Vocational guidance for women—United States—Problems, exercises, etc. 3. Women executives—United States. 4. Women executives—United States—Problems, exercises, etc. I. Catalyst, inc. II. Title.
HF5382.5.U5U68      650.1'4'024042      81-4967
ISBN 0-03-056163-9         AACR2


First Edition


Designer: Lana Giganti

*Printed in the United States of America*
10  9  8  7  6  5  4  3  2  1

328698

# Acknowledgments

Catalyst gives special thanks to the Celanese Corporation for their generous support, which clearly demonstrates their commitment to the full participation of women in the work force in a manner that is maximally productive for both women and employers.

# Contributors

This book was conceived and produced by the staff of Catalyst.

The publications staff includes Elizabeth A. Niles, Director of Publications; Larayne Gordon, Senior Editor; and Melinda S. Walsh, Editorial Assistant. The book was written by Jacqueline Thompson. This project was initiated under the direction of Carol Day, former Director of Publications. Contributing editor was Maria L. Muniz. Pamela Miller, Gail Fleckner, Kate Rohrbach, and Amanda Linn assisted with the research and preparation of the manuscript.

We would like to give special thanks to Betsy Jaffe for her valuable suggestions in reviewing the manuscript, to the Catalyst library staff for their help with our research, and to everyone else who gave so willingly of their time, advice, experience, and most of all, encouragement.

# Contents

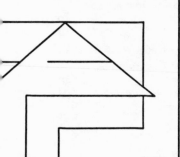

# Foreword

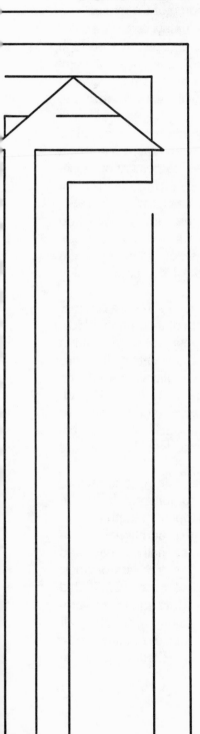

In the four years that I have been editor-in-chief of *Working Woman*, I have watched career-oriented women gain experience and confidence in their ability to perform well—better than well, superbly—in their chosen careers. I have seen where the obstacles and barriers have fallen, opening new paths for women, and where the barriers have been reinforced, slowing down women's progress.

The enormous number of women flooding the labor force is nothing less than a social revolution. The causes are multiple and still not wholly clear. Certainly among them are smaller families, higher education levels for women, independence, self-fulfillment, inflation, and plain old necessity.

Whatever the causes, in my opinion this social revolution is not going to go away. We women are in it for keeps. The statistics underline that fact. In 1950 there were 17.3 million women who worked for pay full-time or part-time outside of the home. In 1980 there were almost 45 million women in the labor force, and by 1990 the projection is 57 million. I believe there will be periods of constraint. We may suffer brief reverses. But nothing will quench the need and desire of women to participate directly in the economy of this nation.

At a time when skilled, well-educated employees are essential to the productivity of a country ever more dependent on high technology and service industries, the productive power of women cannot be demeaned or ignored. Men *and* women, equal in ability and in value to the work force, will work to revitalize America.

Do I dream? So far, yes. We all know that women earn less than men in equivalent jobs. The disheartening fact I read most recently was that, although women now fill 25 percent of managerial slots, they earn only 55 percent as much as managerial men. Yet, I don't believe it has to stay that way. On June 8, 1981, the Supreme Court of the United States ruled that women who are paid less than men are entitled to sue their employers, whether or not the jobs performed by the two sexes are identical. On that day the cause of equal pay for work of comparable value took a long step forward.

It is up to us to make the dream come true so that we can participate fully and equitably in the labor force of this country. How do we do this? We must recognize how powerful we are within the United States' economy. As a full 42 percent of the labor force, we women produce almost a trillion dollars' worth of the gross national product; a sum that is larger than the GNP of almost every other nation in the world. We need to understand our own worth and stand up for it. The time is quickly coming, I believe, when only cowards need to settle for less than they are worth.

The way women are raised in this country has programmed us at many levels to fail. But take heart. It's not inherent. It's not in our genes. We must look at our vast untapped strength and reorient ourselves. We may need retraining or additional education. We may need to break out of traditionally female and overcrowded job fields and into the less familiar, less obvious, but more promising, lucrative, and presently male-dominated areas of business, science, and technology. More and more women are beginning to realize this. In 1981, slightly over half of all the undergraduates enrolled in colleges and universities were women, and the percentage of women enrolled in graduate schools—every kind, from law to dentistry—edges up each year.

As the baby boom dwindles, we will have six million fewer en-trants into the labor force at the end of this decade than at the beginning—but more than half of that labor force will be women. The country cannot do without us. The ultimate question then will be, Do we as women consider ourselves in our secret hearts to be the second sex, or do we have the courage to be equal to men?

*Upward Mobility* is a sound and useful guide to seeing your-self as you really are: your real strengths, your real weaknesses, your real style of working and being. Therefore, I implore you to pay attention to the work sheets in the first chapters of this book. Remember, the questionnaires and checklists are strictly be-tween you and you. No one is grading; no one is judging. The more serious and probing you are willing to be with yourself, the more value you will gain from these exercises in self-analysis. And, of course, the more clearly you understand who you are and what you want, the better you will *experience* the material in this book at the level where it will make a lasting difference. You can read enormous amounts of good advice, but if you have not experienced that information as it relates to your own personal life and ambitions, it will do you little good.

This is a solid source book, one to turn to whenever you need career-related information or reliable techniques by which to ex-amine your career decisions. A good resource that can serve as well as the instrument of progress and development in your ca-reer has value beyond the ordinary. Get into it. Work with it. Let it work with you. Good luck.

Kate Rand Lloyd
Editor-in-Chief, *Working Woman*

# Preface

## Catalyst: What It Is, Why We Wrote This Book

*Catalyst*: something that brings about a change, that initiates a reaction and enables it to take place. Catalyst, the national nonprofit organization dedicated to expanding career and family options for women, has been making new inroads for the working woman since it was founded in 1962 by its president, Felice N. Schwartz, and five college presidents. Today, with a staff of thirty full-time professionals and long-standing contacts in the corporate and professional community, Catalyst has a comprehensive national program that:

- Informs women, employers, counselors, educators, legislators, and the media about issues of common interest through its multimedia information center, open to the public.

- Offers career information and guidance to women at all stages of their careers through its books, filmstrips, videotapes, and series of career booklets.

- Provides counseling to nearly one million women through its network of more than 240 affiliated resource centers nationwide.

- Helps corporate women advance in their careers and employers respond to their needs through special programs and research studies.

- Offers corporations outstanding women candidates for corporate directorships and assists them with their search through its Corporate Board Resource.

- Addresses the specific needs and problems of two-career families and their employers through the Career and Family Center.

Catalyst's current priorities include addressing the needs of the undergraduate woman, the upwardly mobile woman, and the two-career family. Our role is to facilitate the growing partnership of employers and women by helping women plan and develop their careers and by helping business and industry identify and develop the talent and leadership they need.

# Introduction

## Your Career Problems... Are They All in Your Head?

Corporate affirmative action provides an important function, but it is no substitute for personal affirmative action. Personal affirmative action—a concerted effort to succeed using all the self-help tools at your disposal—is the only real solution for women who want to advance in their careers.

This book is intended to help you take positive steps toward a more stimulating job, a position that will give you a paycheck and status commensurate with your abilities.

Before you begin, however, take some time to examine your attitudes toward your career. You may not realize it, but you may have some totally erroneous ideas about advancement or unrealistic expectations that could impede your chances of success.

Barbara Boyle Sullivan, co-founder of the management consulting firm Boyle/Kirkman Associates, says women often unknowingly sabotage themselves. They don't know how to sell themselves in the job market or bargain for better salaries and raises; they set too low a price on their skills; they lack confidence and often they let their concern for security blind them to career opportunities, which like all lucky breaks involve some risk.

To find out if fallacies and myths or other obstacles are holding you back, ask yourself the following questions:

*How reasonable are my career aspirations?* Many women fantasize about "the dream job," failing to realize that "the dream job" doesn't exist for anyone—not even those well-groomed, self-satisfied male and female executives whose stories grace the pages of magazines month after month.

Everyone has to contend with job frustrations. The difference is that some people *do* something about their job problems and other people *dream* about doing something about their job problems. If you fall into the latter category, you've probably never conducted a systematic study of the aspects of your job you dislike, analyzed what you could do about them, or—going a step further—figured out what type of job would be more suited to your temperament, skills, and level of education.

True, there are job frustrations that you'll have to live with, but the aim is to find a job in which the rewards are sufficient to keep these frustrations in perspective. You must look at your situation realistically. Analyze what you have to offer, study your alternatives, and formulate definite goals. Then go after them!

*Am I afraid of success?* In the 1960s, Dr. Matina Horner, an experimental psychologist and currently president of Radcliffe, conducted a study to explore the differences in the way men and women viewed personal achievement. The results were startling: Dr. Horner concluded that achievement motivation in women is much more complex than it is in men. "For women," she wrote, "the desire to achieve is often contaminated by what I call the *motive to avoid success*. I define it as the fear that success in competitive achievement situations will lead to negative consequences, such as unpopularity, and loss of femininity."

Dr. Horner discovered that extremely bright, competitive women lost their resolve when required to compete openly with men. Without realizing it, these women were thwarting their own efforts to succeed. The lack of external support and encouragement also plays a crucial role in discouraging women from achieving career success. Cynthia Fuchs Epstein, associate professor of sociology, Queens College, City University of New York, explains:

> Men also face the problems of making important life decisions and experience anxiety about competition and the drive to success, but they have the firm approval of a society that says, "Yes, you are on the right course, aim high, be something!" That is quite different from the message given to women: "Explain why you want to be something and make sure your reason is a good one." Women do not hear insistent voices saying they *must* do as do men.
>
> Both men and women are probably afraid of the heights of ambition, achievement and accomplishment. . . . But men are forced to face their fears. Women are not challenged to face their fears and thus never lose them and remain self-doubting. Without the support to do their best, most of those [women] who could make it don't.

These explanations of why women may shy away from achieving success in their careers are not intended to discourage you but to alert you to the potential of unconsciously sabotaging your own efforts. By recognizing that these fears may indeed be real deterrents to your career advancement, you are already on your way to dealing with them. As they say to the men, "Aim high, be something!"—and when you achieve your goal, don't forget to applaud.

*How confident am I in my abilities?* Your confidence level needs a boost if . . .

- You often allow yourself to be put on the defensive.

- You require constant words of praise and signs of approval from friends and superiors.

- You make a habit of saying and doing things specifically to please others.

- You feel inadequate compared to your friends and co-workers.

- You passively accept any unilateral decisions made by others despite the fact that these decisions may have a negative effect on your future.

- You stop listening and become defensive the moment anyone criticizes you, even if it's constructive advice.

- You think a failure to perform a certain task well lessens your value as a human being, instead of accepting the fact that you do some things better than other things.

- You allow self-doubt to interfere with your ability to make even simple decisions.

- You are filled with blame and guilt.

- You feel trapped, at the mercy of "the system," other people, and circumstances beyond your control.

You *can* reverse this self-defeating pattern and begin to develop confidence in your abilities. A positive self-image is acquired by: (1) setting goals for yourself, minor ones at first; (2) achieving those goals; and (3) receiving praise from others about those accomplishments. Schematically, such a "circle of accomplishment" looks like this:

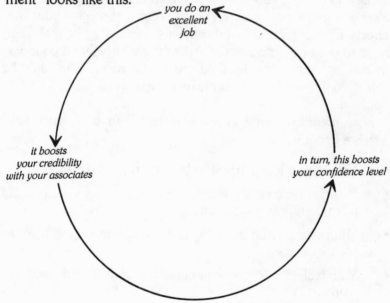

*you do an excellent job*

*it boosts your credibility with your associates*

*in turn, this boosts your confidence level*

Although the diagram makes this remedy look easy, it takes initiative and perseverance to succeed. It's up to you to set the circle of accomplishments in motion by starting out with goals that are realistic and attainable. With each success and the reinforcement you receive from others, your confidence will grow. But it's a cumulative process and takes time.

Eventually you will outgrow your dependence on external sources of praise and learn to rely on your own judgment. The knowledge that you've done a good job and your inner sense of achievement will be all the feedback you need.

Says Dr. Horner: "You have to understand your own inner resources. It isn't having to do a whole analysis of your strengths. It's more liking yourself, having some self-confidence so that you don't always have to depend on external validation. Part of the isolation at the top is that you won't always get external validation and you shouldn't expect to. You have to develop a sense of yourself."

*How do I diffuse sexual discrimination?* Sexual discrimination exists, and if you are an ambitious working woman, you're probably going to encounter it (if you haven't already). So you might as well learn to deal with it in the most effective manner possible.

The most effective way to deal with discriminatory behavior is not to take it personally. Recognize that because of your gender, you face special obstacles. While these obstacles do affect you as an individual, they are not really directed at you at all but at an entire class of human beings—*women!*

If you react hysterically every time a male associate makes some slighting remark, that male associate has, in effect, won the day. He's proved that you're: (1) highly emotional, (2) easy to manipulate, and (3) inclined toward Pyrrhic victories (i.e., winning skirmishes while losing the war). Knowing when and how to make an issue of an action or a remark is important. Often a cold stare, silence, or refusal to acknowledge a discriminatory remark or behavior is an effective response. On the other hand, never asserting yourself, constantly brooding, and complaining about unjust treatment to people who are in no position to help you are just as bad—and twice as destructive psychologically—as overreacting.

When faced with discriminatory barriers, it's better to maintain your cool and channel your anger into a long-term game plan that will advance your career and vanquish your enemies in the process. Anger, after all, is nothing more than negative energy. Convert that negative energy into a positive plan that can do you some good.

There are situations, however, in which legal action against discrimination is warranted. But before you yell "they're discriminating against me," ask yourself a few hard questions:

- Am I being passed over for this promotion because I'm a woman or because the other person did a better job?

- Have I shown initiative and accepted responsibility?

- Have I analyzed the skills required for advancement in my company and taken steps to acquire them?

- Do I know how to work with people I don't personally like?

- Do I have a poor self-image and get treated poorly as a consequence?

- Have I learned how to make requests and suggestions in an effective, businesslike manner?

And, above all . . .

*Do I make my career aspirations known to my superiors?* Too many women are embarrassed to admit they're ambitious, that they want to get ahead. They also foolishly believe that the business world is a meritocracy, that if they work like demons and strive to please, they'll eventually be noticed and rewarded. Unfortunately that's not the way it works in the real world, at least not usually.

Your superiors are not mind readers. They expect that employees who want to advance will make their aspirations known. If you sit at your desk typing furiously every day and act like you're perfectly satisfied, that's what you'll end up doing every day for the rest of your working life—typing furiously.

Dr. Margaret Hennig, co-author of the pioneering book *The Managerial Woman*, calls this reticence on the part of women "the waiting-to-be-chosen syndrome." Dr. Hennig cites the example of a woman who feels she should be paid more, but doesn't ask. Instead she thinks, "I'm so good I should be rewarded." She keeps her mouth shut and inevitably ends up with a piddling raise.

"She thinks it's because the boss doesn't like her," says Dr. Hennig. "But he assumes she's satisfied because she doesn't say anything. After all, he's a man and a man would simply ask for a raise."

When you want something in the business world, that's what you must do too—*ask for it* (preferably right after you've pulled off some coup and become the office heroine for a day).

*How comfortable am I discussing salary or other money matters with my boss?* If you can't learn to talk forthrightly to your superiors about the quantitative worth of your skills, you'll continue to be shortchanged. Attorney Mary S. Hirschfeld feels that many women are paid less than they're worth because they, and therefore others, don't put a high enough price tag on themselves. Ms. Hirschfeld, who earns a six-figure income in private practice, says, "Until women start looking at themselves as what is being sold, they are going to remain a bargain."

Male bosses know that women are uncomfortable discussing money matters. That's one reason why a man might say to his peers, "Let's hire a woman for this job. We won't have to pay her as much." The company won't have to pay her as much because *she* won't demand as much as her average male competitor.

Learn to bargain and recognize that the salary being offered is not the final word, but a starting point for discussion. You've got to know the value of your abilities in the marketplace and then strive to make your salary match it. Never be embarrassed to admit to your boss that money is one of the primary reasons why you work. It is, isn't it?

*How do I view the exercise of power?* Power is one of the things that business is all about. If you think power is a dirty, masculine word, maybe you don't belong in the business world at all. On the other hand, maybe you *do* belong in the business world. You just need to revise your view of power.

Dr. Jerald Jellison, professor of psychology at the University of

Southern California, who specializes in interpersonal relations and conducts power-management seminars for women, explains in a *Self* magazine article (October 1979) that "you need power because you need other people to help you reach your goals. If you can't alter behavior effectively you can't get people to cooperate with you." He believes women often get caught in the "competence-compassion" trap. "Women are expected to be nurturing, caring, and protective of everyone but themselves. It's not that women instinctively have more compassion than men, but people keep forcing women to take the compassionate role. Sometimes compassion stands in the way of making a good business decision."

As an executive, your first responsibility is to the business enterprise. If an employee has a personal problem but keeps making costly mistakes, you must find someone else for the job. If after you've given the employee a chance to shape up things don't improve, it would be a bad business decision to keep him or her in that job. Such decisions are difficult but necessary. However, they don't have to be executed in a heavy-handed, uncaring manner. As women rise to the top levels of management they will be in positions to exercise power with responsiveness and concern for people.

David G. Winter, an associate professor of psychology at Wesleyan University and author of *The Power Motive*, offers this advice to the power-motivated career woman:

> Women have to pass on to other women the lore of how to succeed at power. First, a woman who is interested in power should just go out and work for it like a man. It's nothing to be apologetic about. Second, if she doesn't find the macho syndrome attractive, she shouldn't attempt it. . . . Third, she needs to get as much training as she can in the skills that go with power . . . such as how to delegate, how to organize, how to monitor results, how to use skilled experts instead of doing everything herself.

*Am I willing to take risks?* Drs. Margaret Hennig and Anne Jardim, co-authors of *The Managerial Woman*, maintain that women and men view the concept of risk in entirely different ways: "Men see risk as loss or gain, winning or losing, danger or opportunity. Women see risk in negative terms: loss, danger, injury, ruin. They see it as something one avoids if possible."

This fear of taking a chance is another reason why women find it hard to advance in the business world. While men are willing to gamble now in order to achieve some long-term goal, women tend to see risk only in terms of the here and now. To them, risk means losing what they have already achieved.

Psychiatrist Dr. David Viscott suggests a healthier way to view risk taking. He says that risk taking is unavoidable. No matter how hard you try to play it safe, sooner or later you're going to be forced to take a chance. And if you've never had to deal with risky situations before, you're in trouble. "If people postpone taking risks, the time eventually comes when they either will be forced to accept a situation they do not like or to take a risk unprepared. Because risk involves growing, continually postponing risks leaves one childish, fearful and mistrusting."

*Have I made an accurate assessment of my abilities?* So what if you flubbed it when your first boss sent you out on a sales call? Who wouldn't have? You were new to the job, you'd had absolutely no sales training, and you were given a half hour's notice.

Such an experience might shake your confidence momentarily, but it's no reason to conclude that you could never make it as a saleswoman. One bad experience hardly justifies writing off a career in sales. However, people often have a tendency to generalize about their abilities based on an isolated incident that may have happened years ago. Usually, it's an incident that no one else in the world even remembers.

Maybe sales or bookkeeping or public relations isn't your strength. But don't make a definite judgment about those fields until you've studied them thoroughly—and know yourself thoroughly. Chapter 1 ("Me: Where Am I Coming From and Where Am I Going?") will help you with the latter.

Letty Cottin Pogrebin, book publicist/author/columnist, summed up the dilemma of the ambitious, entry-level working woman when she wrote: "For a woman in a man's world, the longest, most arduous journey is from the cold steel typing table to the warm walnut desk of an executive. If you become too ensconced at the first, you may never get the chance to feel comfortable and cozy behind the second."

By following the advice in this book, you can propel yourself out of that low-woman-on-the-totem-pole job into a position that makes you happy to get up every morning. However, following the advice in this book means accepting the fact that ultimately you are responsible for what happens to you in the working world.

Upward
Mobility

# Me: Where Am I Coming From and Where Am I Going?

> *Success is a matter of will and work. It also helps if you know who you are.*
> —Eleanor Holmes Norton, Director, Equal Employment Opportunity Commission

Before we go any further, it will be necessary for you to observe closely and question carefully the one person who will have the greatest impact on your career development—you. Can you specifically state which work activities you like or dislike? In what type of working environment are you the most productive? What about those "significant others" in your life—your partner, your parents, your friends, your co-workers—are they helping or hindering your quest

**1**

for career advancement? What kind of person are you anyway?

This chapter will help you increase your self-awareness—that is, self-awareness as it relates to goal setting and career and life planning. This chapter is comprised of five sections. Each contains either a quiz, exercise, or series of questions to help you learn about yourself and your career needs and aspirations.

You can't "fail" any of these tests or quizzes. There are no right or wrong answers. The "results" will not map out your career for the next fifteen years, nor will they tell you whether you'll be an "inspired" executive or a mediocre manager at best. They are merely tools to help you with your self-analysis.

Peter Drucker, an author and management specialist, has said that managers are made, not born. "There has to be systematic work on the supply, the development, and the skills of tomorrow's management. It cannot be left to luck or chance."

Don't leave your career development to luck or chance. As we've said before, *you* are responsible for what happens to you in the working world. So take control and get to know yourself a little better.

## A Self-evaluation Test to Pinpoint Your Likes and Dislikes

☐   ☐   ☐   ☐

*Your interests, wishes and happiness determine what you actually do well more than your intelligence, aptitudes, or skills do. . . . If you do work you really enjoy, and at the highest level that you can legitimately claim, you are bound to do an outstanding job.*
—Richard Nelson Bolles, *What Color Is Your Parachute?*

In short, it is important that you try to make your vocation match what you enjoy most in life. Otherwise, you'll probably end up spinning your wheels but never reaching your ultimate destination: success in your chosen career.

To help you pinpoint your likes and dislikes—both personal

and professional—we have put together a series of checklists. The first one concentrates on activities, some of which you undoubtedly enjoy and others that you may actively abhor. The other checklists spotlight various kinds of working conditions, human relationships, work pace, and your self-image as an employee.

## Checklist 1

### Activities I Enjoy

☐    ☐    ☐    ☐

Put a check next to those items that bring you the most pleasure in life.

I like . . .

1. ✓ working with ideas.

2. ✓ working with people.

3. ___ working with things (e.g., tools, equipment, collectibles and other objects).

4. ✓ engaging in mental work more than physical work.

5. ___ engaging in physical work more than mental work.

6. ✓ combining work that is about 50 percent mental and 50 percent physical.

7. ___ organizing, making order out of chaos.

8. ___ making short-term plans.

9. ✓ making long-term plans.

10. ___ working with details.

11. ___ following step-by-step instructions.

12. ___ implementing the decisions of others.

13. ✓ making decisions and setting policy, leaving the implementation to others.

**14.** ✓ working on my own projects where I can determine the goals and set the pace.

**15.** ✓ expressing myself through some type of performance (e.g., singing, acting, public speaking).

**16.** ✓ expressing myself through the written word.

**17.** ___ expressing myself visually or through other forms of nonverbal communication.

**18.** ___ solving problems (e.g., making new connections between disparate ideas).

**19.** ___ calculating and quantifying things.

**20.** ✓ researching and learning new things.

**21.** ✓ observing and analyzing people and/or events.

**22.** ✓ using my imagination to create or invent something.

**23.** ✓ teaching, motivating people.

**24.** ___ giving people orders.

**25.** ___ negotiating or bargaining with others.

**26.** ✓ persuading and influencing others.

**27.** ✓ helping, being of service to others.

**28.** ___ listening and offering advice to others.

**29.** ___ inspecting and tinkering with machines.

**30.** ✓ operating machines.

**31.** ___ building, fixing, or assembling objects.

**32.** ✓ collecting and categorizing objects.

**33.** ___ working with foods and/or cooking.

**34.** ✓ observing physical beauty.

**35.** ✓ traveling, discovering new people, places, and things.

Fill in any additional activities you enjoy:

_____

_____

# Checklist **2**

## Work Environments I Enjoy

☐ ☐ ☐ ☐

Put a check next to the characteristics that describe your preferred work environment.

I prefer . . .

**1.**___large office environments.

**2.**✓medium-sized office environments.

**3.**___small office environments.

**4.**___large factory or other machine-oriented environments.

**5.**___small factory or other machine-oriented environments.

**6.**✓working in and around homes.

**7.**___working indoors.

**8.**___working outdoors.

**9.**✓combining indoor and outdoor work.

**10.**✓working in a city.

**11.**___working in a town.

**12.**___working in a rural or suburban area.

**13.**✓working in a room by myself, but with others nearby.

**14.**___working in a shared—although not crowded—space.

**15.**___working alone in totally isolated surroundings.

**16.**___working in familiar surroundings each day.

**17.**✓working in new surroundings each day.

**18.**✓working in a combination of familiar and new surroundings each day.

**19.**✓working in environments that are more plush and luxurious than functional and efficient.

5

**20.**___working in environments that are more functional and efficient than plush and luxurious.

**21.**___working in chaotic surroundings.

**22.**✓working in orderly surroundings.

List other environments you enjoy:

_____

_____

_____

_____

## Checklist 3

Types of Interpersonal
Contact I Enjoy

☐　　☐　　☐　　☐

At work, I prefer . . .

**1.**___predominantly one-on-one interaction with people.

**2.**___predominantly group interaction with other people.

**3.**✓a combination of one-on-one interaction and group interaction.

**4.**___having constant contact with other people each day.

**5.**✓having limited contact with other people each day.

**6.**___interacting with strangers.

**7.**___interacting with familiar people.

**8.**✓interacting with both strangers and familiar people.

**9.**✓acting in an advisory or helpful capacity toward others.

**10.**___acting in a supervisory or managerial capacity toward others.

**11.**___acting in a peer or teamwork capacity with others.

**12.**___acting in a support (i.e., carrying out orders) capacity to others.

**13.**✓acting independently of others.

**14.**___competing openly with others.

List other types of interpersonal contact you enjoy:

_____

_____

_____

_____

## Checklist **4**

### The Work Pace I Enjoy

☐     ☐     ☐     ☐

I prefer ...

**1.**___to work under constant pressure.

**2.**___to work under pressure about 75 percent of the time.

**3.**___to work under pressure about 50 percent of the time.

**4.**✓to work under pressure about 25 percent of the time.

**5.**___to work at a job with little or no pressure.

**6.**___routine work where the pace seldom changes each day.

**7.**✓flexible and diversified work where the pace often changes from day to day.

**8.**✓work that leaves plenty of time for coffee breaks or on-the-job socializing.

**9.**___work that leaves little time for coffee breaks or on-the-job socializing.

**10.___** to work at a steady, even pace.

**11.___** work that involves intense bursts of activity with alternating rest periods.

**12.___** to concentrate my work in the morning hours, when I am most productive.

**13.___** to concentrate my work in the afternoon hours, when I am most productive.

**14.___** to concentrate my work in the evening and night hours, when I am most productive.

**15.___** to work a regular nine-to-five schedule.

**16.___** to let my feelings dictate my work schedule on any given day.

**17.___** not to work any overtime because my personal life is very important to me.

**18.___** one lengthy vacation a year.

**19.___** shorter vacations interspersed throughout the year.

List other preferences concerning pace and work habits:

_____

_____

_____

## Checklist 5

## The Image I Project

☐　　☐　　☐　　☐

At work, I see myself as a . . .

**1.___** leader, boss, manager.

**2.___** loyal subordinate, a person who carries out orders.

8

**3.**__star performer, the best at her job.

**4.**__steady, dependable worker.

**5.**✓person who puts the needs of the organization ahead of her own personal goals.

**6.**__go-getter who puts her personal goals ahead of the needs of the organization.

**7.**✓loner who works best by herself.

**8.**__team player who works best when interacting with others.

List other status roles you enjoy at work:

_____

_____

_____

_____

When you have completed these checklists, take a blank sheet of paper and write down all the preferences you have checked. Then set the list aside for now. We will return to it in chapter 3 when we get to the section called "Does Your Cluster of Personality Traits Match Your Chosen Occupation?"

## Your Values in the Scheme of Things

☐   ☐   ☐   ☐

You are probably surprised to find an essay on values in a book about how to get ahead in business. What—you are asking yourself—is it doing here?

Actually, your personal value system has a lot to do with how you feel about your work, especially if it is important to you to pursue an occupation that makes you feel worthwhile and like "you are part of the solution instead of part of the problem" in this world.

Your value system is the cluster of beliefs that governs your outlook on life. This belief system was formed early in life. Now that you are an adult, the idea that your behavior and opinions are dictated primarily by a value system buried deep in your subconscious is perhaps a strange one to you. In fact, you'd undoubtedly be hard pressed to pinpoint your unique set of values if asked.

One way to bring some of your subconscious beliefs to the surface is to engage in some fantasizing. Ask yourself this question: If I were handed $50 million tax free, how would it change my life? Where would I live? How would it affect my relationships with others? How would I fill my time? Would I ever have a job again? Would I give a lot of my money away? If so, to whom or what causes?

Spend some time—maybe a couple of days—fantasizing about this possibility and see what you discover about yourself. You may be surprised.

To help you decide where your deeply held beliefs place you, rank each of the qualities listed below in terms of its importance to you. Rank the highest (1) and the lowest (19).

You will find this exercise easier to complete if you first rank the values most important and least important to you. Beginning with the two extremes will make it easier for you to complete the more difficult task of ranking your middle values.

|  | | Your Ranking |
|---|---|---|
| **1.** | Honesty | 6 |
| **2.** | Open-mindedness | 12 |
| **3.** | Friendliness | 16 |
| **4.** | Loyalty to others | 13 |
| **5.** | Flexibility | 3 |
| **6.** | Cooperativeness | 4 |
| **7.** | Independence | 5 |

| | | Your Ranking |
|---|---|---|
| 8. | Idealism | 18 |
| 9. | Pride in performance | 9 |
| 10. | Sense of humor | 8 |
| 11. | Self-confidence | 1 |
| 12. | Ability to take the initiative | 17 |
| 13. | Openness, spontaneity | 2 |
| 14. | Compassion | 10 |
| 15. | Pleasure in learning something new | 7 |
| 16. | Generosity | 11 |
| 17. | Coolness under stress | 14 |
| 18. | Critical attitude toward authority | 19 |
| 19. | Satisfaction in creating something new | 15 |

This list of values is drawn from Michael Maccoby's book *The Gamesman*. Maccoby uses the list to enable his readers to compare their value priorities to that of the average American industrial corporation.

Below you will find the same list of values you have just ranked except that two new columns have been added. Column I shows the value system that the "Corporation" imposes upon employees. Columns II and III will help you determine the extent to which your values mesh with those of the "Corporation."

**Scoring** (A) In Column II, enter your rankings from the previous page. (B) Subtract the higher number from the lower number, and enter the difference in Column III. (C) Add all the numbers in Column III and enter the total.

| | | The Corporation's Ranking | Your Ranking | The Difference |
|---|---|---|---|---|
| 1. | Honesty | 8 | 6 | 2 |
| 2. | Open-mindedness | 4 | 12 | 8 |

| | | The Corporation's Ranking | Your Ranking | The Difference |
|---|---|---|---|---|
| 3. | Friendliness | 15 | 16 | 1 |
| 4. | Loyalty to others | 12 | 13 | 1 |
| 5. | Flexibility | 5 | 3 | 2 |
| 6. | Cooperativeness | 7 | 4 | 3 |
| 7. | Independence | 14 | 5 | 9 |
| 8. | Idealism | 19 | 18 | 1 |
| 9. | Pride in performance | 2 | 9 | 7 |
| 10. | Sense of humor | 11 | 8 | 3 |
| 11. | Self-confidence | 3 | 1 | 2 |
| 12. | Ability to take the initiative | 1 | 17 | 16 |
| 13. | Openness, spontaneity | 13 | 2 | 11 |
| 14. | Compassion | 17 | 10 | 7 |
| 15. | Pleasure in learning something new | 10 | 7 | 3 |
| 16. | Generosity | 18 | 11 | 7 |
| 17. | Coolness under stress | 9 | 14 | 5 |
| 18. | Critical attitude toward authority | 16 | 19 | 3 |
| 19. | Satisfaction in creating something new | 6 | 15 | 9 |
| | | | Total | 90 |

How closely do your values mesh with those of the "Corporation"? The greater your total, the greater the disparity between you and the theoretical "Corporation" in this exercise. Unfortunately, the greater the disparity between your values and those of the "Corporation," the more likely you will experience stress, dissatisfaction, lack of success, and less happiness than you may desire. Fortunately, not every American corporation falls into the values mold depicted in this exercise. Although this particular value ranking may be typical of many large organizations in this country, there are still many other companies whose priorities, when it comes to hiring employees, are quite different. You will learn more about the personalities of various companies and industries in the first two sections of the next chapter.

## Give Your Ego a Money Boost

☐    ☐    ☐    ☐

How do you feel about the size of your paycheck? More importantly, what role does money play in your life?

"Money is one of the most powerful symbols in our society," says Dr. Joyce Brothers. "The way we feel about it and the way we use it reveal a great deal about our characters."

In this section, we want to help you to gain a better perspective of yourself and your career and to find out how money fits into your life. We also want you to gain a better understanding of how you *feel* about money—whether earning it makes you feel elated, on the one extreme; unworthy, on the other; or whether money is simply irrelevant to your circumstances and goals in life.

According to Dr. Brothers, the average person views money as "a form of frozen energy. Liquified, it provides security, pleasure, and comfort; helps others; makes the world a better place." In short, making money is not a goal in itself. It is, rather, a means to other ends, a commodity that makes other goals possible. As Somerset Maugham put it: "Money is like a sixth sense—and you can't make use of the other five without it."

We all work for a complex variety of reasons. Among them: to

**13**

gain some ego gratification, some sense of accomplishment at the end of the day; to feel we are fulfilling a worthwhile "societal" goal; and, of course, to earn money. And unless you've got a lot of money already, working is *not* its own reward. *Money is vital in our society and don't let anyone convince you otherwise.*

The desire to earn more money each year is not something to be ashamed of—especially not in the United States, where the size of a person's paycheck is very often viewed as a measure of that person's worth as an individual.

In this capitalist country of ours, the equation is: paycheck = worth in the eyes of others = self-esteem. Now this may strike you as a false value system. Perhaps it is. But until something catastrophic happens to change our collective value system, the paycheck/self-worth equation will retain its hegemony. And women are quickly beginning to learn this lesson.

In a recent study of 1,000 working women, University of Michigan psychologists Jean Manis and Hazel Markus discovered that the amount of money these women earned had boosted their self-esteem more than any other single factor, including their marital and maternal status.

What this means to you on a personal level is that your status in the working world will remain what it is today until you start earning more money. This is absolutely true in the corporate world, although somewhat less true in the world of nonprofit institutions. In other words, don't accept a promotion that isn't going to put more money in your pocketbook no matter what seemingly plausible rationale your employer offers you. A succession of fancy titles won't mean a thing unless they are accompanied by successively more lucrative compensation packages. That's the way the corporate game is played in America.

But, you say, what should I do if the title I'm being offered is very prestigious but the boss says I can have it only on the condition that I wait six months for the raise that goes with it? What you should do is fight for both *now.*

If you find haggling about money degrading, you are not alone. Plenty of people do. However, we strongly recommend that you learn to overcome these feelings if you want to get ahead in the business world.

The first step is to examine why you find discussions of money so unsettling. Here is an exercise to help you explore your feelings about money.

## Exercise

Pretend that you haven't had a raise in a year and now you want to ask for one. On a piece of paper, write down all the reasons why you deserve a raise. Memorize them.

Next, role-play the meeting you would have with your supervisor and tape-record your salary pitch. Try to distance yourself emotionally by pretending to be a fund raiser who is raising money for a worthy cause—except, in this case, *you* are the worthy cause.

When you are through, play back the tape and relive the experience of saying those things. How did it make you feel to ask for money? How did you sound? Apologetic? Demanding? Or logical, rational, and justified? If you felt negative during the interview, your argument and tone of voice undoubtedly mirrored your negativism.

Now play back the tape once again, except this time, pretend to be your boss. Sit in the boss's "chair" and imagine that you are looking back at yourself.

As the boss, how do you feel about this person's request for money? Are you angry at her? Does her request make you uncomfortable? Or do you think her request is justified? Do you respect her for speaking up?

Many women are reluctant to ask for salary increases because they are afraid that the boss will think less of them for placing such a premium on money. In fact, the reverse is probably closer to the truth; your boss will probably think less of you for not speaking up about money when it's warranted. And the more concerned your boss is about her/his own paycheck, the more she/he will empathize with—although not necessarily grant—your request for a raise.

It took years of conditioning for you to arrive at your present feelings about money—and they can't be changed overnight. But your consciousness about money—and all that it symbolizes—can be raised little by little. Examine your attitudes over a period of time and, gradually, you should be able to put the subject in a more constructive perspective.

# What Personality Type Are You?

☐   ☐   ☐   ☐

Are you an introvert or an extrovert? A risk-taker or overly cautious? Too passive or too aggressive? The presence—or absence—of any one of these personality traits can have a decided impact on your career development.

The following multiple-choice quiz is designed to help you get a clearer picture of your basic personality orientation. For each question, circle the letter—A, B, C, or D—that applies to you. If the situation described is totally foreign to your experience, don't ignore the question. Instead, try to put yourself in that situation and imagine what your response would be.

## Personality Quiz

**1.** My boss has asked me to work overtime for a one-month period and I agree. However, on some nights I'm staying as late as 10 P.M. and I don't like taking public transportation home after 9 P.M. I would:

**A)** not say anything to my boss but become increasingly angry that my employer has not offered me taxi fare.

**B)** hint broadly to my boss about the unsafe conditions on public transit after 9 P.M.

**C)** assume that how I get home is my problem and not speak to my boss about my fears.

**D)** ask my boss for taxi fare for any night that I work later than 9 P.M.

**2.** Of all the meetings I've had with my boss to discuss my performance, salary, or job problems, how many of these encounters did I initiate?

**A)** none

**B)** 0–25 percent

**C)** 25–50 percent

**D)** over 50 percent

**3.** I accepted a promotion out of the secretarial pool in my company because the new job would involve more responsibility, money, and "only light typing if any at all." For the first two weeks at the new job, all I've done is type. I would:

**A)** complain bitterly, but only to my peers.

**B)** keep quiet, hoping that in time things will change.

**C)** remind my boss that the job I'm doing is *not* the job that was described to me.

**D)** do as indicated in (C) and end the meeting by refusing to do any more typing until I am given the other responsibilities I was promised.

**4.** A project meeting is being held in a small, airless conference room, and after a half-hour there, I find myself concentrating more on the uncomfortable conditions than on what is being said. I would:

**A)** keep quiet until the meeting is over and then suggest other arrangements for subsequent meetings.

**B)** keep quiet and try to pay attention.

**C)** interrupt the proceedings at an appropriate opportunity to see what can be done to make the remainder of the meeting more comfortable.

**D)** keep quiet but use body language to indicate how uncomfortable I am.

**5.** Two of my peers have left the company and my employer is making no move to replace them. In the meantime, I am expected to shoulder their work load as well as my own. I would:

**A)** do the work, reasoning that this is my chance to prove I am a real go-getter.

**B)** suggest to my employer that I be given a promotion, a raise, and an assistant; and between the two of us, do the job that once took three people.

**C)** say nothing for a while and hope that the replacements will be hired eventually.

**D)** speak up immediately and find out what my employer intends to do about the extra work load.

6. My boss makes some unjust criticism of my work and it infuriates me. I would:

**A)** speak up immediately, let my anger show, and then try to forget the whole incident.

**B)** try not to say anything but eventually get so angry that I explode days later when my boss can no longer remember what she/he said.

**C)** speak up soon after my boss made the remark but after I have calmed down somewhat myself.

**D)** swallow my indignation and keep my mouth shut.

7. A co-worker is attempting to take credit for an idea of mine that is saving my department a lot of money. I would:

**A)** point out to my best friends at work what the co-worker is doing, hoping the truth will get around.

**B)** say nothing and congratulate myself for being modest.

**C)** ignore my co-worker and go straight to my boss with proof the idea was my creation.

**D)** confront my co-worker about her/his dastardly act.

8. My position as project director requires that I supervise a number of assistants. One of my subordinates—an extremely gregarious woman whom everyone likes—is not performing her job up to par. I would:

**A)** decide to be patient a while longer with the intention of calling her on the carpet eventually—when she does something really awful.

**B)** look the other way indefinitely, since I fear this woman might rally her co-workers to her defense and I don't want to alienate anyone.

**C)** call a formal meeting with the woman to discuss why her work is not up to par and ask her what she intends to do about it.

**D)** get the message across to her indirectly—during informal conversations or water-cooler chats—that I am unhappy with her work and expect some improvements.

**9.** When I express anger over something that displeases me at work, do I:

**A)** mask my anger for several days and finally explode over another smaller matter?

**B)** explode immediately and say exactly how I feel about the matter at hand?

**C)** explode immediately but claim to be angry about a different issue?

**D)** become sullen and rely on facial expressions and other non-verbal signals to get my message across?

**10.** I am job-hunting for a better position. On my first interview with XYZ Company, I am offered a terrific-sounding position, but no mention is made of salary. I would:

**A)** subtly hint at the subject rather than bring it up directly.

**B)** bring up the subject of money early in the meeting.

**C)** ask about the salary range for this job toward the end of the meeting.

**D)** say nothing and hope the salary turns out to be as terrific as the job.

**11.** To cover a gap in my employment history, I am advised to lie on my résumé about the dates I worked for a certain company. There is about a 50 percent chance that I will be caught in the lie by a prospective employer. I would:

**A)** lie but worry about it.

**B)** not lie under any circumstances.

**C)** lie, not worry about it, and not bother to make up an explanation unless I am caught.

**D)** lie, but think up another plausible excuse to cover myself in case I am caught.

**12.** I have a sum of money to invest. I decide to:

**A)** put all of my money in a "safe" investment involving no risk but a low return on investment.

**B)** put two-thirds of my money in a high risk/high return investment and the remaining one-third in a "safe" investment with lower returns.

**C)** put all my money in a risky investment that could pay very high returns.

**D)** put two-thirds of my money in a "safe" investment with a low return and the remaining one-third in a risky investment that could yield a very high return.

**13.** If a co-worker asks my opinion about a superior I dislike, I would:

**A)** ask her/his opinion before stating mine, modifying my remarks accordingly.

**B)** express my negative opinion as diplomatically as possible.

**C)** probably evade the question or, if pressed, refuse to discuss it.

**D)** bluntly say what I think.

**14.** I have to make an important career decision. There is no time limit on it. I would probably:

**A)** be so slow and cautious about it that the day of reckoning never comes.

**B)** be quick about my decision, relying almost 100 percent on intuition and "gut" feelings.

**C)** research all possible alternatives, then rely on instinct to help me make the right decision at the right time.

**D)** take enough time to research all the alternatives, then force myself to choose by a certain deadline.

**15.** How do I feel about trying something new or changing a long-standing habit?

**A)** I don't seek out change, but when faced with it, I adapt myself and sometimes even enjoy it.

**B)** I love change and arrange my life to accommodate plenty of it.

**C)** I don't usually like it but seldom fight a change if it seems inevitable.

**D)** I hate it and actively fight it.

**16.** While employed at a Fortune 500 company where I make $25,000 a year, I am offered a more responsible job in a small but rapidly growing company. I am offered $25,000 in salary and 1 percent of the company's stock. The company is about to go public. I would:

**A)** consider the offer but probably turn it down.

**B)** probably accept the offer.

**C)** come up with a counterproposal: I'd take $20,000 in salary for 2 percent of the stock.

**D)** not even consider the offer.

**17.** I am at the racetrack and I have $20.00 to bet. I would:

**A)** place ten $2.00 bets on sure winners that would probably pay me a fast $.80 each.

**B)** place four $5.00 bets on sure winners that might pay me a fast $2.00 each.

**C)** place ten $2.00 bets on long shots that could pay as much as $50.00 each if the horses win, although the odds are not very favorable.

**D)** place two $10.00 bets on long shots that could return as much as $500.00 each, although the odds are stacked against a win.

**18.** I am offered an exciting, better-paying job but I know I am somewhat underqualified for it. The employer doesn't realize it, however. I would:

**A)** point out my deficiencies to the employer and hope the job—with modifications to accommodate my lack of experience—is still offered to me.

**B)** take the job and try to fake my way through it.

**C)** jump at the opportunity and make certain I do whatever is necessary to plug up the gaps in my knowledge.

**D)** turn down the job.

**19.** I haven't been happy at the ABC Company and am leaving my job for a better position elsewhere. Under prodding during my exit interview, I would:

**A)** confront my boss with everything I previously felt afraid to say for fear of losing my job.

**B)** deny I was ever dissatisfied at the ABC Company even though that was definitely the case.

**C)** try to be noncommittal in my comments about my employment with the company and my relationship with my superior.

**D)** reiterate the dissatisfactions—which my boss is well aware of from earlier meetings between the two of us—that made me start job-hunting.

**20.** When I am confronted with a particularly difficult career decision that involves some risk, I usually:

**A)** ask all my friends for their opinion, but allow myself to be guided only by those opinions that seem the most informed.

**B)** ask only friends who have had to make similar decisions and let their collective experience dictate my decision.

**C)** ask only friends who have had to make similar decisions, but not necessarily be guided by their experiences, since they are not me.

**D)** ask all my friends for their opinions, tally up the score, and do what the majority suggest.

**21.** When a co-worker has done something I admire, I:

**A)** make my congratulatory remarks short and sweet and only engage in a more extended conversation on the subject if the person wants to.

**B)** compliment her/him in passing—say "Congratulations" or "Great job!"—and walk on quickly.

**C)** probably won't say anything but smile and nod agreement when someone else congratulates her/him.

**D)** compliment her/him effusively whether or not it embarrasses her/him.

**22.** When I feel a strong emotion, I:

**A)** always let others know how I feel on the spot.

**B)** need time to identify that emotion before I can even consider talking about it to others.

**C)** sometimes talk about how I feel immediately, but other times I wait awhile.

**D)** savor that emotion and talk about it only in retrospect, after it's passed.

**23.** Around strangers, I am usually:

**A)** moderately comfortable and talkative.

**B)** silent until the other person starts a conversation.

**C)** reserved; I don't say much.

**D)** poised, confident, and gregarious.

**24.** At work, I tend to:

**A)** engage in an average amount of social banter throughout the day.

**B)** be the nose-to-the-grindstone type with little interest in informal chitchat with colleagues.

**C)** engage in non-work-related conversations only when someone else initiates them.

**D)** be very sociable, always willing to drop whatever I am doing for a momentary chat.

**25.** Small talk:

**A)** comes easily to me.

**B)** is impossible for me.

**C)** is something I don't do particularly well.

**D)** is something I am proficient at when I set my mind to it.

**26.** I feel strongly about a certain issue. In percentage terms, how likely am I to change my mind based on the equally strong opinions of my friends?

**A)** 75 percent and above likelihood

**B)** 50 percent–75 percent likelihood

**C)** 10 percent–50 percent likelihood

**D)** under 10 percent likelihood of change

**27.** During a departmental meeting, my boss launches into a five-minute monologue about my excellent performance on the job. I feel:

**A)** happy about the praise but unhappy it had to be delivered in such a public fashion.

**B)** secretly proud but reserved about expressing it.

**C)** openly proud and elated.

**D)** extremely uncomfortable and wish the floor would swallow me—or her/him—up.

**28.** To get ahead on the job, I believe the best policy is to do my work exceptionally well and:

**A)** call attention to myself on a company-wide basis whenever possible.

**B)** never make any waves; my reward will come in time.

**C)** take a bow for some coup I've pulled off only if someone else forces me into the limelight.

**D)** seek to gain attention for myself with my boss or department head if I've pulled off a legitimate accomplishment of some sort.

**29.** During job interviews or performance-appraisal meetings with my boss, I usually:

**A)** do a fair amount of talking, but always let the other person remain in the driver's seat.

**B)** do about 50 percent of the talking, sometimes going so far as to introduce a new topic.

**C)** talk only when asked a direct question.

**D)** do most of the talking.

**30.** I find making new friends:

**A)** an uncomfortable, almost impossible task.

**B)** more pleasant than unpleasant.

**C)** a chore, but not impossible if I set my mind to it.

**D)** extremely easy and fun.

**Answer Key** Give yourself the indicated number of points for each of your answers.

Note that the questions have been grouped into three categories: questions 1–10, questions 11–20, and questions 21–30. Add up your score in each of these categories. The maximum score for each group of ten questions is 30 and the minimum 0.

**Questions 1–10**

| | | 1. | | 2. | | 3. | |
|---|---|---|---|---|---|---|---|
| **1.** A. | 1 | **2.** A. | 0 | **3.** A. | 1 |
| B. | 2 | B. | 1 | B. | 0 |
| C. | 0 | C. | 2 | C. | 3 |
| D. | 3 | D. | 3 | D. | 2 |

**4.** A.   2
    B.   0
    C.   3
    D.   1

**5.** A.   0
    B.   3
    C.   1
    D.   2

**6.** A.   3
    B.   1
    C.   2
    D.   0

**7.** A.   1
    B.   0
    C.   3
    D.   2

**8.** A.   1
    B.   0
    C.   3
    D.   2

**9.** A.   0
    B.   3
    C.   2
    D.   1

**10.** A.   1
    B.   3
    C.   2
    D.   0
    Total:     

Questions 11–20

**11.** A.   1
    B.   0
    C.   3
    D.   2

**12.** A.   0
    B.   2
    C.   3
    D.   1

**13.** A.   1
    B.   2
    C.   0
    D.   3

**14.** A.   0
    B.   3
    C.   2
    D.   1

**15.** A.   2
    B.   3
    C.   1
    D.   0

**16.** A.   1
    B.   2
    C.   3
    D.   0

**17.** A.   0
    B.   1
    C.   2
    D.   3

**18.** A.   1
    B.   3
    C.   2
    D.   0

**19.** A.   2
    B.   0
    C.   1
    D.   3

**20.** A.   1
    B.   2
    C.   3
    D.   0
    Total:     

**Questions 21–30**

**21.** A. 2  B. 1  C. 0  D. 3

**22.** A. 3  B. 0  C. 2  D. 1

**23.** A. 2  B. 1  C. 0  D. 3

**24.** A. 2  B. 0  C. 1  D. 3

**25.** A. 3  B. 0  C. 1  D. 2

**26.** A. 0  B. 1  C. 2  D. 3

**27.** A. 1  B. 2  C. 3  D. 0

**28.** A. 3  B. 0  C. 1  D. 2

**29.** A. 1  B. 2  C. 0  D. 3

**30.** A. 0  B. 2  C. 1  D. 3

Total: _____

## What Does It All Mean?

**Questions 1–10**  Your answers to this series of questions roughly demonstrate your ability to take the initiative in various situations. The opposite of taking the initiative is passivity, of course, and this is *not* a quality that is going to help you get ahead in business.

If you scored less than 14 points in this category, your responses to situations, particularly business situations, probably tend to be passive ones. You may have a hard time identifying your feelings and acting appropriately. Unfortunately, like oil and water, passivity and career advancement do not mix. Studies have shown that the most successful workers are people who are friendly, outgoing, and not afraid to voice complaints occasionally. If you scored below 14, ask yourself: "Am I naturally quite passive, always denying my own needs in an attempt to please others? Or am I a split personality, able to express my opinions and desires in my personal life but unable to do so on the job?"

Either way, your job probably causes you to suffer a great deal of inner turmoil, since you simply put up with things that displease you rather than speak up about them and express your anger. Furthermore, this stockpiled anger can later surface as blowups over small, unrelated incidents at inappropriate times.

Clearly, this kind of behavior will get you nothing but demerits for having a sour attitude. It would be better for all concerned if you would express your unhappiness immediately, and then go on with your work and forget about it. Repressed emotions have a way of contaminating your performance. When you let this happen, you place yourself in the unfortunate position of being criticized not just for uncooperativeness, but for poor work as well. In short, passivity sets up a spiral of bad vibes. And you will be the one who eventually suffers.

An effective method for overcoming passivity is a course in assertiveness training. You can join one of the many classes in assertiveness training offered at YWCAs, women's centers, and in adult education schools around the country.

On the other hand, your problem may be just the opposite: you err in the direction of voicing too many complaints too often and too vociferously. If you scored 26–30 in this category. this may be your problem. You may be an initiator all right, but an initiator to the point of being downright obnoxious and aggressive. And there are times when tact and diplomacy are more effective than direct confrontations. People who are too aggressive can also benefit from assertiveness training: they can learn when and how to express themselves in a way that doesn't offend others.

A score of 15–25 means that you probably have the ability to assert yourself without overdoing it. You are in touch with your feelings about things that happen to you at work, and you're not afraid to speak up when necessary.

**Questions 11–20** These questions were designed to test your penchant for risk taking. If you scored 0–14 in this category, you tend to be cautious. You don't like to rock the boat and you cling to the status quo for dear life. Extreme conservatism when it comes to taking risks can indicate a lack of confidence.

Your desire to avoid failure may be stronger than your drive to achieve success.

A score of 15–25 indicates you are a person who probably has a healthy attitude toward risk. If you scored 26–30, however, you may be a risk-taker to the point of being foolhardy.

**Questions 21–30** These questions are designed to highlight your introvert or extrovert characteristics—particularly in business situations. A score of 0–14 indicates that you are more introverted than outgoing; a score of 15–30 indicates just the opposite.

There are places for both the introvert and extrovert in the business world. We are not going to recommend that the inward personality become more gregarious or vice versa. Rather, we want you to know where you fall on this spectrum so that you choose a vocation that is in line with your natural tendencies. Otherwise, you will find yourself in conflict with your basic nature—and possibly performing poorly in your job. A true introvert should not try to make it as a saleswoman, nor should an enthusiastic, people-loving extrovert confine herself to a solitary occupation like library researcher.

# Significant Others in Your Life: Supporters or Subverters?

☐   ☐   ☐   ☐

Ideally, we'd all like to have parents who encourage us to be the best at whatever we choose to do in life, whether it is to pursue a career, raise a family, or to try and combine both. We all wish we had partners who would double as part-time career counselors, confidants, homemakers, and friends. Unfortunately, many of us don't. This lack of support from "significant others" concerning our careers can be a source of gnawing internal conflict in our lives.

What kind of support—both emotional and physical—do you get from your partner concerning your ambitions? What kind of encouragement do you get from your friends? Your children? Your parents?

The following true/false test will help you decide how much support you are getting from those "significant others" in your life. Skip the questions that do not apply to you.

| | True | False |
|---|:---:|:---:|
| **1.** My friends make me feel good about myself and my job. | ☒ | ☐ |
| **2.** My parents make me feel good about myself and my job. | ☒ | ☐ |
| **3.** My partner makes me feel good about myself and my job. | ☒ | ☐ |
| **4.** My family has high expectations for me in the working world. | ☒ | ☐ |
| **5.** My partner and I share all important decisions about such things as: where we live, our life-style, whether to have children, child rearing, amount of contact with in-laws, social life, when and how to have sex, and how to spend money. | ☒ | ☐ |
| **6.** In our family, we share all household chores more or less equally. | ☐ | ☐ |
| **7.** My partner often wants to celebrate after I've just scored a triumph at work. | ☒ | ☐ |
| **8.** My parents often want to celebrate when I have just scored a triumph at work. | ☐ | ☒ |
| **9.** My friends often want to celebrate when I've just scored a triumph at work. | ☒ | ☐ |
| **10.** My friends, parents, and/or partner are successful in the working world and, thus, good role models for me. | ☒ | ☐ |

---

| | | |
|---|:---:|:---:|
| **11.** After I have just scored a triumph at work, my partner sometimes develops psychosomatic symptoms of illness. | ☐ | ☒ |

**True  False**

**12.** If I'm the center of attention at a social gathering, my partner often tells a joke or abruptly changes the subject to try to refocus attention elsewhere. ☐ ☒

**13.** Whenever I tell friends a story that reflects well on me, my partner immediately follows with a similar story about himself. ☐ ☒

**14.** When I complain about being overworked, my partner usually says, "Look, honey, if it's too much for you why don't you quit? We'll manage without the extra paycheck." ☐ ☒

**15.** My partner demands praise from me about even his smallest business triumphs, but he seldom returns the praise when I succeed at work. ☐ ☒

**16.** My partner verbalizes his support for my career, but his actions often indicate just the opposite. ☐ ☒

**17.** My partner makes frequent reference to the comparative size of our respective paychecks. ☐ ☒

**18.** I feel the tension and competition growing between my partner and me. ☐ ☒

**19.** As I get more and more successful at work, my partner and I seem to have less and less sex. ☐ ☒

**20.** At home, I feel tired, cranky, and resentful much of the time. ☐ ☒

---

**21.** My partner tells me I have become too competitive/pushy/controlling/aggressive/domineering since I started working or succeeding at work. ☐ ☒

|  | True | False |
|---|---|---|

**22.** My parents tell me I have become too competitive/pushy/controlling/aggressive/domineering since I started working or succeeding at work. ☐ ☒

**23.** My friends tell me I have become too competitive/pushy/controlling/aggressive/domineering since I started working or succeeding at work. ☐ ☒

**24.** When I complain about being tired or overworked because my partner refuses to help around the house, he snaps: "I didn't ask you to go to work." ☐ ☐

**25.** My homemaker friends make overtly hostile comments about my career, especially in front of the men in our lives. ☐ ☒

**26.** My partner compares me unfavorably to women he considers "superwomen" (i.e., women who appear to combine a demanding job and the demands of a well-run household effortlessly without asking for extra help from the men in their lives). ☐ ☒

**27.** My partner makes all the major decisions in our life, usually without consulting me. ☐ ☒

**28.** My partner trivializes or refuses to discuss my problems at work, although he expects me to participate in discussions of his problems. ☐ ☒

**29.** My friends trivialize or refuse to discuss my problems at work, although they expect me to listen to all their problems. ☐ ☒

**30.** I feel increasingly trapped, as if my marriage or other love relationship were a prison. ☐ ☒

**Scoring**   If you answered "true" to a majority of questions 1–10, you are a fortunate woman. You probably have a strong support system behind you in your quest for career satisfaction and advancement.

However, if you answered "true" to a majority of questions 11–20, your situation may not be as rosy. The significant others in your life feel ambivalent toward your career and could be trying—perhaps unconsciously—to undermine it. Their tactics are probably very subtle, but they are conflicted and determined to weaken your resolve all the same.

"True" answers to a majority of questions 21–30 indicate somewhat overt hostility on the part of your partner, friends, and/or parents. They are not very willing to lend you any emotional or physical support to lighten your burdens. If the significant others in your life fall into this category, their lack of encouragement and cooperation is probably obvious and persistent.

**Tips for Dealing**   If the people in your personal
**with Subverters**   life who are supposed to be
supporters turn out to be subverters, you must do something about it or you may end up a nervous wreck trying to resolve all the conflict—overt and covert—in your life. Here are some suggestions for improving your situation:

- Don't assume others know what your career and personal needs are. Tell them how you feel.

- Describe any complaints you have about others' negative attitudes toward your career or your success in terms of your own feelings. For example, if you tell your partner you just got a promotion and he walks away with hardly a word of congratulations, don't accuse him of being jealous. Instead, tell him, "I'm hurt that you aren't more enthusiastic than that about my success . . ."

- Try to involve significant others in your career problems by making any discussion of the subject into a strategy session. Discuss, dispassionately, what tactics will work and what won't. Do not overload discussions of career problems with excessive self-pity or purely subjective observations. That kind of talk is boring whether the other person is predisposed to help you or not.

- If you are trying to combine homemaking with working, get rid of any perfectionist streaks that compel you to do everything superbly. There are very few (if any) bona fide "superwomen" in this world and you shouldn't risk your physical or emotional well-being trying to be one of them. Select carefully those aspects of your life that deserve 100 percent of your effort and dare to be "average" when it comes to less important things.

- Get other family members—your partner and/or children—to share in the daily household chores. Unless other family members are incredibly selfish, this should not be impossible, although it doubtless won't happen overnight. If other family members have become used to putting their feet up when they get home at night while you do all the chores, you may be sure they'll initially resist changing this comfortable routine. Persistence on your part should pay off. As Dr. Helen Singer Kaplan, director of the Human Sexuality Program at Payne-Whitney Clinic in New York, expresses it: "When you're on a team, or in a family group, or in love, then your ego is no longer a solo ego. It organizes itself around the needs of the other person." If you need help, the people who love you will eventually see the light and offer it.

  However, if your family continues to balk, examine the possibility that you secretly covet the role of family martyr. Ask yourself, "Do I have a hidden investment in maintaining the status quo for some reason? Will they love me less?"

- If getting emotional support from your family for your career seems an impossibility, seek support elsewhere. By networking (described in chapter 9, "Hitch a Ride on a Coattail!"), you can join forces with your peers, who can bolster your deflated ego, swap career advice and the names of influential contacts with you, and generally make you feel better about your situation.

- Learn to accept the notion that your career is very important to you—even if it isn't important to others in your life. Once you really believe it, you'll find you are less defensive when others try to undermine your career efforts. You'll start seeing it as *their* problem instead of *your* problem. Remember what Eleanor Roosevelt once said: "No one can make you feel inferior without your consent."

# 2

# Them: Your Industry, Company, Boss, Competitors, and Other More Intangible Obstacles

One very important point: You'll never work alone. Your ability to work with others is one critical element of career success. Individual input is important, but teamwork is the essence of most business positions above the clerical level. Even in the typing pool, cooperation—if not actual teamwork—is a necessary aspect of daily worklife.

This chapter will focus on the people you work with between nine and five every day. Using checklists and quizzes, you will discover whether you should consider changing industries, the biases of your company's management, how to discover who really has power in your company, how

**36**

to decide whether your boss is a helpmate or hindrance, cut-throat colleagues to guard against. We will also outline some un-ethical practices companies have been known to pull on their employees as well as consider the effect an economic slump may have on your career and what you can do about it.

# Like People, Industries Also Have Personalities

☐ ☐ ☐ ☐ What do we mean by indus-tries having personalities? Well, you know that all Wall Street lawyers wear Brooks Brothers suits and white shirts, speak in well-modulated tones, and have a special affinity for mahogany. Everyone in advertising talks in slogans, has brilliant flashes of inspiration, believes in creative clutter, and gets fired 1.5 times per year. All publishing people yell a lot, are talented and under-paid, run their lives on deadlines, and go to lots of cocktail parties.

Of course, these are exaggerated stereotypes of particular in-dustries, but we do associate specific industries with specific im-ages. And although there are many exceptions to the "image" or "personality" of any one industry, by doing some research and soul-searching, you can match a job's personality to suit your own.

Why is that so important? Having a personality clash with your job can lead to job dissatisfaction and confusion regarding career choice. Perhaps you think you hate accounting, but what you really might hate is dressing conservatively and adhering to a strict nine-to-five routine—all characteristics of your present em-ployment situation.

You must learn to decide whether the dissatisfaction is with *what* you're doing or *where* you're doing it.

You could be in the right *job function* but in the wrong *indus-try*. Accounting, sales, administration, general management, production, data processing—all these are examples of job functions. But people performing those job functions could be employed in any industry. An industry is a distinct group of companies with something in common. For example, there's the automotive equipment industry, which is comprised of companies that supply both auto manufacturers and consumers with all types of automotive parts for vehicles. There's the retailing industry, which is made up of companies that sell goods directly to consumers, or the public relations industry, which includes those firms that are retained by organizations or companies to promote their public image.

Keep in mind that some terms like *public relations* can refer to both a job function—a public relations officer or speech writer employed by a Fortune 500 company, for instance—or an industry. *Accounting* is another such term. You could be an accountant—more specifically, a bookkeeper or financial vice-president employed by any kind of firm—or an accountant who works specifically in the accounting industry. Peat, Marwick, Mitchell & Co., Price Waterhouse, and Arthur Andersen are all accounting firms within the public accounting industry. These firms provide outside accounting, tax, and auditing services to clients, usually large corporations or extremely wealthy individuals.

So here you are: you're a certified public accountant (CPA), but unlike many of your colleagues, you do not thrive in the conservative atmosphere of your present employer. So why not get a job as a comptroller for a film-production company, which may be more to your liking? There will be trade-offs to consider, of course. You will get more professional respect from your fellow CPAs if you stay within your own industry, particularly if you work for one of the prestigious Big Eight accounting firms. You'll probably be paid better as you progress up through the ranks in one of the larger accounting firms, too. However, if you aren't moving up at an accounting firm or the environment doesn't suit you, it might be better for you to consider an accounting job on the corporate side.

Assuming that you have already settled in an occupation (i.e., job function) that you enjoy, you should know the following information before deciding on the industry within which you would like to be employed. Consider the industry's:

- *Age.* Mature industries, such as the steel or investment banking industries, are generally more conservative than younger industries such as high-technology computer manufacturing or solar-energy-equipment manufacturing, for instance.

- *Growth Rate.* Rapidly expanding industries are likely to offer more rapid advancement opportunities than slow or no-growth industries.

- *Size.* If the industry is small, you will have fewer options should you decide to change jobs.

- *Location.* Many industries are clustered in one major city or geographic location (e.g., most of the large publishing companies are in New York), while others (e.g., the insurance industry) are located throughout the country. This may make a significant difference to you: Are you committed to a particular locale, or do you want the flexibility to relocate?

- *Prosperity.* High profit margins in an industry generally yield higher salaries.

- *Orientation.* An industry is either people-oriented (e.g., many service industries, such as management consulting), data-oriented (e.g., computer software or publishing industries), or product-oriented (e.g., appliance manufacturing or the garment industry). Which do you prefer?

- *Response to Recessions.* Should the economy take a downturn, how badly will this industry be hit? For an extended discussion of this topic, see page 63, "Is the Economy the Real Culprit?"

- *Receptivity to Women.* In 1979, Heidrick & Struggles, the executive recruiting firm, surveyed 223 women officers of the nation's leading industrial corporations, banks, retail chains, transportation companies, and public utilities. (The majority were employed by nonindustrial companies, however.)

    Which industries did these officers feel were the most receptive to women? Thirty-four and one-half percent felt that banks and other financial institutions offered the greatest opportunities for women; 32 percent voted for retail organi-

**39**

zations; 17 percent for consumer-products manufacturing; 11 percent for insurance; 1 percent for utilities; and .5 percent for capital-goods manufacturing. They also felt that large companies were a better bet for the aspiring woman than smaller companies, although a significant number of the women said company size had nothing to do with advancement.

The next section will help narrow your focus from the industry level to the specific type of company that would best suit you.

## How's the Air Up There?

☐ ☐ ☐ ☐ Stanford University's business school newsletter once ran a short piece satirizing four well-known companies that do a lot of on-campus recruiting. The ostensible purpose of the article was to outline what answers business school students should give to standard interview questions asked by recruiters. But the article also succeeded in giving a very amusing picture of how these companies differ from one another in terms of their organizational personality.

The message that came through was this: If you want to work at Morgan Stanley, a Wall Street investment banking firm, you'd better like wearing three-piece suits, have a distinguished family lineage and, ideally, a relative or ancestor who worked for the firm. On the other hand, if your goal is a job at General Mills, you'd better love Minneapolis, salesmanship, and junk food, in that order. At Citibank, your main problem will be distinguishing yourself from the bank's 9,999 other MBAs. And at Booz, Allen & Hamilton, the management consulting firm, you'll get heavy experience in how to live out of a suitcase and go without sleep for days on end.

In the last section, you learned that industries have personalities. The same can be said for individual companies within an industry. For instance, take the management consulting industry. It is well known that management consulting is one industry that requires heavy travel and long hours. However, Booz, Allen & Hamilton, the firm mentioned above, requires perhaps the heaviest and longest hours because it pursues new business so aggressively and is growing so fast that it can hardly keep up with its staffing needs. Although management consulting firms, as a group, are more like each other than many other kinds of companies, they still differ from each other in small but perceptible ways.

IBM is another company with a strong corporate personality. In the classic 1950s study called *The Organization Man*, William H. Whyte, Jr., depicted the computer giant as a quasi-military organization in its mores and hierarchy. "Success here," one company official said, "are guys who eat and sleep the company. If a man's first interest is his wife and family, more power to him— but we don't want him."

That statement said a lot about the climatic conditions imposed by IBM's management in those days. While the weather report out of IBM these days is certainly brighter for women and minorities—and corporate wives as well—the old cloud cover hasn't entirely dissipated. Many people still think of IBM as the place where all the men have to wear white shirts on pain of being fired.

The stereotype of IBM is a perfect example of why you shouldn't blindly accept the standard shibboleths about a company. When you want to know what it would be like to work for a particular company, you should do your own in-depth investigating.

How do you go about it? There are a number of ways, some obvious and some more inventive.

The first step is to get all the company's public relations handouts—its annual report, recruiting literature, product brochures, and so on. These publications will tell you the basics: the organization's size, age, profitability, growth rate, industry position, and the image it is trying to project. If you want to be even more thorough, research and read any feature articles about the company that have appeared in *Fortune*, *Business Week*, *Forbes*, or the

*Wall Street Journal.* If possible, try to get the company's house organ or employee magazine. Company publications can be very enlightening concerning management's willingness to allow a free flow of information not only from the top down, but also from the bottom up.

Next, find an excuse to visit the company's headquarters. (Better yet, try to go with someone who actually works there.) In the lobby of the building or in the elevator, notice the way the company employees dress and behave. Do they appear relaxed and happy or uptight and harried? Is the reception area done in traditional or modern decor? What are the age and demeanor of the receptionist? (Don't think the company's management didn't think about that when it hired him or her.)

Finally, try to arrange an informal chat with several current and former employees of the company. From them, try to ascertain the organization's attitude toward women, its promotion policies—both official and unofficial—its collective value system, its pattern of rewards and punishments, its freedoms and restraints.

After you've done your homework, use the checklists below to solidify what you've learned.

**Checklists for Diagnosing a Company's Health**  These checklists are designed to help you evaluate your current employer or prospective employers. After you finish filling in the words *yes*, *no*, or *maybe* in the blanks provided, you should have a good idea of how you feel—or would feel—about working for the company in question.

## Checklist 1
### Attitudes Toward Women

☐  ☐  ☐  ☐

  **1.**__Are women employed in responsible positions at all hierarchical levels and in all functions—not just in the traditionally female occupations—throughout the company?

**2.**___If not, are there indications that the company is moving rapidly toward that ideal?

**3.**___Does the company promote women from within?

**4.**___Excluding understandable places like the men's room, are all areas of the company or factory accessible to women?

**5.**___Are women included in off-hours socializing as equals?

**6.**___Are women employees encouraged to network (i.e., join professional organizations and find mentors)?

**7.**___Do any women employees supervise or manage men?

**8.**___Are there any women senior managers or partners in the company or firm?

**9.**___If not, is there a high-ranking woman who reports directly to the chief executive officer or managing partner?

**10.**___Does the highest-paid woman earn as much as her male counterparts?

**11.**___Are there women holding jobs that involve travel?

**12.**___If the company recruits at colleges, does it go to women's colleges?

**13.**___At coed schools, does it interview about the same number of women as men?

**14.**___Are medical insurance, sick leave, overtime, and pension plans the same for men and women?

**15.**___Is time off for childbirth treated the same way as any other temporary disability? (This is now required by law of any employer who has fifteen or more employees.)

## Checklist 2
### Personnel Policies

☐    ☐    ☐    ☐

**1.**__Are career paths within the organization open and flexible? (Almost any job can be considered a stepping-stone to a better job, even a job in an unrelated area, provided the worker has gotten the proper training to qualify.)

**2.**__Does the company have a tuition assistance or internal training program?

**3.**__If either of the above exist, will you qualify?

**4.**__Is the company's top personnel officer considered a member of senior management?

**5.**__Is the development and promotion of subordinates a formalized part of a manager's job to the point where managers are rated on this on their performance appraisal forms?

**6.**__Does the company have a formal performance appraisal program that includes employees at all levels?

**7.**__Does the company have a formal job-posting program so that all employees can learn about openings and apply for them?

**8.**__Does the company have a flexitime (employee can choose what hours of the day she wishes to work) or compressed-time (employee can opt to work a forty-hour week in four days instead of the usual five) policy?

**9.**__Are employees' salaries reviewed at regular intervals, or at least once a year?

**10.**__Is there enough flexibility built into the company's salary administration program to encompass special cases that do not fall within the usual strictures?

**11.**__If it is a large organization, are there mechanisms in place for resolving personnel and labor disputes (e.g., internal review boards, ombudspersons, unions)?

12.___Are people of all racial, ethnic, religious, and class backgrounds represented in sufficient numbers among the employee population?

13.___Are people of all racial, ethnic, religious, and class backgrounds in the pipeline for advancement throughout the company?

14.___Are people of all ages represented in sufficient numbers among the employee population?

15.___Are people of all ages in the pipeline for advancement throughout the company?

# Checklist 3

## Political Climate

☐    ☐    ☐    ☐

1.___Does ability, experience, and training—vs. other more subjective criteria—determine whether employees are promoted?

2.___Do employees socialize—both during and after work hours—across hierarchical lines?

3.___Does management clearly outline its policies and goals through formal methods of communication (e.g., newsletter and other company publications, bulletin boards, closed-circuit TV programs, regular employee-management meetings)?

4.___Do employees generally feel secure in their jobs?

5.___Are the types of people holding the "visible" jobs (e.g., public relations spokespeople, consumer relations officers) representative of the people who wield the real power within the company?

6.___Is there stability within the top management ranks? (For example, does the promotion and retirement of senior officers proceed in an orderly fashion, or is it hard to anticipate due to high turnover and constant policy changes?)

## Checklist 4

Organizational
Development

☐      ☐      ☐      ☐

**1.**___Is the organization or company profitable?

**2.**___Is the organization considered one of the leaders in its field?

**3.**___Is the organization well managed in terms of having clear-cut goals and realistic strategies for reaching them?

**4.**___Is the company future-oriented, and does it react reasonably fast to new challenges, technological developments, and other opportunities?

If you answered "yes" or "maybe" to a majority of these questions, you probably enjoy—or would enjoy—working for this type of company.

---

## Hierarchies and Power: What the Organizational Chart Won't Tell You

☐      ☐      ☐      ☐          You've heard of pyramid power? Well, judging from the structure of most modern business organizations, you'd think they all subscribed to its supposedly mystical powers! Believe in it or not, the pyramid is the symbol most often associated with a business hierarchy because there is usually one "chief" wielding the ultimate power at the apex of a hierarchical organization and successively more "Indians" to do his or her bidding at the lower levels. Power filters down from the top through a specified chain of command.

Why does the power of a hierarchy flow from the top down? "The functional logic is simple," writes Betty L. Harragan in her book, *Games Mother Never Taught You.* "When a task is too big for one person, divide it. . . . The intent of hierarchical organization is to subdivide large and complex tasks into manageable components . . . to insure that no task exceeds the ability of its performer."

This is the theory behind a formal organization chart. Any company that employs more than twenty people probably has an organization chart. It is a schematic representation—it often looks like a family tree—of the lines of authority within the company. Using job titles rather than people's names, the chart tells who reports to whom.

In truth, every organization has two power charts—the formal one and an informal one. The informal organizational chart is "invisible," and only close observation will uncover it. Basically, this power chart is determined by a series of unwritten albeit strong relationships between individuals in a company. It is this invisible power network that often determines who gets hired, fired, and promoted.

Don't ignore the informal organization chart where you work just because it takes a concerted effort over a period of time to figure out what it is. Many on-the-job problems are caused by not understanding this sub-rosa communications network within a company and not learning to use it to your advantage. Keep in mind that the stronger the informal organizational chart is within your company, the more political your company probably is. And if you're proceeding on the theory that merit alone will eventually get you that promotion when your company is actually a highly political organization where *who* you know is as important as *what* you know, you're proceeding on the wrong theory. And that's why you may never get promoted. (More about manipulating office politics to your advantage in "The Rules of the Game: Office Politics," pages 243-55.)

How can you map out an informal organizational chart for your company? The following questions should give you enough insight into the personalities in your organization—and the inter-relationships among those personalities—to enable you to sketch your company's (or department's or division's) true power chart:

- *Who always seems to have the inside scoop on corporate policy changes before they are announced?* We are not referring to the people who gossip a lot and guess a lot about coming changes, but are seldom right. We are talking about the people who always seem to have reliable information. The people who are invariably right must get their information directly from a corporate policymaker or from the next best thing, one of the policymaker's aides. Either way, these people are "connected" and that's a distinct advantage in any organization. Draw lines between these people and their probable sources on your private organizational chart.

- *Who has a mentor?* Relationships between peers are one thing. But relationships between people at different hierarchical levels within a company are the ones to watch. For the subordinate person, a relationship of this kind is often the springboard for fast promotions within the company.

  An influential "friend," above you on the company's formal organizational chart, who helps boost your career is variably known as a "mentor," "rabbi," "godmother," or "godfather" depending on her/his gender. Anyone with a mentor has one leg poised on the next step of the corporate ladder. Draw a line between this person and her/his mentor on your informal organization chart.

- *Who socializes with whom outside the office?* The ties forged between employees after work hours carry over into their office relationships. Such people will generally be more loyal to each other and more likely to help each other should any power struggles occur. They also exchange useful information on a regular basis.

  Again, subordinates who socialize with senior executives—or anyone several levels above them on the formal organizational chart—are at an advantage. The reason for the social tie is immaterial. It could be the result of a long-standing friendship, an old school tie, a relationship between their respective spouses, or the fact that they happen to belong to the same club or live in the same town. Whatever the reason, the existence of the relationship is what matters. Draw a line between such people on your organizational chart.

- *Which employees have power that extends far beyond what their titles indicate?* Usually, these are longtime employees who have quietly built themselves an empire. The source of their power could stem from "knowing where the corporate bodies are buried," or from something as simple as a clerical technicality. For example, many bookkeepers have maneuvered themselves into positions of power by insisting that they must initial any go-ahead memos concerning new projects or expenditures within the company. Thus, they can effectively "kill" a project by letting the memo sit on their desks, uninitialed, for months. That's negative power. But it is power all the same. Place such individuals near the apex of your informal organizational chart.

- *Which employees, if any, have relatives in the executive suite?* This source of power needs no explanation. Draw lines between such employees and their relatives.

- *Which employees are having an affair?* Obviously, plenty of emotional support, advice, and information is going to pass between two people who are intimately involved. Draw a line between them on your chart.

- *Who has the most credibility among their peer group?* The person who has credibility—whom other employees *believe* has the power to achieve results—is a person to watch. According to Rosabeth Moss Kanter, author of *Men and Women of the Corporation*, "People with credibility can take greater risks and make more mistakes because others believe they will produce." She concedes, however, that credibility upward, among your superiors, is more important to possess than credibility downward, among your subordinates. "To have it downward, with subordinates, managers must first have it with their own superiors and the executives they work with in the rest of the company."

  Place employees with credibility higher up on your organizational chart.

- *Who occupies the "power offices" in your company?* Michael Korda set forth a theory of corporate power based on a company's physical layout in his book *Power: How to Get It, How to Use It.* He advises the corporate power-seeker to view the layout of each floor in a company as a kind of game board. The offices that people occupy on that game board say a lot about how much power the occupants wield.

  Korda claims the corner offices, because they tend to be larger and have two walls of windows, are the primary seats of power. The people who occupy them are the kingpins. On the other hand, the closer a person is situated to the physical center of an office layout, the less power he or she has. "Offices in the middle of a row are less powerful than the ones at either end. Power, therefore, tends to communicate itself from corner to corner in an X-shaped pattern, leaving certain areas as dead space, in power terms, even though they may contain large comfortable rooms with outside windows."

  You must judge if Korda's thesis applies to your company, for it isn't applicable everywhere, at least not in companies whose office space consists of a series of nooks and crannies rather than a square or rectangular space.

It's crucial for you to map out an informal organizational chart for your company. With your "road map" to office power sources to guide you as you make your moves, you'll stand a better chance of weathering power struggles threatening to unseat you, and of moving up when positions you covet become vacant.

## Is Your Boss a Helpmate or a Hindrance?

☐  ☐  ☐  ☐    Whether or not you advance in your present company depends, to a large degree, on your boss. Does your boss want to see you gain a promotion, or is she or he jealously guarding you to see that no other managers entice you into a bigger and better job elsewhere in the company? If you've become indispensable to your boss, the latter may apply. However, it is a pretty insecure boss who lets any subordinate become *that* indispensable.

Naturally, there are many other reasons why your boss might not be willing to support you in your efforts to move ahead in your career. Your boss may honestly believe you don't deserve a promotion because you lack the necessary skills or because you have a negative attitude. Maybe your boss just plain doesn't like you. (This is what is euphemistically referred to as a "personality clash" and it happens often in business.) Or your boss may have emotional and psychological problems that preclude her/him helping others. Maybe it took your boss so long to get where she/he is today that she/he resents anyone else climbing the corporate ladder in a quarter of the time.

In short, boss trouble is universal. All working persons have at some point encountered superiors they don't like, or who don't like or appreciate them, or promote them; or who are not as smart as they are, or less conscientious, or—perhaps worst of all—don't think women belong in any job that doesn't require typing.

Here is a quiz for you to test whether your boss belongs in the helpmate or hindrance category. Consider carefully before you put a check in the column headed "Frequently," "Occasionally," "Seldom," or "Never."

| Your boss . . . | Frequently | Occasion-ally | Seldom | Never |
|---|---|---|---|---|
| **1.** appears to be an emotionally and psycho-logically secure person. | ☐ | ☐ | ☐ | ☐ |
| **2.** is accessible to her/his subordinates. | ☐ | ☐ | ☐ | ☐ |
| **3.** is fair-minded (and doesn't play favorites). | ☐ | ☐ | ☐ | ☐ |

| | Frequently | Occasion-ally | Seldom | Never |
|---|---|---|---|---|
| **4.** is good at the technical aspects of her/his job. | ☐ | ☐ | ☐ | ☐ |
| **5.** is good at the managerial aspects of her/his job. | ☐ | ☐ | ☐ | ☐ |
| **6.** has the respect of her/his subordinates. | ☐ | ☐ | ☐ | ☐ |
| **7.** has the respect of her/his peers. | ☐ | ☐ | ☐ | ☐ |
| **8.** has the respect of her/his superiors. | ☐ | ☐ | ☐ | ☐ |
| **9.** has clout in the company beyond what her/his title would indicate. | ☐ | ☐ | ☐ | ☐ |
| **10.** is a good role model for you. | ☐ | ☐ | ☐ | ☐ |
| **11.** delegates authority by encouraging subordinates to take the initiative and use their judgment in making decisions. | ☐ | ☐ | ☐ | ☐ |
| **12.** retains a sense of humor about office problems and crises that arise. | ☐ | ☐ | ☐ | ☐ |
| **13.** is organized (establishes objectives and sets priorities for her/his subordinates). | ☐ | ☐ | ☐ | ☐ |

**14.** believes in the sink-or-swim method of supervision—that is, when

| | Frequently | Occasion-ally | Seldom | Never |
|---|---|---|---|---|
| she/he assigns you a project, she/he explains it carefully once and then doesn't want to hear about it again until it's completed. | ☐ | ☐ | ☐ | ☐ |
| **15.** does what's necessary to ensure high morale among her/his subordinates. | ☐ | ☐ | ☐ | ☐ |
| **16.** admits when she/he doesn't know something. | ☐ | ☐ | ☐ | ☐ |
| **17.** is aware of her/his deficiencies and takes action to correct them. | ☐ | ☐ | ☐ | ☐ |
| **18.** accepts a moderate degree of conflict between her/himself and a subordinate as a fact of organizational life. | ☐ | ☐ | ☐ | ☐ |
| **19.** believes that gender has nothing to do with a person's abilities. | ☐ | ☐ | ☐ | ☐ |
| **20.** encourages creativity and innovation among her/his subordinates. | ☐ | ☐ | ☐ | ☐ |
| **21.** concentrates more on substance than form in rating subordinates' work. | ☐ | ☐ | ☐ | ☐ |
| **22.** spurns sycophants, bootlickers, brownnosers, yes-people, and others of this ilk. | ☐ | ☐ | ☐ | ☐ |

| | Frequently | Occasion-<br>ally | Seldom | Never |
|---|---|---|---|---|
| **23.** is on a fast track in the company. | ☐ | ☐ | ☐ | ☐ |
| **24.** ignores minor errors unless they happen too often. | ☐ | ☐ | ☐ | ☐ |
| **25.** places a higher value on merit and hard work than on her/his subordinates' savvy political maneuverings. | ☐ | ☐ | ☐ | ☐ |
| **26.** is supportive of the women in the company. | ☐ | ☐ | ☐ | ☐ |
| **27.** is cordial and diplomatic in her/his relations with others at all levels in the company. | ☐ | ☐ | ☐ | ☐ |
| **28.** is a risk-taker without being foolhardy. | ☐ | ☐ | ☐ | ☐ |
| **29.** puts the interests of the individuals who work for her/him above blind corporate loyalty. | ☐ | ☐ | ☐ | ☐ |
| **30.** demands loyalty from subordinates but, in turn, will go to bat for subordinates with her/his superiors. | ☐ | ☐ | ☐ | ☐ |
| **31.** communicates with subordinates face-to-face rather than through memos. | ☐ | ☐ | ☐ | ☐ |

**32.** believes in motivating subordinates with

| | Frequently | Occasionally | Seldom | Never |
|---|---|---|---|---|
| rewards rather than through fear and punishment. | ☐ | ☐ | ☐ | ☐ |
| **33.** is known for bringing her/his protégé(e)s along with her/him on the journey up the corporate ladder. | ☐ | ☐ | ☐ | ☐ |
| **34.** asks subordinates' opinions before making a major decision that will affect the whole department. | ☐ | ☐ | ☐ | ☐ |
| **35.** maintains a flexible, open mind about solving any problems or crises— professional or personal —that may arise. | ☐ | ☐ | ☐ | ☐ |
| **36.** passes on any information she/he gets via the grapevine (e.g., news of job openings, political maneuverings, compliments on your work) that could influence your career. | ☐ | ☐ | ☐ | ☐ |
| **37.** credits you for any good ideas you have or projects you successfully develop. | ☐ | ☐ | ☐ | ☐ |
| **38.** consults you if she/he must make a decision that will affect you directly. | ☐ | ☐ | ☐ | ☐ |

| | Frequently | Occasion-ally | Seldom | Never |
|---|---|---|---|---|

**39.** expects you to take responsibility for mistakes you've made, but once you've done so, she/he won't dwell on them.

□ □ □ □

**40.** takes responsibility for her/his subordinates' mistakes in front of superiors—in short, doesn't pass the buck.

□ □ □ □

**41.** gives you informal appraisals of your performance so you know where you stand in her/his estimation.

□ □ □ □

**42.** discusses a formal written performance appraisal with you—giving you a chance to rebut any negative comments—before she/he sends it on to the personnel department.

□ □ □ □

**43.** tells you *what* to do but not necessarily *how* to do it.

□ □ □ □

**44.** is tolerant of subordinates whose work habits differ from hers/his.

□ □ □ □

**45.** is quick to praise subordinates for a job well done.

□ □ □ □

**46.** seems pleased—rather than threatened—

| | Frequently | Occasionally | Seldom | Never |
|---|---|---|---|---|
| by a subordinate's excellent performance. | ☐ | ☐ | ☐ | ☐ |
| **47.** allocates work fairly among subordinates. | ☐ | ☐ | ☐ | ☐ |
| **48.** considers your special requests—professional and personal—carefully before rendering a decision. | ☐ | ☐ | ☐ | ☐ |
| **49.** carefully considers and often accepts your ideas. | ☐ | ☐ | ☐ | ☐ |
| **50.** encourages the career development of subordinates, including women, even if it means losing them to another department. | ☐ | ☐ | ☐ | ☐ |

**Scoring** Give your boss 3 points for *every* check you placed in the "Frequently" column, 2 points for *every* check mark under "Occasionally," 1 point for *every* check under "Seldom," and 0 points for *every* check under "Never." How does your boss add up? Well, we can't promise to give you a precise psychological portrait of your helpmate/hindrance, but some broad pictures can be drawn.

For instance, if your boss got a score of 50 or less, she/he will probably not be of much help to you in your quest for career advancement. Your boss may be suffering from symptoms of a "Theory X manager"—an executive who is domineering, dictatorial, unwilling to listen to criticism, and even less willing to listen to other people's ideas about how things should be done. Such a boss is constitutionally incapable of delegating authority and believes communication is a one-way street—her/him giving other people her/his opinions but never vice versa. If you're saddled with this type of boss, you'll have to work around her/him if you're ever going to gain a promotion from your current job.

A score of 51–100 indicates that you probably have an average boss. Your boss may not actively promote your career but she/he won't actively stand in your way either. Most bosses fall into this category.

A score of 101–125 singles out your boss as above average in her/his willingness to help you get ahead. You're lucky.

---

## Evaluating the Prospective Boss

☐ ☐ ☐ ☐    During a job interview, it is important to evaluate your prospective boss in terms of what she or he can do for your future career development. Obviously, based on a one-hour meeting—maybe less—your judgments about a person will be composed of nine parts instinct and one part solid knowledge. However, there are several suggestions we can offer you for critiquing a potential boss:

- Do you get the sense that you are talking to a decisive person? Does she or he have the authority to hire you or must she/he consult a superior? Is this person vague about the scope of your job—an indication that "someone upstairs" calls the shots in her/his department? The last thing you want to do is work for a boss who has no power within an organization. If your boss is powerless, imagine where you'll stand in the corporate hierarchy.

- During the interview, try to steer the conversation around to a discussion of your future boss's management style. Is she/he a Theory X or a Theory Y manager? In short, is she/he authoritarian, democratic, or a combination of the two?

---

But you're even luckier if your boss scored between 126–150; that boss is exceptional, a real gem. In addition, your boss is a "Theory Y manager," a boss who encourages teamwork and open communication among her/his employees. If you can't advance with this type of boss supporting you, you'd better take a long hard look at your own attitude and qualifications. (The terms "Theory X" and "Theory Y" managers were used by Bernard Haldane in *Career Satisfaction and Success*.)

- Look around you. Does the office appear to be efficiently run? Or do you get a sense that your prospective boss thrives on crisis management? Do the other employees look relaxed yet busy, or harried and overwrought? If you like working in a hurricane atmosphere, fine. If you don't, make sure calm seas are what you'll be getting.

- On a gut level, do you respect this person? Do you feel you could learn a lot from her or him? If you feel the least hesitancy about answering yes to these two questions, try to analyze why. If, after careful thought, you still feel negative, you probably shouldn't accept the job. If you don't have respect for a boss, you won't develop a constructive relationship with her/him. Remember, you don't have to *like* someone—and want to have her or him as a lifelong friend—to *respect* her/him. Liking a person and respecting a person are two different things. You're much better off respecting an authority figure such as a boss rather than liking her/him, although the two are not always mutually exclusive.

# Cutthroat Colleagues and Other Office Monsters

☐ ☐ ☐ ☐ There are many factors that can result in a person losing or quitting her/his job. But one major reason often cited by management consultants is personality conflicts—not just personality conflicts with bosses, but run-ins with peers also. As one job counselor put it: "In today's job world, acceptance is more important than competence. Every enemy you make, even if he's a pygmy with a toothpick, will hinder you. Every ally, no matter how insignificant, will smooth your way and help you."

It may be going too far to say that acceptance is more important than competence; however, the point is well taken. Moving ahead is hard enough without having to battle "enemies" actively plotting your downfall.

California management consultant Robert M. Bramson has studied the behavior of some 400 managers and other workers at dozens of companies and public agencies. His conclusion: In the average office, 10 percent of the employees are troublemakers; 70 percent are rattled by this difficult minority and can't cope with them effectively; and the remaining 20 percent aren't bothered by the troublemakers. Why are 20 percent able to maintain their equilibrium? Because they have constructed workable strategies for neutralizing their bothersome colleagues.

"People who are difficult have learned that behavior precisely because in the short run it has worked for them," Bramson explains. "The reason the bad behavior works is that it elicits predictable, typical reactions from other people."

However, such bad behavior does *not* elicit predictable, typical reactions from the 20 percent in every office who learn to cope with it effectively. Bramson calls these coping strategies "managing your own behavior." In essence, he recommends "doing something different from what comes naturally" when you are dealing with a difficult co-worker. "Being candid and assertive are always worth trying once, but they won't always solve the problem."

**60**

One strategy that definitely won't solve the problem is running to your boss each time a co-worker pulls a fast one. Indeed, your boss may be the reason behind the problem. If daily guerrilla warfare is the norm in your office, it would be fair to assume that your boss thrives in this atmosphere, perhaps even pitting one subordinate against another on purpose in the mistaken belief it will bring out the best in them. Another possibility is that your boss is just plain incompetent. She/he either hates conflict and pretends not to see it, or has lost control over the situation completely. In either case, it's useless trying to get your boss to intercede for you in office squabbles. To succeed in any organization, you must learn your own corporate survival tactics.

Here is a small sampling of the Cutthroat Colleagues you are bound to encounter at some point in your career—and some suggestions for neutralizing their threats:

- *The Friend You Left Behind You.* You are ambitious and your "best friend" in the office is not—at least that's what she/he claims. But for a person who is supposedly satisfied with her/his lot in life, she/he certainly acts jealous of you. On the surface she/he may sound and act nice enough, but the helpful little comments she/he makes to others about your performance on the job will hardly win her/him the Ms./Mr. Congeniality award.

  If you're an achiever, you will have to become adept at dealing with jealousy among your peers. The first step in coping with the jealousy of others is to recognize it exists. Don't be fooled by a lot of gushing praise and seemingly helpful advice. Some of the peers you leave behind in a cloud of dust would love to see you fall flat on your face. Obviously, their "helpful" suggestions should be viewed for what they really are—comments intended to subtly undermine your self-esteem and others' perceptions of your abilities.

  Psychologists Muriel Goldfarb and Mara Gleckel point out that "people who attain their goals are people who have a strong self-image and are willing to accept change in their lives. Others' lack of support can't deter them. If you are in the secretarial pool and you get promoted to supervisor, obviously some of your former co-workers aren't going to like it. Consider the fact that you may have outgrown many of your old buddies in the typing pool anyway, and it's time to give them up and move on."

It is true that when we progress or make changes of any kind in our lives, we have to give up something—or leave someone behind. Often it's people we've called friends. But look at it this way—"friends" who want to see you stay just where you are will hardly fit into the definition of what a friend truly is: a trusted companion, an ally.

- *The Work Off-Loaders.* These are peers who chronically push their work off onto someone else. Anyone else will do as long as *they* are relieved of the burden.

  There are generally three reasons why people try to get others to do their work: either they've also been continuously dumped on, they're just plain lazy, or they're incompetent. If they've been promoted too far too fast, the last reason is probably the case.

  It's best to stop an Off-Loader in her/his tracks. A smile and the answer "I'm sorry, I don't have the time" are the best ways to thwart this co-worker's aims. If the Off-Loader uses high-pressure tactics and your resolve disintegrates, leaving you with a pile of her/his work on your desk, then you've taken responsibility for it by default. If you ignore the work and it's important, your neck will be in the wringer when the boss finds out about it. Besides, once you let an Off-Loader get away with this tactic, she/he is likely to try it again and again. So if you don't want to put up with this nuisance, it's best to stop it cold the first time around.

  Should the Off-Loader be clever enough to get the boss to assign you some of his or her work, your strategy should remain essentially the same. Do not get furious, do not get defensive, do not attack your co-workers. Just state your case simply. A frank discussion with your boss about the division of work and responsibility will get you further than whining about being overworked and misused. There are times when it pays to be direct—and this is one of them.

- *The Idea Thief.* Idea Thieves are generally people bereft of any ideas of their own. That's why they're so intent upon stealing yours.

**62**

The best ways to guard against idea thievery are to: (1) keep your ideas to yourself in the germination stage— that is, don't go around bouncing all your spur-of-the-moment thoughts off everybody in sight, and (2) put your ideas in memo form once they are fully formulated. Even if you plan to present your idea verbally to your boss in her/his office, or to a group of colleagues in a meeting, have a memo outlining your plan ready to pass out the moment you are through speaking. Launching an idea verbally without a written backup invites theft. Remember, once someone else moves in on your idea and assumes the credit, it is extremely hard to set the record straight. Our advice is not to give an Idea Thief an opening in the first place.

These are just three of the Cutthroat Colleagues to look out for in an office setting. There are many others. (You can make a game of spotting the cutthroats in your office.) We will come back to this topic again in chapter 12, "The Rules of the Game: Office Politics."

## Is the Economy the Real Culprit?

☐  ☐  ☐  ☐
You are having a difficult time advancing in your career. No matter how many night-school courses you take, or how many power-structure charts you draw, or how many savvy political maneuvers you orchestrate, you are going nowhere fast. What's wrong?

Perhaps nothing is wrong—with *you*, that is. What *is* wrong is a sluggish economy, and it is affecting your and other people's ability to move ahead in your chosen occupation.

There's an old saying: A recession is when other people lose their jobs; a depression is when you lose your job. Perhaps you think that the state of the economy has very little to do with your life. Except in the dire instance that you get laid off, you can see little relationship between the statistical mumbo jumbo delivered by the ivory-tower economists and your own lack of career advancement.

Think again. The state of the economy affects every working woman—indeed, every working person. It affects your job security, your ability to change employers or to get a raise from your present employer, and even your choice of career field.

When you chose your vocation, you may have researched the "hot careers" of the coming decade. The U.S. Department of Labor Statistics makes regular projections concerning the occupations that will be in the greatest demand in the future. These projections take into account a number of variables including the general state of the economy, special factors that will affect a particular industry or job function, and the relationship between the supply of specially trained workers and the number of jobs available in each field.

Suppose you did train for one of these "hot careers." Maybe the field that was red-hot five years ago is only lukewarm today. That's the problem with the economy. It changes constantly and—much to the chagrin of economists—often unpredictably.

We live in a free-enterprise system that vacillates between periods of boom and bust. There is seemingly no way to avoid this up-and-down motion in our economy, although the federal government attempts to keep the peaks and valleys from becoming too extreme.

Unfortunately at present, the economic picture is definitely on the bust side. Recession is the word on everyone's lips and some prophets of doom are even hinting at a depression. While in the past Americans looked forward to a better, brighter future, many today would be happy if they could just hang on to the status quo and keep it from getting worse. They wonder how they can keep up with rapidly rising consumer prices when salaries creep up slowly and the value of the dollar is shrinking. (Can anyone remember the "good old days" in 1967 when inflation was at 3.0 percent?)

Recession, double-digit inflation, rising oil prices, not to mention government mismanagement, have all contributed to the current state of affairs. And, of course, the worse the economy, the tighter the job market. Experts are now predicting the fiercest competition for jobs since World War II. The picture for the eighties and nineties is sobering indeed. Here are just some of the factors that will be shaping the job market in the decades ahead:

- According to the Bureau of Labor Statistics (BLS), 114 new civilian job categories will be created by 1990. However, over half will be routine, low-paying jobs. For instance, the BLS estimates that there will be twice as many job opportunities for clerks as for managers in the eighties.

- Higher education has become a given in this country and in the job market. The old belief in a college degree as a sure ticket to a better-paying, more "rewarding" job no longer holds true. The BLS estimates that there will be a greater supply of college graduates than of jobs requiring a college degree in the eighties. The result? One out of four graduates will have to take a job below her/his educational qualifications.

- Technological advances will both create new jobs and eliminate others. For instance, the rising use of computers has created a tremendous need for systems programmers, analysts, technicians, and computer salespeople. At the same time, the increased use of computers and the movement toward "paperless" offices will also lessen the need for employees such as file clerks, bookkeepers, and bank tellers.

- The labor population will develop a decided midriff bulge in the eighties and nineties. And it won't be for lack of exercise. Why? Demographics. The changing size, age, growth, density, and distribution of the U.S. population will have a very definite impact on the economic picture to come. During the seventies, the "baby-boom generation"—everyone born after World War II between 1946 and 1965—entered, and will continue to enter, the work force in droves. As a result, in the 1980s, half the working population will be in the twenty-five-to-forty-four age bracket—the prime years for promotion and career advancement. Experts predict a severe struggle will develop as nearly sixty million workers compete with each other for the top jobs.

The oldest members of the baby-boom generation—

those who entered the labor force in the late sixties—had a distinct advantage. To their good fortune, they arrived on the business scene when executive groups in many fields were nearing retirement. At the same time, the economy was expanding rapidly and the newcomers were sucked into high positions. Promotions came quickly.

Those born at the tail end of the baby-boom years—the late fifties and early sixties—won't have it so good. The same demographics that helped the earlier group are going to work against those entering the job market now. For these Jane/Johnny-come-latelies, the quick path up the corporate ladder is blocked by people who are equally well educated but only a little older—people who will be in the work force for another twenty-five to thirty years. In short, many highly qualified workers will find all the rungs on the corporate ladder occupied for quite some time.

The baby-bust crowd—those born after 1965 when birth rates declined—will have an easier go of it, at least initially. Since there will be fewer young people entering the labor market for the first time, the competition for entry-level jobs is expected to decline. However, where they go from there is anyone's guess. With the large numbers of baby-boomers still very much in the picture, corporations will no longer be able to deliver the rapid promotion prospects of the past.

Changes in the age structure of the population will also affect the demands for goods and services, which in turn affect the need for workers in certain occupations. For instance, educational services will be hard hit as the number of young people needing basic educational services declines. At the same time the baby-boom population will be needing more housing and services such as health care, thus creating more jobs for workers in those fields.

- Women in particular face a rough challenge ahead. The women who entered the labor force in such large numbers will be heading for middle- and upper-management positions in the coming decades along with a few million male baby-boomers also ripe for promotion. Competition will get even tougher as women, minorities, and male employees in general struggle up the corporate ladder simultaneously. Carnegie-Mellon University economist Arnold Weber predicts that the 1980s will be "a time of increased tension and potential conflict among the various groups in the labor force."

How does all this affect your own career? When it comes to career planning, there are certain economic truths you should weigh whether you are a young adult formulating career plans for the first time, or a woman who would like to change her career after fifteen years in the same profession. For instance:

- Service sector jobs (e.g., health care, auto repair, business and financial services) are generally more immune to economic fluctuations than production jobs. Even when money is tight, sick people will still need health care, and everyone always needs sanitation and police protection services. However, service firms that are narrowly specialized—for instance, a consulting firm that specializes exclusively in aerospace matters—will experience more instability than those firms that have a diversified clientele. Furthermore, the service sector of the economy is currently growing so fast that it already employs over twice the number of workers than the manufacturing sector or agricultural sector does—a ratio of 63.7 million workers to 30.1 million workers. The Bureau of Labor Statistics estimates that employment in the service sector will grow about 30 percent by 1990, although growth will vary among the individual industries comprising this sector.

- During bad economic times, industries involved in the production, wholesaling, and retailing of "necessity" goods and services (e.g., food, basic clothing items, mass transportation, health care) will fare better than industries producing "discretionary" goods and services (e.g., cars, jewelry, furs, vacations).

- During bad economic times, personnel cutbacks occur first in a company's "spending" departments (e.g., staff positions such as public relations, consumer relations), and last in its money-making departments (e.g., line positions such as marketing and manufacturing). It would be wise to set your sights on the line. For more on line vs. staff positions see chapter 3.

- When an economic slump hits one industry particularly hard, the weakest companies are generally forced out of business while the industry's leaders endure. Being employed by an industry leader can give you a little extra "insurance" during economic downturns. Also keep in mind that smaller companies owned by large conglomerates are often able to weather bad economic slumps by staying under the umbrella of the "Big Brother" conglomerate.

So, you ask, who will survive all the gloom and doom? Well, according to economic experts, if you are an engineer with a specialty in energy, hold an additional degree in computer science, run a plumbing business on the side, are flexible about where you live, and belong to a union that has negotiated a contract with built-in cost-of-living escalators, you've got it made—at least through the eighties!

If you don't happen to fall into this category, don't panic. If you are among the best, brightest, and most brilliant you'll probably be okay. Corporations will still be paying top money for top talent. However, even the less "superior" among us will likely weather the storm. There's no need to start having nightmares about standing on a bread line. Brooding over doomsday scenarios can only lead to inertia—and that's the one thing you cannot afford to indulge in.

You can start by paying more attention to the economic news and trends. Read the *Wall Street Journal, Business Week, Fortune*—these and other business publications run inflation updates and "Ways-to-Beat-Inflation" articles. You've heard of forewarned is forearmed? Well, forewarn yourself. Understand about the inner workings of the economy and how it impacts each and every worker. A course in basic economics wouldn't hurt. Learn to look at the broad picture. Don't just worry about getting through today, but plan on how to get through the next five, ten, twenty years. In the meantime, we have a few tips for you:

1. As we've said before, begin to take control of your career right *now*. With many people competing for a limited number of top jobs, there won't be much room for error. Formu-

late your career plans carefully. Evaluate your strengths and determine where they can be put to best use—*and* where they will be noticed.

2. Try to gain as much experience in as many areas as possible. Generalists are always needed; very narrow specialization can lead to quick obsolescence. Build upon your training as much as you can. The more skills you possess, the more options you will have. Advanced education and continual self-development will be mandatory for career advancement.

3. Don't get locked into the one-career-per-lifetime syndrome. Indications are that workers in the coming decades will be changing careers two or more times in their lives. Like cats, these people always land on their feet when they fall—even when they've been pushed by the economy. That's because they're adaptable. Learn to think in terms of transferable skills that can be used in a variety of vocational settings.

4. People are heeding the advice to "Go West young [wo]man"; they're also shifting to the South. According to the BLS, by 1990 over half the population will be living in the southern and western areas of the United States. Individual geographical areas experience their own particular periods of boom and bust in specific occupations. Those persons who have the foresight to spot the "boom towns" and the flexibility to move around will have better employment possibilities.

5. In the you've-got-to-be-kidding category: eschew class and status and go for the money if you have to. Guess who'll be in great demand during the eighties and nineties? Highly skilled manual workers—electricians, plumbers, pipe fitters. And guess whose salaries are moving up just as quickly? You guessed it. For a lot of people, these jobs are going to present very viable alternatives. And the financial compensation won't be anything to sneeze at.

6. If you are considering a career change, play futurist. No, we don't mean setting yourself up as a fortune-teller. But think in terms of what the population will be needing five to ten years from now. For instance, jobs involving energy man-

agement, conservation, and alternative energy sources are likely to be good bets for the future. (Ever thought of becoming a solar energy technician?) Videotape and satellite communications are also promising. And let's not forget the computer field. Colleges just can't keep up with the demand for computer scientists. The computer is here to stay; even kids have their own computer toys. The demand for workers in all phases of the computer science field is expected to remain high—and stable—for quite some time.

7.  Finally, and we know you'll be shocked to hear it, admit to yourself: I may not make it to CEO. Now, we're not saying you won't, or that you shouldn't fight for it, or that it's futile to try. All we're saying is that we're going through an economic period when advancement for many will be slow and tough going. Don't tie your self-worth to how high you sit on the totem pole. Remember to look for rewards both in and outside of work.

In a nutshell, what will it take to make it through the eighties and beyond? Aggressiveness, flexibility, training, foresight, and yes—a little luck.

# Don't Be a Sucker: A Dossier of Dirty Tricks Perpetrated by Some Not-So-Nice Employers on Their Employees (Particularly Women)

☐  ☐  ☐  ☐  Your employer—or prospective employer—has got to be pretty low to pull any of the following shenanigans on employees. Although most of you, we hope, won't encounter these dubious maneuvers during your career, it pays to be forewarned. At the very least, understanding these dirty tricks may help you to block them before they're put into effect. At the other extreme, you could consider legal action. The specific circumstances will dictate exactly how you deal with any of the following problems:

- *Age discrimination.* Many companies won't hire people—at least for lower- or middle-management jobs—who are over age forty-five or fifty. Why? Because their pension benefits will be payable sooner.

  A related ploy is to force a mature employee to resign just before she/he reaches retirement age, when she/he can finally collect her/his pension. For "voluntarily" resigning, the employee is usually given a lump-sum payoff that is never as large as what she/he would receive in pension benefits, of course. (Companies intent on "conserving" their pension funds in this way are clever enough not to fire only mature employees because such a move would lay the groundwork for an employee lawsuit. Also, it might not have the desired effect on the company if the employee is already fully vested in her/his pension—that is, she/he can get out of the pension fund 100 percent of what is due her/him.)

  Just like sex discrimination, age discrimination is against the law. Unfortunately, of all the equal employment opportunity legislation passed in the last fifteen years, the Age Discrimination in Employment Act of 1967 (ADEA) is probably the most ignored and least enforced. Since ADEA has no affirmative-action provision, it is relatively easy for companies to ignore its basic intent—to promote the hiring of qualified "older" people (between forty and sixty-five years old) and to outlaw any arbitrary discrimination against that age group. However, when the baby-boom generation moves into middle age in the 1990s, this issue is sure to surface and be fought in the courts with the same vehemence now given to sexual-discrimination suits.

- *Technological displacement.* Suppose you are a typist in a secretarial pool. Your company decides to revolutionize its office procedures by installing a highly sophisticated word-processing system. Instead of retraining you to use this equipment, you are fired and someone who is already familiar with the equipment is hired. Or no one is hired to take your place because automated equipment requires fewer people to run it. You are a victim of technological displacement.

In all fairness to employers, technological displacement is not so much a dirty trick as a fact of business life; in the long run, it saves time and money. But it *is* a dirty trick to fire you instead of retraining you. In the case of word-processing systems, most word-processing vendors offer to retrain existing clerical workers to use the new equipment. This retraining program is included in the price of the equipment.

- *Firing you for a trumped-up cause when the real reason for the dismissal is your high salary.* If you haven't been promoted in years yet you've continued to get incremental pay raises annually, you'll eventually be priced out of your job classification. For considerably less money, your employer can hire someone from outside the company to do your job, perhaps not as well but competently. At a certain point, it becomes financially feasible for your employer to consider this option even at the risk of a lawsuit from you. If this happens, you might consider a lawsuit but only if the ostensible reason for the firing is an obvious, *provable* fraud. Far better, however, to go ahead and get a job elsewhere.

- *Relying on job-enrichment gimmicks to compensate for meager wages or raises.* The employer who tries to convince underpaid employees that an interesting job, a pleasant place to work, and congenial colleagues are worth much more than a hefty paycheck is doomed to failure. That kind of fast-talk lays the groundwork for giant-sized morale problems in any company. Unless your company is in such severe financial trouble that it will fold unless all employees across the board agree to wage freezes or wage cuts, there is no rationale for this kind of employer sweet-talk. You and your co-workers should mount a collective campaign to combat it.

- *Forcing you to take a polygraph test as a condition of employment.* Alan Westin, an expert on privacy and the author of *Whistle Blowing! Loyalty and Dissent in the Corporation*, says you must take an employer-required polygraph unless you are lucky enough to live in one of the eighteen states that have slapped a ban on the use of lie-detector tests in hiring. It's also legal for a prospective employer to ask you to submit to the test in a state where such tests are legal, while actually offering you a job in a state where they're not legal. Check your own state's laws on this matter. Even in states where polygraph testing is legal, there are often restrictions. For instance, some states allow only government and law-enforcement agencies to use or administer such tests. Other states forbid employers to make such tests a mandatory part of the hiring process.

- *Trying to pass off a job-rotation program as a management-training program.* Sometimes management trainees fail miserably when they're moved into actual management posts. Often, it's not their fault, for they haven't been trained for anything except a series of rather routine jobs.

  To save money, some companies put their high-potential employees through a bogus management-training program that is really nothing more than a job-rotation program. The "trainees" are shuffled through a series of entry-level positions in various departments but are never given any real exposure to management-level problems or decision making. Thus, it's not surprising that they can't handle management-level work when they finally get it.

  Employers who are dead set against having women in their management ranks sometimes use this bogus management-trainee ploy on purpose. They single out token women, put them through so-called management training, watch the women fall flat on their faces in real management-level jobs, unceremoniously fire them, and then use those women as examples to justify why there are no females in the executive suite.

This last trick is just one of a battery of dirty tricks aimed solely at women. The others include:

- Shunting women into jobs with different titles and carrying lower pay than equivalent male-dominated positions that pay more.

- Not giving women the same scope and diversity of responsibility as are given to men in comparable jobs.

- Failing to use the same criteria for evaluating women as men.

- Paying women less than men who hold the *same* job title and perform the *same* job functions.

- Insisting on upward mobility through the secretary route rather than through a training program.

- Excluding women from whole categories of positions and thereby blocking their access up the corporate ladder via conventional career paths.

- Not inviting executive-level women to join social and business clubs that would facilitate their acceptance into management ranks.

- Requiring women to submit to aptitude tests that were obviously designed for men; and then using the women's lower scores to justify not hiring or promoting them.

- Asking women illegal interview questions such as "When do you intend to have children?" or, even worse, "What form of contraception do you use?"

- Pressuring women to submit to sexual favors as a condition of employment or of keeping their present jobs.

If you can prove any of the above charges, you have the basis for a strong sexual-discrimination suit. Whether you need to go that far to get the practice eliminated or changed depends, of course, on the circumstances. But before you hire a lawyer, you should consider the long-term pros and cons very carefully. Will a sexual-discrimination suit give you immediate revenge and a sense of gratification while destroying any hope of a successful career in your field? These are the kinds of questions you must weigh. They will be discussed in depth in "Will a Discrimination Suit Ruin Your Career?", pages 99–101.

# Reality: Your Current Prospects for Moving Up

Now we want you to take a good hard look at your present situation. This chapter will help you to assess precisely what your chances are of advancing through the ranks at your present company or in your chosen vocation. To do this, you will have to ask yourself questions such as:

- Does my firm discriminate against women?

- Is my image—my dress, speech, body language, or my manner—working against me?

- Am I willing to accept the trade-offs that accompany my occupation?

On the other hand, after reading chapters 1 and 2 and doing the exercises and quizzes, perhaps you've decided the reason you aren't progressing is that you're in the wrong vocation. Your likes and dislikes and cluster of personality traits indicate that you might be much happier in another occupation or industry.

This chapter will force you to focus on these tough questions and make some sound, long-range career plans.

# Does Your Cluster of Personality Traits Match Your Chosen Occupation?

☐      ☐      ☐      ☐

*In order that people may be happy in their work, these three things are needed: They must be fit for it. They must not do too much of it. And they must have a sense of success in it.*

—John Ruskin

There are few agonies worse than spending your whole working lifetime in the wrong vocation, one that does not suit you temperamentally or make the best use of your interests or skills.

If you're in the wrong occupation, you probably know it, at least on a subconscious level. Your occupational mismatch could explain why you get depressed every Sunday evening, for example. Maybe you've been late to work a lot recently, because a part of you is resisting those eight hours every weekday. Or perhaps your work has become increasingly slipshod. The reason: You take little or no pride in what you do for a living. You may be experiencing a feeling of utter futility, a feeling that life isn't really worth living after all. In short, you feel trapped and you don't know what to do about it.

Well, you *can* do something about your predicament. This section will help you explore your vocational alternatives and guide you to a more suitable occupation—if, indeed, that is the answer to your problem. First, let's make sure that a new occupation is really the cure for the malaise that you feel. The following check-list should help you decide. Check the statements that apply to you.

**1.**___I never consciously chose my present occupation. One thing led to another and I "drifted" into my present situation.

**2.**___When I compare my likes/dislikes list (compiled in chapter 1) with the requirements of my occupation, I find the two often conflict.

**3.**___I know everyone has a "work identity" and a "private identity," but mine are so different, they have so little to do with each other, that I feel like a split personality.

**4.**___To advance in my occupation, I will have to adopt a life-style (i.e., friends, social life, marital status, type of home, behavior, dress) I do not like or feel comfortable with.

**5.**___To advance in my occupation, I may have to live in a region of the country I do not like.

**6.**___I can't identify anyone in my field whom I really admire or would call a role model.

**7.**___The prevailing values in my industry run counter to my own.

**8.**___My occupation requires a larger commitment of my time and energy than I am willing to make.

**9.**___I am basically an _____ personality but
    introverted/extroverted
my occupation requires opposite characteristics.

**10.**___I am basically a _____ personality
      passive/aggressive
but my occupation requires the opposite trait.

**11.**___I am basically a _____ but my
      non-risk-taker/risk-taker
occupation requires the opposite characteristic.

**12.**___Making a lot of money is important to me but my occupation is relatively low-paying.

**13.**__The significant others in my life—people whose opinions I value—have little or no respect for my occupation.

**14.**__I am one of the few _____
women/minorities/Ivy League grad-

_____
uates/unmarried individuals/Catholics/Protestants/Jews/

_____
political liberals/political conservatives/individuals in my age

_____ in my occupation, and this feeling of isolation
group
makes me extremely uncomfortable.

**15.**__I have studied the typical career ladders in my occupation and I am not enthusiastic about pursuing any of them.

**16.**__Even if I am successful and follow my occupation as far as it is likely to take me, I probably won't feel fulfilled.

**17.**__Job security is important to me and my occupation does not offer enough of it.

**18.**__I'm sure I cannot make my occupation more enjoyable, challenging, or interesting merely by changing employers.

**19.**__I'm sure I cannot make my occupation more enjoyable, challenging, or interesting merely by changing industries.

**20.**__Status considerations are important to me. My occupation does not carry enough prestige or clout in my eyes or in the collective opinion of others.

**21.**__My occupation is still relatively closed to women and I do not have a trailblazer's ability to cope with the constant roadblocks in my path.

**22.**__My image (dress, speech, body language, manners) is not appropriate for my occupation, yet I'm unwilling to conform because doing so would make me feel as if I were betraying the "real me."

If you checked more than half of these, you may well be mismatched to your present occupation. However, if you didn't check too many of the above statements, and you are definitely unhappy about your job, consider the possibility that you may be caught up in a "career crisis." A career crisis can be brought on by any number of factors; for instance, when you:

- Have reached a dead end in salary or promotions at your present place of employment.

- Are stymied in your attempts to move ahead.

- Realize that the job you thought was ideal has its drawbacks as well.

- Realize your boss has been hindering your efforts to move ahead.

- Realize your boss has a bad opinion of you that even your best efforts cannot change.

- Are caught in the middle of two battling political factions.

- Have doubts about whether excellent job performance will get you further in your organization than Machiavellian political maneuvering will.

- Have conflicting feelings about the sincerity or reliability of all your "friendly" colleagues.

Job burnout, the feeling that mentally and physically you just "can't stand it anymore," is another problem that can cause you to feel frustrated or disillusioned with your occupation. Like a career crisis, burnout can be the result of a number of factors: too heavy a work load, lack of cooperation from co-workers, or excessive monotony of tasks, to name just a few. Burnout can manifest itself in physical symptoms such as continual fatigue, tenseness, or excessive fluctuation in weight. It can also have emotional and psychological symptoms like excessive daydreaming, memory lapses, irritation with other people and their problems, or low morale. There are indications that certain jobs or work environments—for instance, high-stress situations or jobs that require a lot of people contact—have a greater tendency to produce burnout.

The list of circumstances that can precipitate a career crisis or burnout is endless, but both problems have one thing in common: they cause you to experience pangs of self-doubt. With your self-esteem thus shaken, you may confuse your unhappiness about your specific situation with unhappiness over your occupation in general. Job dissatisfaction and vocational dissatisfaction are two different things. A job can be changed, a work environment can be altered. Switching to an entirely new field, however, is very serious business—and not easy.

Before you decide to abandon your occupation and start afresh in another field, try to analyze exactly what is making you unhappy. Too much work? Perhaps what you really need is a time-management course that will teach you how to set priorities to better manage your work load. Too much stress? Maybe a class in stress-management techniques can help alleviate the situation. Boredom? Try to think of ways to make the job more interesting and challenging. Show some initiative, think up a project that you would enjoy—and would benefit your employer—and fight for permission to institute it. If you are turned down, don't give up. Come up with another idea and keep doing so until you do prevail. Or make a conscious effort to advance using some of the methods outlined in later chapters of this book. Discuss other possibilities with your boss; she or he may already be aware of your dissatisfaction and be willing to help you come up with new ideas.

If you've exhausted these possibilities and are still discouraged, consider changing employers—or industries. Maybe your problem is that you are currently in a staff job when you would be happier in a line job. You don't necessarily have to change occupations to remedy that problem. An editor who puts together the monthly magazine for a large consumer-products company is in a staff job. Should that person become an editor at a publishing house, she/he is instantly transformed into a line employee and may thrive on her/his newfound responsibility.

However, if you have considered all these alternatives and are still convinced that a complete change of occupational scenery is the only solution to your career problems, read on. Below is a bibliography of sources that will tell you.

**How to Translate Your Unique Cluster of Skills and Interests Into a Specific Occupational Goal** There's no magic about this process. You are probably going to have to pay several visits to your local library and spend a good many hours reading through career literature. Another option is to consult a career counselor who can help you "see" your skills in various occupational settings. But before you spend any money on a professional counselor, see if a little self-directed counseling won't do the trick.

The federal government can be a good source of career information. The fourth edition of the *Dictionary of Occupational Titles* (*DOT*), published in 1977, is your first stop. It lists over 35,000 job titles utilized in over 23,000 occupations. To make the best use of the information in the *DOT*, you should also spend time reading the *Guide for Occupational Exploration*, a companion work. The *Guide* contains an interest inventory test designed to help you match your skills and personality traits with specific vocations. Next, the *Guide* introduces you to 12 broad "interest areas," which are in turn broken down into 66 "work groups." These work groups are ultimately segmented into 1,200 specific jobs that are numerically coded and cross-referenced to the job titles listed in the *DOT*. These two publications should be available at any library or you can purchase copies by sending $12.00 for the *DOT* and $11.00 for the *Guide* to Superintendent of Documents, Government Printing Office, Washington, D.C. 20402.

By writing to the same address and enclosing $8.00 you can purchase another valuable career reference, the *Occupational Outlook Handbook 1982–83*. (This volume will also be found in most libraries.) The *Handbook* is more expository and less statistical in nature than the *DOT*. It describes several hundred occupations in thirty-five major industries. For each occupation, it discusses the nature of the work; typical places of employment; earnings and working conditions; necessary training, qualifications, and advancement potential; the employment outlook; and sources of additional information. A companion booklet called

"Matching Personal and Job Characteristics" is available free from any of the regional offices of the U.S. Bureau of Labor Statistics. It defines 23 occupational characteristics and requirements—for instance, "physical stamina," "problem-solving ability," "jobs widely scattered," "works as part of a team"—and then lists them in chart form with 281 occupations. The chart enables you to compare your personal interests, capacities, and educational qualifications with characteristics usually associated with certain occupations or groups of occupations.

If you are a recent college graduate, the *Occupational Outlook Handbook for College Graduates* is a good overall source. It, too, is available from the Superintendent of Documents in Washington, for $4.50, or at many libraries.

Five other privately published aids should also prove helpful. *The Self-Directed Search Program*, compiled by Dr. John L. Holland of Johns Hopkins University, classifies personality/skill traits into six categories: realistic, investigative, artistic, social, enterprising, and conventional. The author has you answer a series of questions that will tell you which category or categories pertain to you. You will end up with a three-letter summary code that is keyed to occupations listed in a companion booklet. In less than an hour, you should have a basic list of occupational possibilities, which you can then investigate further elsewhere. One complete specimen set of *The Self-Directed Search Program* is available for $2.00 from Consulting Psychologists Press, 577 College Avenue, Palo Alto, Ca. 94306.

The *Career Information Questionnaire* is a booklet that covers in easy-to-read form every consideration that should go into choosing a vocation. The booklet focuses on considerations such as the demand for workers in a chosen field, how fast a field is growing, any geographic limitations, employment security, opportunities for self-employment in the field, and acceptance of women and minorities. It is available for $1.25 by writing to the National Career Institute of Career Planning, 521 Fifth Avenue, New York, N.Y. 10175. The booklet is designed to accompany Dr. Charles Guy Moore's book, *The Career Game*. It is available in some libraries or for $12.95 by writing to the same source.

Two Catalyst publications can also be of help to you. *What to*

*Do with the Rest of Your Life: The Catalyst Career Guide for Women in the '80s* (New York: Simon & Schuster, 1980) is six guidebooks in one: a guide to planning your career, a guide to health careers, a guide to science and engineering careers, a guide to government and law careers, a guide to the skilled trades, and a guide to business careers. After surveying each field, the book explains how to go about job-training and job-hunting in that field. Profiles of women already in each field and a comprehensive list of basic resource agencies to consult for further information are also included.

*Marketing Yourself: The Catalyst Women's Guide to Successful Resumes and Interviews* (New York: G. P. Putnam's Sons, 1980) tells you how to write a winning résumé. It also covers various hypothetical interview situations and gives you step-by-step strategies for handling them.

The paperback *What Color Is Your Parachute? A Practical Manual for Job-Hunters and Career Changers* (1981) by Richard Nelson Bolles has become a classic career-guidance work. It is everything the subtitle implies. The book is available in most bookstores or by writing directly to the publisher, enclosing your check for $6.50 to Ten Speed Press, Box 7123, Berkeley, Ca. 94707.

Once you've narrowed down your occupational alternatives to five specific vocations—ten at the most—we advise you to write directly to the trade associations in each field for more information. You can get the names and addresses from your library's copy of the *Encyclopedia of Associations*, published annually by the Gale Research Company.

Using the association's career literature, formulate a chart with these headings:

- Occupation
- Prerequisites (i.e., education, skills, employment experience)
- Geographical/Life-style Requirements
- Typical Career Path(s)
- Earnings Potential

- Demand
- Acceptance of Women
- Other Important Considerations

For each vocation, fill in the information on the chart. Then compare the occupations. Which appears to offer you the best deal? Which would require the least amount of retraining? (This is an important consideration if you are over age thirty.) Take out the list of your likes and dislikes that you compiled in chapter 1 and make sure these vocations conform to your personal requirements. Try to assess which occupation gives you the best "gut" feeling. Finally, talk to people already in the field; try to get a feel for what working in an occupation is really like.

Remember, the hardest part of any career change is actually deciding to do it. Once you make the decision, you'll probably feel as if a great weight has been lifted from your shoulders. But it's up to you to cast off this burden. As Ezra Pound put it: "A slave is one who waits for someone else to come and free him." Don't spend your life enslaved in the wrong occupation.

## Your Choices

☐　☐　☐　☐
You make choices, or tradeoffs, in every area of your life, and your career is no exception. You're dreaming, for example, of a job in a glamorous industry like television that pays $40,000 a year, is low pressure, and yet still offers good potential for advancement. You might get two of those assets in one job, but never all four. No job will *ever* satisfy *all* your needs, but you can strive for a job that will accommodate many of them.

In this section, you will examine some of the choices you must consider in the process of identifying the job or occupation best suited to your needs. You will have to balance these choices against your own needs and wants before you can decide which trade-offs you are or aren't willing to make.

**84**

**Choice A: High Pressure/High Pay vs. Low Pressure/ Less Money** The dictionary is the only place where *success* comes before *work*—specifically, hard work. There's an old saying that can be applied to the business world: "There's no such thing as a free lunch." In short, don't expect the reward of high pay without assuming some of the stresses that accompany hard work. Employers, being hard-nosed pragmatists, operate on the theory that the more unpleasant the job, the more they will have to pay to get someone to do it. In white-collar occupations, "unpleasant" generally means stressful. So if you know that you can't tolerate pressure or cope with stress, then you're going to have to scale down your monetary goals and dreams of advancement somewhat. To put it succinctly, if you can't stand the heat—get out of the boiler room.

It's a fact that the men and women who achieve the greatest success in business are those who have a single-minded devotion (some would say obsession) to their careers—and the emotional and physical stamina to withstand great amounts of stress. Dr. Joyce Brothers points out that "psychologists retained by large corporations to test men and women being considered for promotion to executive ranks look for one quality more than any other. . . . This pivotal quality is total commitment, the ability and desire to work to top capacity. They want people who scoff at 40-hour weeks, who work 60-, 80-, and 100-hour weeks because they find their work exciting and rewarding and they are seeking success. Total commitment is the common denominator among successful men and women."


**Choice B: High-Status vs. Low-Status Occupations** Status is a tricky and very personal consideration. Like beauty, status is very often in the eye of the beholder. Definitions of "status" occupations will vary among individuals. Generally speaking, however, the occupations that are considered high status are those that require the most education and preparation. They also tend to pay well. For instance, doctors, lawyers, and dentists are usually high up on the status totem pole. However, high pay does not always accompany high status. Clergymen, university professors, and high-school teachers usually score high on occupational status surveys. But these professionals are notoriously underpaid in relation to other high-status, advanced-degree professionals.

At the low end of the job-status spectrum, there are similar anomalies, due in part to the rise of powerful labor unions. Most people would put the job of garbage collector near the bottom of the status heap. But today, many sanitary engineers have achieved pay parity with some construction workers and other higher-status blue-collar workers; indeed, they have surpassed some white-collar occupations in terms of wages. And as we pointed out in chapter 2, in the future, many jobs considered "low status" by the college-educated group will pay as well or better than white-collar "status" jobs simply because there will be such high demand for these services.

So, what determines status—high pay, education, "genteel poverty"? Well, we'll leave that up to you. Depending on your own attitudes, status may or may not be a vital consideration when choosing your life's work.

### Choice C: Government Service vs. Nonprofit Institutions vs. Private Industry

If you are talented, hardworking, and *male*, you definitely stand a better chance of moving onward and upward faster in private industry than in the nonprofit or governmental sectors. If you are talented, hardworking, and *female*, this may be true also, provided you work for an enlightened company that does not discriminate against women.

However, working for Uncle Sam can feed more than just your patriotic fervor. Practically every job in private industry has an equivalent within the federal system.* Most federal jobs are regulated by the Civil Service Commission, although there are

---

*For purposes of comparison, this section discusses only federal jobs. Generally speaking, federal jobs offer more advancement opportunities, higher pay, and better benefits. Moreover, each state has its own personnel and merit system. Your state and city employment agency or civil service agency can give you more information about local government jobs.

some agencies that have their own merit appointment systems: the FBI and the Postal Service, for instance. Only about 2,000 jobs in the federal government result from political appointments. Civil service jobs are filled through a competitive merit system. Each civil service job carries a specified government-service (GS) rating and salary. The pay levels go from GS–1, which might be a clerk's job, to GS–18, which is always a position requiring a highly skilled and educated professional.

So what's so great about a job with the Feds?

- *The Pay.* Government salaries at the entry and middle-management levels tend to be quite good—in fact, higher than some comparable positions in private industry. There's never any dickering about salary or raises either. That's strictly a matter of what GS level you've attained. (There are ten salary grades within each GS level and periodic merit raises are usually given across-the-board, regardless of whether a worker truly merits it or not.) In addition, government wage scales for white-collar positions are the same for every area in the country. Therefore, if you live in an area with a lower cost of living, you might actually be "earning" more than someone with the same salary who works in a city where housing and food costs are higher.

- *The Benefits.* Health and pension benefits within the federal system are generally excellent. Federal pensions are indexed; that is, cost-of-living adjustments are made to pension benefits twice yearly. Another advantage for many working women is that some agencies have flexitime and part-time work schedules.

- *Promotions.* Most government internal training programs are very good. Also, promotion from within is encouraged. The Civil Service has mandated that no candidate will be hired from the outside to fill any job if there is someone already working for the federal government who is qualified.

- *Job Security.* For many people, job security is the biggest single advantage offered by federal employment. It is practically impossible to get fired from a civil service job. In fact, it can take years to fire even an obviously incompetent worker

Sounds like a perfect situation, doesn't it? Well, nothing is perfect. Lest you think that working for Uncle Sam is a bed of roses, here are some "minuses" you'll also have to consider:

- Getting hired can be a time-consuming and difficult proposition. The Federal Job Information Center in your area can give you the best information on job availability, forms, and exams. Basically, the system works this way: first, you fill out a myriad of forms including the SF 171—the government's version of a résumé. (Depending upon the GS level of the position you apply for, you may also have to take the Professional and Administrative Career Exam [PACE].) Based on your qualifications, you are then given a rating and your name is placed on a register. The closer your SF 171 matches any particular job description, the higher up you'll be. When a job opening occurs, the employer picks names from the register and—voilà—a job is filled. Sounds pretty easy; all you have to do is wait. In theory, maybe. But let's put it this way—if you sit and wait, the band will go home before you're even asked to dance. In other words, to get a federal job (particularly at the higher levels), you'll have to do a little extra maneuvering. There are many more applicants than job vacancies. This is where your networking skills can come in handy. The more "inside" people you know or can get to know, the better your chances. These employees often know of unlisted jobs and they also get prior notice of listed positions. (Remember, we said that promotion from within is encouraged.) And although they still have to follow civil service procedures, these insiders can help you tailor your SF 171 to match a job description as much as possible.

- Although it's difficult to get fired from a civil service job you are still subject to some of the same economic downturns as private-sector employees. If the federal, state, or city government suffers a loss of income, employees are laid off. (Veterans with preference are the last to be laid off.) Jobs that result from political appointments have their own hazards. A change in administration in an election year can put you out of a job.

- The same merit and promotion system that provides security for the talented also protects the inept. As a supervisor, you may have to put up with a less-than-adequate subordinate simply because you'd probably have to spend years of your life trying to get her/him fired. The reverse also holds true; you won't have as much leeway in hiring your personnel as you would in private industry or in the nonprofit sector.

- While benefits such as health and pension plans are quite good, civil service employees don't have other "perks" such as profit-sharing plans, savings plans, or stock options.

- Finally, remember that as a federal employee you are working for The Bureaucracy. Red tape and triplicate forms are a fact of life. Nothing ever moves quickly. You'll have to have (or develop) a high tolerance for paperwork and regulations.

Well, you've considered the Feds; what about the nonprofit sector—those foundations, charities, schools, universities, church groups, cultural organizations, and associations that have tax-exempt status with the Internal Revenue Service? With the exception of positions at the senior management levels, nonprofit jobs seldom pay as much as comparable jobs in private industry or, for that matter, comparable civil service jobs. (A nonprofit institution's top officer probably earns the equivalent of the CEO of a small to medium-sized company. Secretaries, clerks, and middle-management personnel generally earn less than they would elsewhere.) These institutions also offer somewhat less job security than government jobs, since they depend so heavily on outside funding and contributions—both of which can be unpredictable.

However, don't dismiss nonprofit institutions out of hand. There are other reasons why you might want to work for one. In the nonprofit world, the goals of the organizations are, theoretically at least, more humane, altruistic, and "socially redeeming" than the goals of corporations. A publicly held corporation's ultimate goal, after all, is profit.

If you are somewhat of a crusader by nature, nonprofit work might appeal to you. Also, the pace of nonprofit work is often slower and less pressured than private industry. Although chances are that you won't find stock options, pension plans, and tuition-refund programs in your benefits package, there are compensations. Many nonprofit institutions do provide good health and life insurance benefits and other perks such as more generous vacation time and flexible work schedules. So, even if the organization won't pay for the class, you may at least be able to get the time off during the day to attend it.

Working for a nonprofit institution may get you more responsibility sooner, since staffs tend to be smaller than in large corporations. Often you are able to acquire experience in several areas of an institution's services and programs, thus broadening your skills even further. Also, because the organization of a nonprofit institution is not as rigid or structured as that of a corporation, you may have latitude in defining your job and more autonomy in planning and developing new projects.

Finally, there is less competition for jobs and promotions in the nonprofit world. (Indeed, many people who work for nonprofits do so strictly on a volunteer basis.) However, if you spend a good part of your career working in the nonprofit sector, it is often very difficult to enter the corporate world later.

In capitalist America, top dollar is still reserved for those who can make a go of it in the corporate world. Generally, the larger and more prestigious the corporation, the fiercer the competition for jobs, the greater the stress you will experience, *and* the greater the monetary rewards if you are successful. Most corporations have excellent benefits packages and executive perquisites, particularly at upper-management levels.

Unfortunately, job security in this sector of the economy is practically nil unless, of course, you belong to a union. The business world didn't get dubbed the "corporate jungle" for nothing. Although there's some deadwood in the corporate world also, Darwin's "survival of the fittest" theory can generally be applied here.

### Choice D: Glamour vs. "Dull" Industries

Most people consider anything to do with the media (magazine, newspaper, or book publishing; radio-TV; films; theater; recording; modeling; advertising) glamorous. And because people feel this way, the competition is tough for entry-level jobs at companies like Random House, CBS, Twentieth Century-Fox, and J. Walter Thompson. This type of thinking creates a "buyer's market," allowing so-called glamour-industry employers to pay less for lower-level personnel than other industries while continuing to attract talented people. Of course, glamour jobs have their own perks—if you like hobnobbing with celebrities or attending lots of "media events," you may consider this a worthwhile trade-off.

Keep in mind also that glamour-industry pay scales become more competitive with those of other industries at the middle- and upper-management levels. So if you begin your career at a "glamour" company and can put up with the "starvation" wages until you begin moving up, you can probably look forward to earning a decent salary in the future.

**Choice E: Line vs. Staff Jobs**   A line position is any job that is directly concerned with producing or selling whatever goods and services the company deals in. Thus, line jobs have a direct impact on the bottom line: they generate profits. Staff positions, on the other hand, are located in service departments such as personnel, customer relations, and public relations. These departments are staffed with specialists in assorted fields who assist line personnel. Although staff personnel make a vital contribution to an organization, they don't generate income. They are a drain on profits, pure overhead. However, line personnel, if they are doing a good job, increase profits. Thus, is it any wonder that staff personnel are the first to get laid off if there's a recession. And, not so coincidentally, staff areas have the greatest concentrations of women employees.

Line and staff personnel differ in one other important way: line managers set policy; staff managers are empowered only to carry out policy.

In her book *Games Mother Never Taught You*, Betty L. Harragan refers to line functions or departments within an organization as "the front-line fighting forces, the money-making units: sales and production." She also points out that what constitutes a line function in one industry may be a staff function in another. "In retailing, for instance, the 'production' branch is buying; buyers and merchandise managers literally 'produce' the goods the stores sell. In banking, however, the profit-making product is money; one sector produces it by collecting it from depositors, the other loans it at higher interest rates."

Of course in an industrial company the distinction between line and staff functions is perhaps the most clear-cut. Anyone involved in manufacturing or marketing the company's product is part of an operating unit or profit center—that is, a line function. Everyone else is involved with staff operations or functions—for instance, purchasing, accounting, and research.

Clearly, it's much easier to measure the output of a line employee than it is to measure that of a staff employee. All you have to do is count the number of widgets that were produced in X amount of time under the line employee's supervision or the number of widgets that were sold by the line employee within a specified period of time. But how do you quantify the output or the effectiveness of a public relations employee? A personnel worker? A purchasing agent? You can guess at her/his contribution to the bottom line, but you can't prove it. This is precisely why staff personnel often feel that they are expending great effort in the performance of their jobs and getting very little reward—monetary, emotional, or otherwise.

By now it should be dawning on you that the way to advance in most companies is through the line ranks. As a line employee, you'll be paid more, get more appreciative feedback on your work, and have more decision-making power. And experience in the marketing and production areas of a company is generally held to be essential for any senior management position. There's one catch, however. The line positions in most companies are still filled overwhelmingly by men. Sure, women have been allowed to move up in business—up through the staff ranks, however.

Although we said earlier that every job you take should be successively better and pay more, there is one exception. When you move from a staff into a line position, you will probably be making a lateral move. It's a career decision that should pay great dividends in the future. But for the moment, you'll have to be satisfied with the same salary or possibly even less. After all, to make such a move, the company will have to retrain you—possibly enroll you in its management-training program—and during this process, you'll be costing the company money. But if you turn out to be a top performer in a line job, it will certainly have been worth the company's while—and your own. Not only will you eventually earn far more as a line manager, but you'll be on the track that can lead to the executive suite.

## "They're Discriminating Against Me!"

☐ ☐ ☐ ☐ Maybe your employer is discriminating against you—and other women—and maybe not. In this section, we will discuss the practice of sex discrimination and its ramifications for working women today.

Discrimination against working women has been a fact of business life throughout American history. Today, there is less sex discrimination practiced by employers but it has not been eradicated entirely, not by any stretch of the imagination. Journalist Mary Scott Welch discovered this when she got an assignment from *Redbook* in 1977 to do a story on "The Ten Best Companies for Women Who Work." After extensive interviews with working women, the heads of women's organizations, the affirmative-action officers of large companies, and the directors of government agencies handling equal employment opportunity claims, she concluded that no American company deserved the honor of being labeled an ideal, or even satisfactory, employer of women. Instead, she wrote a story called "How Women Just Like You Are Getting Better Jobs." It described several of the large class-action sex-discrimination suits that have been filed against well-known companies in recent years.

Increasingly, women are taking to the courts to redress their grievances against their employers' personnel policies. By 1980, more than 50,000 complaints of discrimination, ranging from sex to age to racial discrimination, were pouring into the watchdog government agencies each year. In some of the cases the charges will be dismissed, but many will be deemed valid enough to warrant prosecution. Of these, most will be settled out of court with the plaintiffs receiving anything from back pay to reinstatement, although the latter is rare. If the suit is a class action—a legal term given a suit in which a few individuals represent an entire class of people—the settlement will probably include a detailed corporate personnel plan for hiring, training, and promoting more women.

Don't assume, however, that such litigation is easy. It's costly in both emotional and financial terms. For example, once your formal complaint of discrimination becomes common knowledge around the office—and it always does—expect your colleagues to treat you as something of a pariah. Even other women co-workers, women who are themselves always complaining about inequities in the company, may no longer want to be seen talking to you. After all, verbalizing dissatisfaction is one thing. Doing something about it is quite another matter.

Furthermore, unless an organization like the American Civil Liberties Union wants to make a test case out of your grievance, expect to pay plenty in legal fees. Even if you can talk a sympathetic attorney into taking your case on a contingency basis— that is, if you win the lawyer gets a percentage, usually a third, of the monetary settlement—you'll still have to pay your attorney's out-of-pocket expenses. These expenses could easily cost you hundreds of dollars.

But before you even think in terms of lawsuits, it's important to know how sexual discrimination is being defined today. Over the years, the definition of sex discrimination has changed and evolved as more legislation is passed and more court decisions are handed down. Today, statute law and case law have identified the following forms of discrimination as unlawful:

- unequal pay for the same work;
- sexual harassment where an employee's response affects whether she is hired, promoted, or fired; or negatively af-

fects an employee's on-the-job performance by creating an "intimidating, hostile or offensive work environment";

- unequal access to internal training programs, such as management-training programs or tuition-reimbursement programs that underwrite individual external training;

- unequal recruitment, hiring, and promotion policies;

- firing of pregnant employees or forced prebirth leaves of absence;

- unequal pension fund payouts;

- inequitable allocation of fringe benefits, including medical and maternity benefits, life insurance, pension, and retirement programs;

- dress codes that require women employees to wear prescribed uniforms but permit men to wear "customary business attire" of their own choosing.

However, as any lawyer specializing in equal employment opportunity (EEO) litigation will tell you, a cagey employer can find a way around these laws—which is one reason that one-third of the country's 43 million working women are stuck in clerical and service jobs that pay less than $9,000 annually. This puts them among the lowest-paid workers in the United States. It's a sobering thought that in spite of the recent and much-publicized progress of women in the work force, in 1977 the average annual earnings of women were $8,618—only 59 percent of men's $14,626.

In fact, employers have become so clever at evading the spirit of the law—if not the letter—that EEO advocates are pressing on with a much broader concept to combat discrimination. Instead of being satisfied with demands for "equal pay for equal work," EEO proponents want legislation enacted that institutionalizes the idea of "equal pay for *comparable* work." Women's rights leaders cite examples of nurses who make less than their hospitals' janitors and secretaries who make less than ditchdiggers to explain why such legislation is urgently needed. But a major stumbling block is how to develop job evaluation systems that present objective comparisons of the skills, effort, and responsibility required to perform vastly different jobs. If anyone does come up with a feasible method for determining the relative monetary worth of jobs and equal-pay-for-comparable-work legislation is enacted, this will only be scratching the surface of the problem. Thomas G. Cody, of the Chicago consulting firm of Lester B. Knight & Associates, estimates that closing the gap between women's and men's pay will cost the nation's employers about $2 billion a year.

With that kind of money at stake, employers will no doubt use all the lobbying power at their disposal to keep such legislation off the books. In the meantime, more and more white- and blue-collar women are learning their job rights and pressing on with suits under the laws that do exist.

But before you decide to do likewise, we suggest you do the following:

- Determine whether sexual discrimination as defined by law does indeed exist. You are protected by Title VII of the Civil Rights Act of 1964, which prohibits discrimination in employment based on sex, race, color, religion, or national origin. According to the Women's Bureau of the U.S. Department of Labor, you have a right to complain if:
  —an employer refuses to let you file a job application but accepts others;
  —a union or an employment agency refuses to refer you to job openings;
  —a union refuses to accept you into membership;
  —you are fired or laid off;
  —you are passed over for a promotion for which you are qualified;
  —you are paid less than others for comparable work;
  —you are placed in a segregated seniority line;
  —you are left out of training or apprenticeship programs; and ...
  —the reason for any of these acts is your sex, race, color, religion, or national origin.

- Try to view your situation objectively. Keep a confidential notebook in which you describe each alleged incident of sexual discrimination. Write down exact quotes—what the other person said and what you replied. Let some time pass and then reread what you've written. Don't wait too long, however, because there are time limits on filing that are specified by law. Does it still sound like a clear instance of discrimination to you? Or were there extenuating circumstances to explain why the other party behaved as she/he did? Accusing someone of discrimination is a serious matter. You should never be hasty in your judgments. However, if your company does engage in a pattern and practice of sex discrimination and you do sue, your notebook can be admitted as evidence in court.

- Never threaten your employer with a discrimination suit because: (1) you may not go through with it and then you'll look cowardly; (2) you may get fired on the spot; (3) it's always better to take the "enemy" by surprise. You may drop broad hints to your employer indicating that you intend to investigate a certain personnel policy further because you think it's illegal, but don't come right out and say, "I intend to file a charge of discrimination against this company."

- Don't file an individual discrimination complaint with the appropriate government agency if it is at all possible to get other women to file with you. Then you will be filing a class action where you allege that other women employees within your employment classification are also being systematically discriminated against by your company. Psychologically, you will feel much stronger about filing under these circumstances. It's the old adage: There's strength in numbers.

- Confide in trustworthy friends outside your company. They are more objective and they can be good sounding boards. Get feedback from them about your predicament. Also, start networking and attending meetings sponsored by feminist groups. You will feel less isolated and alone with your grievances this way. After all, you will need all the moral support you can get if you do file.

- Start collecting evidence *before* you file suit. Your diary is one piece of evidence. Others include promotion lists, transfer announcements, statistical reports—anything that supports your contention that your company discriminates. It's also advisable to keep track of your peers—their salaries (if you can find out), titles, work responsibilities, any differences in the way men and women holding the same job title are treated, and so on.

In addition, write memos—and keep copies—confirming any important discussions that you've had with peers or superiors. All of the above can be admissible evidence. Finally, get a copy of your company's affirmative-action plan and read it. Analyze how your company's stated personnel policies differ from actual practices.

- Interview several attorneys before you select one. Inquire about their experience with cases similar to yours. Ascertain whether they are going to be dictatorial and impose strategy decisions on you, or whether they'll be willing to lay out options and let you decide. Ask if they are willing to let you help them analyze research in order to cut down on their "billable" hours.

  If you're interviewing someone who works for a law firm, find out who actually will handle your case and how accessible the lawyer will be. Also, consider what image the attorney projects, because a person who looks and behaves like a "radical" will come off badly compared to your company's battery of well-dressed conservatives. Finally, you should feel comfortable with the lawyer you select, knowing that she/he is more committed to your cause than to the financial gain or personal publicity that may accrue to her or him because of your case.

# Will a Discrimination Suit Ruin Your Career?

☐ ☐ ☐ ☐

The answer to this question depends on a number of variables:

- the size and stature of your company;

- the nature of your industry—is it geographically contained and gossipy (Wall Street financial institutions, the fashion industry) or large and sprawled all over the country?;

- your rank in the company;

- your long-range career objectives—do you like your line of work or are you in the process of a career change anyway?;

- whether you file an individual claim against your employer or join with other female employees and file a collective claim or class-action suit.

Clearly, a suit against a well-known and respected company is going to cause more comment than a suit against the XYZ Nuts and Bolts Company. Suits against Fortune 500 companies are usually reported in the newspaper. And while the publicity may make you a heroine in the eyes of feminists and working women, it may also brand you a "troublemaker" in the eyes of some personnel people and executive recruiters.

Of course, personnel people and executive recruiters aren't likely to pay very close attention unless your rank is relatively high. The higher you rise in the corporate hierarchy, the scarcer the potential jobs become and the more carefully you will be screened before you are promoted or offered a job elsewhere. During this screening process, any legal actions you've filed against present or former employers are bound to surface. Once such claims come to light, you will have to work twice as hard to convince potential employers of your desirability as an employee. In the higher echelons of power where great value is attached to teamwork, your reputation as a "troublemaker" may be a handicap.

Legal action on your part is even harder to downplay if you work in a small, close-knit industry where everyone knows everyone else. The owners of Seventh Avenue garment manufacturing companies, for example, all tend to know each other and socialize in the same clubs. It would be hard to sue one of these employers without having your name bandied about over cocktails or the eighth hole of a golf course. Even if there isn't any gossip at the time you file your claim, the matter will certainly come up when you try to get a job at a firm down the street from your present company.

If you've had it with your present occupation or industry and intend to seek future employment in a totally unrelated area, you have less to worry about. Employers tend to think along industry lines. If you are making a radical career change, the new employers you approach will place less emphasis on your old jobs and probably make only cursory inquiries—if any—among your former employers.

Once you file a formal charge of discrimination with the appropriate government agency, you are, theoretically at least, protected from retaliation from your employer. This is small consolation, however, if your employer should decide to launch a subtle campaign to make you miserable for eight hours every day. In February 1980, *Savvy* magazine ran an article ("Trouble-Makers: What Happens When a Woman Blows the Whistle on Her Company?" by Janice Prindle and Geoffrey Stokes) reporting how women who had filed sexism charges against their employers felt about it in retrospect. The reporters concluded: "Though an action against on-the-job discrimination can sometimes bring positive results in the long run, not one of the women we talked with—women whose cases we chose at random—hadn't experienced some form of backlash, on the job or off it." The article not only profiled women who had been harassed by the companies they had sued, but also went on to describe cases of women who had waited until they left a company to file suit and even then had suffered negative consequences.

However, one way to institute such a suit and still emerge relatively unscathed is to band together with a group of your confederates and file jointly. The stories of women who have formed groups and then sued are more inspirational.

In the mid-1970s, sixteen women working for the National Broadcasting Company filed a complaint with the New York City Human Rights Commission, and eventually brought suit. Of those original sixteen, seven had left NBC by 1977—"not exactly fired, but not encouraged to stay either," as one observer put it. Of the remaining nine, several have been promoted. The suit was eventually settled out of court, as is typical, with NBC agreeing to a detailed affirmative-action plan covering the recruitment, hiring, training, and promotion of more women; and a boost in female employees' pay to equal the average salary of male employees at the same grade level.

The class-action suit instituted against the Chase Manhattan Bank in 1976 had a similar outcome. Of the thirteen original plaintiffs, three were still at the bank in 1980. Their careers were progressing on schedule and one of the women had even distinguished herself by becoming the first woman the bank had sent abroad to negotiate important contracts. Two other women were eventually dismissed for cause; some left Chase voluntarily for better jobs elsewhere; and a few of the women had never worked for Chase in the first place. They had applied for jobs at the bank and been turned down or refused interviews while men with the same qualifications were interviewed and hired.

Unquestionably, it takes a great deal of courage and perseverance to see a sex-discrimination lawsuit to the end. For many women, the outcome has been worth the struggle. For others, the results have been less than encouraging. It's a serious step— one whose possible outcome and consequences should be discussed and thought out carefully before *any* decision is made.

## For Additional Information on Job Discrimination and Women's Rights

### Two helpful booklets

"A Working Woman's Guide to Her Job Rights"
U.S. Department of Labor
Office of the Secretary/Women's Bureau
Washington, D.C. 20210

"Getting Uncle Sam to Enforce Your Civil Rights"
Clearinghouse Publication #59
Publications Division
U.S. Commission on Civil Rights
Washington, D.C. 20425

### Related publications

*Corporate Experiences in Improving Women's Job Opportunities* (Report Series #755) by Ruth G. Shaeffer and Edith F. Lynton.

*The Economics of Sex Discrimination* by Janice F. Madden.

*Equal Pay in the Office* by Francine D. Blau.

*The Equal Rights Handbook* by Diane T. Eisler.

*Old Boys–New Women: The Politics of Discrimination* by Joan Abramson.

*The Rights of Women: The Basic ACLU Guide to a Woman's Rights.*

*Sex Discrimination and the Law: Causes and Remedies* by Barbara A. Babcok et al.

*Sexual Harassment of Working
Women: A Case of Sex Discrimination*
by Catharine A. MacKinnon.

*Sexual Shakedown: The Sexual
Harassment of Women on the Job* by
Lin Farley.

*What Every Woman Needs to Know
About the Law* by Martha Pomroy.

*Women Winning: A Handbook for
Action Against Sex Discrimination*
edited by Virginia Pendergrass.

*The Women's Guide to Legal Rights*
by Jane Shay Lynch and Sara Lyn
Smith.

## Organizations

American Civil Liberties Union
Women's Rights Project
22 East 40th Street
New York, N.Y. 10016

Campaign to End Discrimination
    Against Pregnant Workers
1126 16th Street, N.W.
Washington, D.C. 20036

Center for Constitutional
    Rights/Women's Rights Program
853 Broadway
New York, N.Y. 10003

Coalition of Labor Union Women
15 Union Square
New York, N.Y. 10003

Equal Employment Opportunity
    Commission
2401 East Street, N.W.
Washington, D.C. 20506

**103**

Federal Women's Program
Civil Service Commission
1900 E Street, N.W.
Room 7540
Washington, D.C. 20415

National Commission of Working
    Women
Center for Women and Work
1211 Connecticut Avenue, N.W.
Washington, D.C. 20008

National Organization for Women
    Legal Defense and Education Fund
132 West 43rd Street
New York, N.Y. 10036

Office for Civil Rights
Department of Health, Education &
    Welfare
Washington, D.C. 20201

U.S. Department of Labor
Office of the Secretary/Women's
    Bureau
Washington, D.C. 20210

Women's Equity Action League
Education and Legal Defense Fund
805 15th Street, N.W.
Washington, D.C. 20004

Women's Legal Defense Fund
1010 Vermont Avenue, N.W.
Suite 210
Washington, D.C. 20005

# Does Your Image Match Your Aspirations?

☐　☐　☐　☐　Everyone possesses a very specific on-the-job image. Your boss and co-workers form a certain opinion of you, and because of that conception, they consequently expect you to behave, dress, and perform in a certain way. Eventually, their conception of your image can become a self-fulfilling prophecy. And that self-fulfilling prophecy can work for or against you.

In this section, we want you to consider whether the picture you present to the world truly reinforces your career aspirations. Maybe you were denied that supervisor's job because you dress more like a secretary than an ambitious, talented career woman. Perhaps your sweet Southern-belle behavior dilutes your effectiveness as a purchasing agent for a major company in a "masculine" industry like steel. Or your slouching posture may be crippling your ability to make a dynamic statement to prospective customers.

Superficial matters like dress and speech do matter in the business world. Certainly competence is more important, but substance without appropriate style and behavior won't get you very far.

Boyden Associates president Carl W. Menk claims that a person's image is crucial to her or his success in the job market. As head of one of the world's largest executive search firms, Menk has personally recruited dozens of top managers for major American corporations. When a man like Menk admits that 20 percent of his final evaluation of a candidate is based on what some people consider superficial criteria—a person's manner of speech, voice, dress—it's worth taking another look at the sometimes maligned concept of "personal packaging."

"Image may seem like an artificial, surface criterion," says Menk, "but don't discount its importance. While you're sitting there in your scuffed shoes the employer will be asking himself, 'Will this person be able to gain the respect of our other employees? Will he or she have the polish to mix with our clients socially? Will this person be pleasant to work with?' "

Are you in need of an image overhaul? You might be if:

- People always assume you are a lot older or younger than you really are.

- People are constantly saying, "Would you repeat that, please?"

- Your co-workers think you are sexy-looking.

- People tend to fidget and look away when they find out what you do for a living.

- You are frequently offered jobs below your ability and training.

- Relative strangers call you "dear," "honey," "sweetie," and similar endearments.

- People mimic your mannerisms and speech habits supposedly in jest.

- You have trouble getting your ideas accepted at work.

Most companies have an image and would like their employees to conform to it. There is also a distinct image or business style that accompanies every profession. A lawyer, for example, is expected to dress and carry herself/himself one way, while a publicity agent is expected to look and act quite differently.

According to image consultant Elaine Posta, president of the Image Institute of New York, one of the most common mistakes working women make is not conforming to their employers' image—indeed, not even knowing what image their company likes its employees to project. The second most common mistake women make is wanting to look like somebody else—someone who is more glamorous, more zany, or more sedate.

To avoid the first mistake, look around you. What are the up-and-coming middle managers in your company wearing? How do the members of the company's top management team dress and behave? Observing these people over a period of time, you should be able to detect a pattern, a definite "look" and mode of behavior shared by the most respected people at the different hierarchical levels within the company.

You can avoid the second mistake, the I-want-to-be-somebody-else syndrome, by working with what image consultant Stephanie Tudor calls the "Image Equation," the sum of three vital image components: (1) a woman's inner beauty and style; (2) her goals, aspirations, and life-style; and (3) her ability to use current fashion, makeup, and hairstyle trends to serve her own ends, rather than as dictates to be blindly followed.

**106**

According to Tudor, working the Image Equation requires two things: introspection and outward inspection.

A clear, unbiased self-evaluation is step one. Begin by listing all your image assets and liabilities in separate columns. Scrutinize yourself in the mirror if you have to, and jot down everything you see—good or bad—no matter how minor. Next to your liability column, leave room for a third column, headed "Ways to Improve." Don't just stop after you've made the list; resolve to do something constructive about your image failings.

For example, if you know that your speech habits are poor, devise a plan of action to improve your speaking "image." Take a public-speaking course; practice with your tape recorder or in front of friends or relatives. Make certain you set aside time in your busy schedule for a daily dose of self-improvement. Keep at it until you and others can see some good results. Use the same methodical approach with all your image problems. *Don't* expect to become perfect overnight, but *do* expect to look a bit better every day.

Look at your asset column. Consider the fact that good things can be made even better. Suppose your hairstyle is just okay. It's not bad and yet it's not really great either. Devote some attention to finding a new hairstyle, using new hair-care or coloring products, or locating a new hairdresser who will give you a more attractive cut. "Just a little more effort in the asset category can take you from okay to sensational," says Tudor.

Step two in working the Image Equation is a look into your future. What are your goals and aspirations? How would you like to be living five years from now? Once you've determined your direction, look for role models—women who are already where you want to be. See how successful women in your field look, and ask yourself if you could adapt their image to fit you—don't *copy*, but *adapt*. Try to observe what image is working for them and why.

Next, consider your personality. What do you feel comfortable wearing? What makes you feel attractive? You'll probably find there's some correlation here with your life-style. Ask yourself, "What type of clothing is most suitable for my daily activities? What types of people do I come into contact with regularly?

What are their expectations?" Throw all this information into your computation.

Step three. Here you must ask yourself if you really keep up with fashion trends or ignore them, hoping somehow that you'll still manage to look all right. Do you understand current fashion and how it relates to you? Keep in mind that fashion ranges all the way from very trendy designer clothes to the most conservative ready-to-wear garb. Even though fashions constantly change, you can still adapt your own look to what is in vogue. You can start by using the fashion magazines as your basic reference materials. Remember that within every fashion trend, there is at least one nook or cranny where each of us can feel comfortable.

"When the best of the 'inside you' meets the best of the 'outside you,'" says Tudor, "that's when a beautiful image is born. Being somebody else never really works. Besides, it's more fun to let somebody else want to be you!"

A full-fledged image overhaul would encompass changes in your appearance, wardrobe, grooming, speech, gestures, and manners. If you want the advice of an expert on changing your image, there are approximately 160 firms in the United States today that offer image-improvement programs with a range of price tags. To locate one in your area, send for the *Directory of Personal Image Consultants* (published by the Editorial Services Co., 1140 Avenue of the Americas, New York, N.Y. 10036). Your employer may be willing to underwrite the cost (via its tuition-reimbursement program) should you decide to attend a group workshop offered by an image consultant. However, before you spend a dime, find out if your company ever retains such consultants for in-house training seminars. More and more companies are hiring image consultants to give training programs for employees. When image consultants are brought in, their general mandate is to transform employees into better team players and to mold them into the company image, whatever that may be.

But before we leave this topic, it is only fair to warn you that a radical change in your image will cause people around you some discomfort for a while. They got used to the "old" you and they won't quite know how to react around the "new" you. Also, there is always the possibility that an image overhaul won't change a poor "job-capability image" at your present company. Human nature being what it is, it's often nearly impossible to get people to rethink a strong opinion they already hold about you. If a bad "job-capability image" continues to haunt you, you should consider a job change so you can start afresh. At a new company, you'll be viewed as a capable, rising newcomer from the very first day.

# Have You Made a Little List?

☐ ☐ ☐ ☐ Musing about priorities and long-term career goals is not enough. You should think about them, yes; but you should also write them down in the form of a Personal Career Plan that you can refer back to a year from now, two years from now, even five years from now. Career and life planning can clarify your thinking and make it possible for you to exert some control over life instead of letting life—or the fates, destiny, whatever you want to call it—control you.

Long-term planning will also help you avoid two of the worst career pitfalls: (1) task-orientation and (2) job-orientation. You are task-obsessed if you get so involved in the minutiae of your job that you lose sight of your job's real purpose. Let's say you are the assistant to the president of a company. As the president's representative, you are expected to present a businesslike, dignified picture to other employees or any visitors to your boss's office. But you have so much paperwork to complete most days that you figure getting that work done comes first, and being gracious to visitors comes second. Wrong. This is an example of misplaced priorities. You lack an understanding of the position's real function. In short, you can't see the forest for the trees.

Focusing on individual jobs rather than a series of jobs that constitute a career is equally detrimental. A job is the way a person occupies her/his time for eight hours every day. A career, on

**109**

the other hand, is a succession of jobs that form a coherent pattern, ideally leading upward. No matter what your specific occupation, your career will consist of these smaller pieces called jobs. Consequently, each job you hold should provide a greater opportunity for growth and advancement. But without a Personal Career Plan, it is easy to lose sight of your ultimate objectives. While it's true that some women do progress without a conscious plan, these women are the exceptions. And most acknowledge that they would have been better off *with* a plan.

Barbara Boyle Sullivan, one of the owners of the New York City–based consulting firm Boyle/Kirkman Associates, admits that for the first dozen years of her working life, she never thought in terms of a long-range career. The career progress she made just seemed to "happen" to her. Boyle joined IBM fresh out of college in 1959, assumed she'd work for a few years and then get married and go back to her hometown to raise a family. However, her life evolved differently. She remained single and continued to advance at IBM. Finally, after eleven years, she was asked to fill out a career form indicating what she foresaw as her next two jobs. Only then was she introduced to the concept of career planning. She recalls researching all her alternatives at IBM and deciding her goal was to be a branch manager. "All of a sudden I was excited and running," she says. "I had more energy to do my work because I had more reason to do it."

In the 1960s, when Boyle was progressing so serendipitously at IBM, people could afford to be more blasé about long-term career planning. Demographics and the booming economy were in their favor. But in today's extremely competitive job market where the postwar baby-boom generation is creating a glut of eager, well-educated workers, no one can rely solely on instinct to get ahead. Some conscious decision making and planning early in one's career are essential.

Ideally, your working life—between the ages of about twenty-two and sixty-five—should follow a pattern somewhat like this: In your twenties, you should concentrate on finding the right occupation, the right field in which to utilize your talents. Age thirty should be a year of taking stock—what have you accomplished so far and where are you headed over the next ten years? You should spend your thirties pursuing those specific goals. Age forty is another time of reassessment and, possibly, redirection. In recent years, there has been a small but growing trend among people in their late thirties and early forties to make mid-career switches. Instead of continuing to pursue the long road upward at a giant corporation, for instance, a person may decide to work for a nonprofit organization, or open up her/his own business, in her or his field.

If you choose to stay with your original occupation, however, the years from forty to fifty should be a time of consolidation. If your aim is the top—the presidency of a company or becoming well known in your field—this is the time to achieve it. By fifty— or fifty-five at the latest—most ambitious people have reached the pinnacle of their careers. And from this point on, after their earlier struggles to make it to the top, the pathway leading to retirement levels off. It's a time when you can reap the benefits of the long struggle.

That's the ideal career scenario. But women are especially prone to detours such as marriage and child rearing. Because of these contingencies, women have to be even more diligent about long-term planning than the average man, whose working life may proceed with very little interruption.

**Devising a Personal Career Plan** A Personal Career Plan is a timetable for advancement. It should answer the following questions:

- What would I like to be doing in five years? Ten years?
- What would I like to be earning in five years? Ten years?
- What kind of life-style would I like to have in five years? Ten years?

When attempting to answer these questions, take your time. It's not unusual to spend two months formulating a career plan. Don't rely purely on logic during this decision-making period. Include your emotions, beliefs, and values in your deliberations.

And don't forget the emotions, beliefs, and values of those significant others in your life.

The answers to these questions will provide you with a list of goals. The next part of your career plan should focus on how you plan to achieve these goals. Suppose you are currently a trainee in a large advertising agency and your five-year goal is to be an advertising copywriter. You might ask yourself:

- What special training will I need to qualify as a copywriter?

- What books could I read on the subject?

- How extensive a portfolio of sample ads will I need to get my first copywriting job?

- What are my chances of moving into the copywriting department at my present company, or will I need to go elsewhere to break into that area?

- How do people usually get their first copywriting jobs? What kind of previous experience do they have?

When you have discovered everything there is to know about how to become a copywriter, your next step is to devise a short-term plan that outlines, in six-month intervals, the progress you expect to make toward your goal during the next five years.

The format of your Personal Career Plan is up to you. In truth, how your plan looks on paper matters very little, but it must be on paper so you can refer back to it periodically, and revise it if necessary.

Keep in mind that the reason for a career plan is to focus your thinking so you can make the most efficient use of your mental and physical energy over a specified period of time. Your objective is to channel your energy into a manageable number of goals, realizing that the smaller the number of goals you try to pursue simultaneously, the more concentrated your energy will be.

# 4

# Skills You Need for Getting Ahead

The higher you rise within any organization, the less you will be using specific vocational skills and the more you will be relying on general management skills such as communicating, planning, organizing, negotiating, and delegating.

This chapter will give you an overview of these important skills. No matter what your occupation or industry, you will need to develop them in order to move ahead.

## Problem-Solving Skills

☐ ☐ ☐ ☐

The accumulation of knowledge in your field and the honing of your technical and professional skills through on-the-job experience are, of course, necessary ingredients for career success. However, there is one other ability that is perhaps equally as important: problem-solving skill.

"No matter how much different kinds of work may vary upon the surface, underneath they have this common base: they deal with one kind of problem-solving or another," writes Richard Nelson Bolles in *What Color Is Your Parachute?* "Universities, community organizations, business—all require people good at problem-solving *no matter what title may be tacked on the man (or woman) they hire in order to justify his/her salary.* Problem-solvers get hired, whether they are fresh out of college, or later in life."

While a mental storehouse of facts and information will certainly not hurt your quest for advancement, the truly valued employee is the one who can go one step further and apply analytical, problem-solving, and decision-making skills to a business situation.

The first step toward solving any problem is to recognize that the problem exists and then define it. This may sound self-evident, but it is surprising how few people are really good at identifying problems. And unless a problem is correctly identified, no workable solution will result. For instance, suppose you are the product manager at a large consumer package goods company. One of the products you are responsible for is not selling well. You decide the problem is that your product is priced too high in comparison with competitive products. So you lower the price to match the competition. The product still does not move. Why? Because the real problem—which you failed to identify—is that your product is inferior in quality. To make up for this deficiency, you will either have to offer your product at a price probably substantially lower than its competition before people will buy or else improve the quality of your product.

After you have identified a problem—not an inconsiderable task, as we pointed out—the next step is to rid yourself of any preconceived notions about how that problem should be solved. Maintain an open mind about how to solve your problem and try not to have any built-in prejudices about the right or wrong way to proceed. In formulating solutions, you should figuratively place your problem on a table and then "walk" around it, viewing it from every angle. Be sure to get ideas from others who are involved or who have special expertise that may help solve the problem. Give your imagination free rein, keeping track of all possible solutions, regardless of how improbable they may seem. Using this brainstorming method, you will come up with some solutions that seem farfetched. But even these should be closely examined, for there may be an element in these "wild" ideas that holds the key to a practical solution.

Write down all your possible solutions. Then research them, keeping in mind the following questions:

- What is my ultimate goal?

- What time restrictions am I facing?

- Do I have the necessary resources available?

- Do I have the authority to implement the solution?

- What costs, both money and manpower, are involved?

- What new problems might this solution create, and how will I solve them?

Your answers to these questions must be rooted in a thorough knowledge of the subject area of your problem. In the consumer product example we used above, the subject is marketing. If marketing is your specialty you're all set, but if it isn't you'd be better off consulting with someone who has expertise in this area.

So far, you have progressed through these steps:

1. Identifying the problem.

2. Brainstorming solutions while keeping a completely open mind and allowing no biases—at least during this stage—to cloud your thinking.

3. Analyzing the feasibility of various solutions, bringing factual knowledge and informed judgment into play.

4. This involves making a decision about which solution to choose. Reaching a decision is a highly individual matter

and will have a lot to do with the kind of person you are. Some people are rational decision-makers. They list the pros and cons that accompany each solution, and then simply select the alternative that has the longest list of pros and the shortest list of cons. Other people are instinctive decision-makers. They steep themselves in knowledge about their problem, forget about it for a while, and then wait for lightning to strike. They play their hunches. However, these are *informed* hunches.

Whatever decision-making style you adopt, you must not delay the process too long. Keep in mind that not coming to a decision is actually a decision—albeit a tacit one. People who drag out the decision-making process indefinitely are usually people who are reluctant to take risks, since *every* decision involves some form of risk. They avoid coming to a decision because once they do, they anticipate that they will feel trapped with an irreversible, and perhaps poor, solution. Others are reluctant to commit themselves to a specific course of action because they feel that decisions are too revealing, telling other people too much about themselves.

The important thing in decision making is not to let indecisiveness paralyze you. The maxim "Do nothing long enough and all problems will be solved for you" is true enough, but it is courting disaster. It also bespeaks an extremely passive way of dealing with life. Inherent in problem solving is the will to take charge of a situation and put it to rights.

Once your decision is made, your next move is to implement it. At this point, problem solving dovetails with two other important business skills, planning and organizing, which are covered in the next section.

# Planning and Organizing Skills

□  □  □  □

You've probably noticed that the busiest-looking person in the office is not necessarily the most efficient. A lot of activity signifies little unless that activity is properly channeled and produces results. The ability to channel energy to produce the most amount of work in the least amount of time is known as planning and organizing skill; it is absolutely crucial in business. (The ability to plan and organize well is also crucial in juggling the roles of wife, mother, and career woman.)

Planning and organizing are actually two different processes. *Planning* is the process of establishing goals. *Organizing* is the process of arranging in sequence the steps needed to achieve these goals. Both these processes result in *implementation*— reaching those goals.

Whether the goals you set at work are long- or short-term will depend on the level you have attained in the organizational hierarchy. *Long-term goals*—policy making, in other words—are set at the senior management level. They are broadly defined objectives that concern the company's future, its strategic or structural plans. *Short-term goals*, on the other hand, concern the operational or tactical steps that go into implementing corporate policy objectives.

No matter what the nature of the goals, the planning process remains the same. The first question you must ask yourself is "What do I want to accomplish?" You should be able to answer that question with one short phrase or sentence. That is your goal. The next question brings organizational skills into play: "How can I accomplish this goal?"

For instance, suppose you are the supervisor of the typing pool in a large company. Management has made the policy decision to install a sophisticated word-processing system throughout the company. The job of planning for the transition from the old, manual typing system to the new, fully automated system is your responsibility.

Your goal is to map out a plan that will make the transition period as smooth as possible. To accomplish that goal, you will have to answer such questions as:

- How long will the transition period last?

- How will the department's staffing needs change due to the installation of this new equipment?

- Assuming we will need fewer workers in the department to run the new equipment, how will we pare down the number of employees? Through attrition? Layoff? Reassignment?

- What impact will the changeover have on my departmental budget? On people's morale? How can I include key people in the transition so that they feel involved in the process?

- At what point should I start scheduling typists to go through the training program introducing them to the new equipment?

- While workers are being retrained, how will I handle the normal departmental work load?

You should always ask yourself broad questions at first and slowly work your way down to the details. If you skip over the general questions and focus on the detail questions too soon, you will feel like you are sinking into quicksand. You will be overwhelmed by the minutiae surrounding your goal. In such an instance, the problem lies not with your analytical abilities but with your method of approach. Thus, Organization Rule #1 is: *Start with the general questions first and later zero in on the details.*

Organization Rule #2 is: *Write your plan down on paper.* Give your plan visual representation, whether that takes the form of a simple, straightforward list or an elaborate flow chart so popular with management consultants. The first draft of your plan will contain your rough ideas, in random order, about how to proceed. Your second draft may also contain ideas in no special sequence, just more of them. However, by your third or fourth draft you should place your ideas in some logical order. Ask yourself such questions as:

- What has to be done first? Second? Third?

- Are there any steps that can be done simultaneously?

- Have I broken down the most complex steps into their component parts and placed them in the proper sequence?

Organization Rule #3 is: *Build flexibility into your plan.* This may mean formulating several contingency plans should key circumstances change or crises arise at the last minute. The good planner sets objectives within a *dynamic* mode that leaves plenty of room for eleventh-hour adjustment. For example, you have charted the basic plan for the word-processing changeover. That plan goes from Step A to Step E; however, Steps B, C, and D are augmented with Alternative Step B, Alternative Step C, and Alternative Step D. You factored these alternatives into your plan at the outset. They are your fallback position should unforeseen circumstances arise. For instance, what will you do if a last-minute project has to be completed and the staff is involved in the training program?

Making these allowances does not change your stated objective—to plan for a smooth transition. Rather, these allowances will provide even more assurance that your goal will be reached. Planning and organizing skills can be learned. Although it's true that systematic thinking comes more naturally to some people than others, planning and organization skills can be learned through diligent study, careful observation of others engaged in the planning process, and by repeated practice. Even if your current job requires very little planning, you can devise small daily planning exercises to familiarize yourself with the process. For instance, take the pile of task-oriented work your boss has given you and make a plan that allows you to accomplish the work in the most efficient manner possible. Build in time for interruptions. Write your plan down, then see where you have to deviate from it during the week as circumstances change. Or you might pretend to be your boss and devise your own plan for a project she/he has just been assigned. Chart your plan *before* you look at hers/his and see how the two differ. If your boss falls into the "helpmate" category (see chapter 2), you might even show your plan to her/him—she/he'll probably be impressed with your initiative—and discuss the merits of her/his plan versus yours. A word to the wise, however: Keep an open mind and learn. Don't be a show-off or you'll defeat your purpose.

# Time-Management Skills

☐    ☐    ☐    ☐

Recent studies show that most people waste as much as two hours a day, a terrible loss when measured as a component of productivity. However, people generally don't realize they are wasting that much time because those two hours drift away in bits and pieces—five minutes spent daydreaming at your desk, eight minutes expended in small talk at the coffee wagon, another fifteen minutes lost in panic over the pile of work on your desk.

The quest for ways to accomplish more in less time is as old as the pursuit of the Holy Grail. There lurks in most of us the nagging suspicion that we are not allocating our time efficiently. We wonder if there isn't something we could do to squeeze more productivity out of the eight (or more) hours we spend on the job each day.

Marvin Rudin, author of *Practical Time Management*, contends that there are a number of things the ambitious woman can do to increase her productivity. Rudin claims that most time-management authorities lead people astray with sophisticated theories on how to plan, organize, and delegate authority when the real culprit is nothing more complicated than *faulty priorities*—not taking the trouble, first, to determine what tasks are the most important; and, second, to concentrate on those tasks rather than the less urgent ones.

This sounds simple enough, but Rudin's own theory is somewhat more complicated. In brief, he believes that to establish priorities, you should weigh the time required to accomplish a task against its potential return. He subjects his tasks to a cost-benefit analysis and assigns top priority to those with the best score. At his harshest, Rudin suggests that you should not "suffer fools gladly" when they drop by your office unannounced for a chat, for example. You should simply ask them to leave because you have more important things to do. However, he does point out that this approach would be wrong should you happen to work in an organization that places a good deal of emphasis on office politics. If this is the case, those casual, unannounced visits with your peers are important and should be assigned a higher priority on your list.

Michael LeBoeuf, another time-management expert and author of *Working Smart: How to Accomplish More in Half the Time*, suggests that each second of your time is so precious that even the most mundane things must be taken into consideration in charting your personal time-allocation plan. Among the tips he gives are:

- Learn to associate sitting behind your desk with *work only*.

- At your desk, think with a pencil in your hand. Thus, as you are writing down ideas, you will already have begun the process of expanding and evaluating those ideas.

- Begin each day by making a "to do" list and rank each item in order of its importance. In short, set priorities.

- Break down overwhelming tasks into smaller assignments. If you don't do this, you may find yourself avoiding the big job because it seems so complicated.

- Delegate trivial tasks to others. Don't waste precious energy better expended elsewhere.

Most important of all, list your objectives, both professional and personal, at the beginning of each week. Assign a value to each one, and then apportion your time accordingly. Consider your moods and daily energy levels in deciding when to tackle the most demanding jobs. Save your most pressing projects for hours when you're at your peak. Finally, try to end your day's work on a high note. If you quit at a point of satisfaction, it will be easier to return to it at some later date and your start-up time will be reduced.

# Communication Skills

☐　　☐　　☐　　☐　　You have worked out a thorough plan to solve a specific business problem, and it has been accepted by management. Now you are in the process of implementing it. At this stage, however, all the problem-solving, planning, and organizing skills in the world will be of little use if you do not have another extremely important business skill—the ability to communicate your needs to your co-workers and to persuade them to cooperate with you.

The effective decision-maker must not only develop thoughts and solutions to a problem, but she/he must also be able to communicate ideas clearly in order to convince subordinates and superiors of their value. In other words, the effectiveness of your planning, organizing, and problem-solving skills is directly related to the effectiveness of your communication skills.

Communication is the process of delivering a message. There are two ways you can get your message across to your colleagues: through either the spoken or the written word. You should develop your skills in both these areas; it is the rare person who reaches the top in business without strong oral and written skills.

It is never too late to learn to communicate better. Nor is it necessary to take expensive and time-consuming writing and speaking courses. Here are some tips that should improve your communication skills.

*Always speak (or write) in the receiver's language.* Seems obvious, doesn't it? But we cannot stress how important this is. Just consider the vast differences between people—their jobs, training, experiences, education, and biases. When approaching people with a proposal or idea, place yourself in their position and try to visualize the proposition from their point of view. Ask yourself: What might appeal to this person? What motivates her/him? What subjects interest her/him?

To be able to answer such questions, you have to be a good listener and observer of people. You must develop the ability to

**122**

read the clues inherent in people's dress, speech (tone, inflection, accent), and body language, as well as to pay close attention to the words they use.

Since you cannot truly function well in any business environment without the ability to relate to people as individuals, you must keep practicing; gradually, good listening and observation habits will become second nature to you.

*Always be precise when expressing yourself.* This rule holds true for both written and verbal communication. Think through what you want to say and then choose words that express your meaning exactly. When people speak or write in generalities, it is usually because they have skipped step one: They haven't established the purpose behind their communication. Strive to express yourself in simple declarative sentences. The longer and more convoluted your sentence structure, the more confused the receiver is likely to become.

*Make certain your verbal and nonverbal messages are the same.* Nonverbal communication can be as "eloquent" as any written or spoken message. Your tone of voice, inflection, posture, or facial expression can dramatically alter the meaning of your message. How you say it is as important as what you are saying.

Here is an example of the transmission of conflicting verbal and nonverbal messages. You tell a male colleague that you will listen to his idea with an open mind even though his recommendation conflicts with yours. Then, as your colleague explains, you lock your arms across your chest, thrust your head forward, and narrow your eyes to slits. Your body language is communicating the opposite message—that you have already made up your mind and he is merely wasting your time.

*Learn to be a good listener.* Listening is an *active* process that involves much more than the purely physical act of *hearing* the spoken word. A good listener must also understand and evaluate a speaker's message before responding. This means listening with a truly open mind, letting the other person speak without interruption, learning to read the nonverbal message that is also being communicated, and taking the time to think over the message before formulating your own response.

**Fundamental Writing Skills**   The ability to write a lucid, compelling letter is one of the key elements in a successful career.
Any woman who demonstrates strong writing skills has an edge
over her competitors.

Marjane Cloke, director of public relations services for The
Mutual Life Insurance Company of New York (MONY), travels
around the country demonstrating the art of effective letter writing to companies, schools, and civic organizations. She firmly believes that any correspondence, even form letters, must be
"human, interesting, action provoking, and easily understood" if
they are to evoke a response in the reader. "Few people are
good letter writers," she claims, "because they:

—don't plan what they are going to say before they write;

—fall into a rut by using the same openings, closings, and
phrases, changing only the facts and figures;

—refuse to write as naturally as they speak;

—are afraid to be original for fear it will not be correct or will
be misunderstood."

To write letters that will jump out of the pile and make the
reader take notice—and action—Ms. Cloke offers the following
rules:

- Write the way you talk, in a natural conversational tone. If
  you can make your letters sound like you are talking, people will be more likely to respond.

- Be yourself. Don't try to imitate someone else's style.

- Ask questions in your letters. As people read your letter
  they will begin to formulate an answer and are more likely
  to reply.

- Use words that are easily understood. Avoid stuffy phrases
  and technical jargon that often obscure what you really
  mean to say.

- Focus on your reader's interests, not yours or your company's.

- Write in terms of "I," not "we."

- Be sincere. Don't make flimsy excuses the reader will not
  believe.

- Be brief. If you don't have much to say, don't fill up the page with excess words.

- Always be polite—even if you are angry or have a legitimate complaint.

- Make people remember you. If you have something in common with the person you are addressing, such as a meeting or conference you both attended or a mutual acquaintance, mention it in the letter to refresh the reader's memory.

"Above all," Ms. Cloke stresses, "let your personality come through in your letters. Everyone has a unique personality but they often tend to lose it in writing. Remember to 'talk' your letters and keep in mind the interests of your reader."

**Fundamental Speaking Skills** Elayne Snyder, director of Elayne Snyder Speech Consultants, finds that most of her clients are concerned with controlling their nervousness when they speak to an audience. "Nervousness is good," she explains, "if you use it to your advantage. . . . Psych yourself by saying: 'I have something worthwhile to tell this audience, I know my subject, I'm prepared, I'm rehearsed.' "

Ms. Snyder claims that speaking to a group of people, regardless of the size, is much less intimidating if you think of speech making as "enlarged conversation." "All the fear and nervousness you feel before giving your speech or in the early moments are worth the 'high' you will experience afterwards. If you approach your speaking invitation with positive anticipation you're more likely to have a positive experience. If you dread it, you'll *feel* dreadful. Expect a 'high' of self-satisfaction and you will have one."

To present yourself positively and command the audience's attention, Ms. Snyder offers the following advice: "When you approach the lectern, stand tall and confident. Position yourself about six to eight inches from the lectern with both feet firmly on the floor. Put your notes down and find a comfortable place for your hands. Placing one hand on either edge of the lectern is both comfortable and convenient (so you can use your hands to gesture when appropriate and natural). Before and during your speech, maintain eye contact with your audience." If using a microphone, be sure to find out how it works and, if possible, test it before the audience arrives.

Once you know how to control your nervousness and how to address the audience, the next step is to present your speech in a compelling manner that communicates clearly your information and holds the audience's interest. Ms. Snyder breaks the speech into three logical components: the introduction, the body, and the conclusion.

She recommends starting with an attention-grabbing introduction, such as an anecdote, a question posed to the audience (stick to questions with "yes" or "no" answers rather than questions that require your audience to think about the answer instead of listening to you), or an impressive fact or statistic.

In the introduction you must tell the audience the subject and purpose of your speech. In the body of the speech develop your points, supporting them with examples, facts, and figures. Limit your coverage to three or four main points, since that is all the audience will be able to remember. It is a good idea to keep a speech file in which you can store information, anecdotes, and examples that can be incorporated into your speeches.

The conclusion of your speech should be a summation of your main points ending with a restatement of your purpose, so your audience will remember it. If you conclude with an anecdote be sure it is germane to your topic.

Ms. Snyder summarizes the three key parts of a speech very succinctly: "In the introduction you tell the audience what you will tell them. In the body you tell them what you promised to tell them. In the conclusion you tell them again what you told them."

Aim to build a good feeling between yourself and the audience. Communicate your message clearly and successfully by using simple words and language meant for the ear. By following these guidelines and practicing at every opportunity, effective speech making will become another of your managerial skills.

# Management Skills

☐ ☐ ☐ ☐

The Peter Principle states that people rise in an organization until they reach their level of incompetence. Many people reach their level of incompetence the moment they move out of a job requiring excellent technical or professional skills and into a job requiring significant supervisory and managerial skills.

The good manager is a person capable of "letting go"—of delegating responsibility to staff members. While this may sound easy enough in theory, it is devilishly hard to do in practice, especially if you have just left a job where you were expected to perform all the necessary tasks yourself. Suddenly you have one person or maybe several people ready to do your bidding, but you can't bring yourself to parcel out some of your newfound responsibilities and power to them.

According to Nathaniel Stewart in *The Effective Woman Manager*, people who can't delegate authority generally fall into one of the following categories:

- *The Inexperienced Manager.* She has moved ahead in business steadily due to her energy, drive, technical know-how, and resourcefulness. She, therefore, assumes that this pattern of solitary endeavor will continue to advance her career even though she is now in a managerial position. She is deluding herself, however. By continuing to do everything herself or—just as bad—giving her subordinates such detailed directions that they cannot exercise any initiative, she will quickly brand herself as a poor manager and motivator of people.

- *The Egotistical Manager.* She is a perfectionist and thrives on the high praise she constantly receives for her exceptional performance. She is loathe to delegate responsibility because she is convinced nobody could do any task as well as she can. Since she can't abide sloppy work, she would rather do it herself.

- *The Insecure Manager.* Generally, this type has reached a permanent plateau in her career. Now she is just "riding it out," although she harbors the hope that someday a challenging project will come along and she will perform so well on it that her career will again take off. Thus, the insecure manager is reluctant to delegate any important project to subordinates who may run with it, advancing their careers instead of hers.

- *The Work Addict.* Also known as the workaholic. Intense expenditure of energy over prolonged periods of time keeps this type of person going. To the workaholic, all tasks are of equal importance. She will not relinquish any part of the work load except the most routine items.

Obviously none of these types falls into the "good manager" category. Just what makes a good manager? Peter Drucker in his massive book, *Management: Tasks, Responsibilities, Practices*, isolates five basic operations that every good manager undertakes. She or he . . .

- *Sets objectives.*

- *Organizes, plans, and assigns activities.*

- *Motivates and communicates*, making a team out of her/his subordinates.

- *Measures performance*, rewards those who are on target, and sees to it that others keep working toward the objectives established.

- *Develops people*, including her/himself.

Drucker's attributes of a good manager bring together three of the very important business skills discussed in this chapter: planning, organizing, and communicating. As a manager it will be your task to fuse these three skills to create a climate in which you can delegate responsibility.

You must first learn to set clear objectives and develop plans that will accomplish your goals. You must also be attuned to the particular aptitudes and limitations of your staff members. Who is best suited to undertake a specific part of a project? Who has specialized knowledge that could be put to good use? How is the work to be divided? Will everyone report directly to you or will you use an intermediary? What kinds of deadlines must be met? An efficient manager must take all these factors into account.

A good manager also communicates ideas and expectations *clearly*. Don't assume that someone will instinctively "know" what you want done—spell it out. And just because you have delegated some work to a group or an individual does not mean your responsibility is ended. You are still the bottom line and you must answer to your superiors for the success or failure of any project. Therefore, it is important for you to monitor the work of your staff as it progresses. Don't wait until something is finished to discover that it has been done wrong. It is critical to give and receive feedback and develop an ongoing communications channel between you and your staff.

Finally, the effective manager will also take the time to carefully evaluate the results of any work delegated to others. Could the project have been organized differently—or better? In the future, who can be called on to perform a particular task well? Whose strengths seem to lie elsewhere? By analyzing and evaluating the end results you will ensure that your people are working on what they do best.

Irving Burstiner, assistant professor at Baruch College of the City University of New York, adds another important attribute to the good manager. He advises would-be managers to increase their breadth of knowledge, transforming themselves from specialists into generalists. One way to do this is by adopting a questioning attitude. "The questioning attitude contributes a good many pluses to its practitioner," Burstiner writes in "Moving Up: Guidelines for the Aspiring Executive" (*Personnel Journal*, December 1974). "For one, it brings him/her a great deal of information—in all shades and varieties—that he/she would not normally get. For another, it helps him/her clarify his/her thoughts and ideas, for he/she measures them against the answers to his/her questions. Still other benefits stem from the 'social interaction' that takes place; we all gain from sharing experiences. Finally, through questioning, we demonstrate our interest in other people, and these people usually wind up feeling that interest and responding in kind!"

Until the point in your career when you move into a supervisory (or lower-level management) position, your technical/ professional skills are all-important—those are the skills that are given the most weight during your periodic performance appraisal reviews. But once you become a supervisor, your "people-skills"—the ability to delegate authority, to motivate your staff to do their best, and to groom them to move ahead in their own careers—will be weighed more heavily than anything else.

These people-skills can be learned. Indeed, many business commentators believe most working women already possess excellent people-skills if they would only apply them on the job and not just at home. Says Dr. Joyce Brothers in *How to Get Whatever You Want Out of Life*: "Women have not learned to capitalize on their special strengths. We are tremendously strong and capable. Unfortunately, the things women are most successful at are things that society does not value highly. But these abilities are transferable. They can be transferred to areas where they will be valued highly."

Dr. Brothers cites a study made of the talents required to run a household efficiently. That study concluded that homemaking involves a broad range of capabilities—from creative to organizational—that business managers also must have in order to be successful. If homemakers-turned-moneymakers applied these same skills at work, they too could be tremendously successful.

The consulting firm of Cresap, McCormick, and Paget, Inc. was retained by Citibank of New York to study how the bank could best meet the needs of its customers. Cresap, McCormick, found that women employees rated significantly higher than men in their desire to help others, and 11 percent higher in politeness and efficiency—the two traits that bank customers considered most essential. The consulting firm strongly recommended that women be assigned the post of "platform officer"—those who deal with the public—whenever possible.

Women are the traditional empathizers, the mediators of conflicts, the nurturers of others. These are precisely the human relations skills that good managers must demonstrate, and more organizations are beginning to realize that these supposedly feminine traits can be used to telling advantage in business.

## How to Handle Disgruntled Subordinates: One Female Supervisor's Formula

☐    ☐    ☐    ☐

Evelyn Anderson is a twenty-eight-year-old production supervisor in a large pharmaceutical plant in Indiana. Her title is Section Supervisor/Packaging Inspection in the company's quality-control division. Every day she oversees thirteen assembly-line workers, most of them men, and interacts with an all-male crew of machinists and mechanics who are responsible for repairing plant equipment.

"The biggest problem women production managers like myself face," says Anderson, "is that male factory workers don't know what to expect from them. They wonder how a woman will react when a piece of machinery breaks down. Is she going to sit in her office and give orders from there? Or is she going to go out on the floor and become part of the operation by actually getting some grease on her hands?"

Anderson, who holds a BS degree in mechanical engineering, does the latter. In the process, she's learned an invaluable lesson in how to relate effectively to fellow workers.

Because Anderson likes to tinker with machines—and is good at it—she often finds herself crouched on all fours helping the mechanical crew repair faulty machinery in the plant. It is a frustrating job under the best of circumstances.

"Once," she recalls, "I was just as stymied as they were so I inadvertently let go with a bit of profanity when my monkey wrench refused to catch. There was a deafening silence. First, the men looked at each other, then they looked at me, and slowly smiles broke out on all their faces as if to say, 'You're human, after all!' My slip of the tongue did not lead to excessive swearing on the job or any other evils. What it did was make the mechanics feel less self-conscious around me."

Anderson maintains that this is another example of men not knowing what to expect from a woman boss—or how to behave around her. "Before that incident, I never realized how uncomfortable the mechanics felt around me. Apparently, they thought I was a very proper young lady in white gloves, who was easily shocked. Since then, I've made it a point to talk to any new group of workers informally and outline what I expect of them and, most importantly, what they can anticipate from me. My message is that women are the same as men when it comes to wanting to get the job done."

Periodically, Anderson still has to contend with discriminatory remarks but, through trial and error, she has found that turning the other cheek is the best response. "If you don't become frenzied and don't run off complaining to everybody about the bad behavior of the individual, I find you earn greater respect. And, as a result, the barbs are cast less and less frequently."

## Business Etiquette

☐ ☐ ☐ ☐

It is said that manners are the body language of a culture, an intimation of its soul. The more civilized a society, the more its citizens observe a code of social "niceties."

Etiquette means knowing how to move through a sometimes hostile or indifferent world with ease and grace. It is a code that is no less important in business than in one's personal life. Courtesy is one ingredient that greases the wheels of commerce and makes them turn smoothly. In order to succeed in the business world, you must be able to meet your associates' business needs as well as their human needs.

How can you meet your colleagues' "human needs"? Quite simply—by extending them every courtesy, by treating them with dignity. Manners are the means to this end.

Below we've isolated the ten most fatal business faux pas committed by both men and women in the course of daily business. If you don't want your business associates to come away from an encounter with you feeling annoyed, awkward, or even angry, be certain you are not guilty of any of the following breaches of etiquette.

**Faux Pas #1: Assuming That All Your Business Associates Prefer to Be Addressed Informally by Their First Names** In a small office, the use of first names among employees is generally decided by the employer. Take your cue from her/him. In a large corporation, expect to be on a first-name basis only among your peers.

**Faux Pas #2: Sending Out Sloppy-Looking Business Letters** Business correspondence full of typographical and spelling errors brands you as unprofessional. Mailing such letters is tantamount to walking into somebody's office for a business appointment dressed in jeans and a T-shirt. By your carelessness, you are saying to the addressee,

---

"I'm not concerned with details or surface impressions." However, in the business world, details and surface impressions matter.

Not only should you eliminate any mistakes from your letters, you should also observe the conventions of business correspondence in terms of format. Also, we recommend you use the best-quality stationery you can afford. The design of your stationery should be clean and modern-looking, unless you have some special reason for it looking otherwise. The owner of a shop called Grandmother's Attic might want her letterhead to give off a cluttered, nineteenth-century air, for instance. But if you are a businesswoman, eschew such oddities and stick with a contemporary design. By all means, make sure your envelopes are of the same quality as your letterhead. Ideally, they should match.

**Faux Pas #3: Mistreating Business Associates' Secretaries** By mistreatment, we refer to any behavior that would make a secretary dislike you. You should always strive to make secretaries your allies. Their proximity to the boss gives them an edge over you. Often, they can make dealing with the boss much easier for you. At the same time, rudeness or unthoughtfulness on your part can make life much more difficult. If a secretary says something disparaging about you to the boss, you will never know it and will not be able to defend yourself. All you will know is that suddenly the boss stops returning your telephone calls and breaks an important appointment with you. Remember, on a subconscious level, many an executive adheres to the old adage: "Anyone who insults my secretary, insults me."

**Faux Pas #4: Displaying a Cavalier Attitude About Business Telephone Calls** When you make a business phone call, always identify who you are and what company you represent. If you are calling a close business associate, you can drop the mention of your company, but you must still identify yourself by name no matter how many times a day you speak with this person. To do otherwise invites confusion and a misunderstanding that could prove embarrassing.

If you are calling a stranger long-distance and she/he is not in, don't ask that person to return your call unless the individual stands to benefit from your subsequent conversation. A journalist might ask a stranger to return her/his long-distance call if he was going to give that stranger some favorable publicity, for instance. A salesperson, on the other hand, would show a decided lack of courtesy if she/he expected a stranger to call her/him back long-distance for the purpose of receiving an unsolicited sales pitch.

Avoid putting anyone on hold because "an important call just came in." That diminishes the importance of the person to whom you are speaking. And *never* simultaneously talk with someone at your desk while trying to keep up your end of a telephone conversation. If you absolutely must speak to someone in your office in the middle of a telephone conversation, excuse yourself politely and cover the phone. And be brief about it.

If you have a secretary, do not have her/him place your calls for you unless you are extremely busy and getting through to the other person would waste a lot of time.

### Faux Pas #5: Laxity About Making and Keeping Business Appointments

Never drop in on a business associate just because you happen to be passing by. Arriving on someone's office doorstep without an appointment is rude, to say the least, and shows a lack of courtesy on your part. By making an appointment in advance—and arriving promptly—you are granting your business associate dignity by assuming that she/he leads a busy, ordered, daily existence.

If you are consistently late for appointments, you cancel out the good impression you made by making the appointment in the first place. Your tardiness says to the person kept waiting, "My time is more valuable than yours." Viewed from this perspective, tardiness is an insult.

### Faux Pas #6: Smoking in the Wrong Places

Most smokers know enough not to light up on the street or in elevators. Unfortunately, too many smokers *do* light up in reception areas and in people's offices where there are no ashtrays.

Do not start smoking and then look around for a receptacle. If there is no ashtray in sight, assume that smoking is prohibited—or at least not encouraged. And just because it is obvious that you can smoke in the reception area, do not mistakenly assume the same holds true in someone's office. Extinguish your cigarette *before* leaving the waiting room. If there is an ashtray in your host's office, ask if she/he minds if you smoke before lighting up. If there is no ashtray, don't even bother to ask permission. It could be embarrassing to you and your host if she/he must deny permission.

### Faux Pas #7: Giving Conflicting Signals About Who Pays the Bill When You Lunch with a Business Associate

The words "Let me take you to lunch at Restaurant X" indicate that you intend to host the meal. Taking command at the table is another indication that you intend to pick up the tab. For example, if you are the one who gives the order to the waiter throughout the meal, your luncheon partner has a right to be chagrined if you don't insist on paying for it. If you extend the lunch invitation because you want an associate's advice on a project or an idea, a favor, or some information, you should expect to pay the bill.

If, however, you just want to get together with the person and your idea is to go dutch treat, the correct way to phrase the invitation is "Let's have lunch together. Where should we go?"

### Faux Pas #8: Talking Solely About Business at a Business/Social Occasion

Although this is a grievous error in this country, it could be a fatal one abroad where managers like to restrict their business dealings to people with whom they feel comfortable. Most foreign executives would rather do business with a person who shares their life-style and values than with a stranger, even if the stranger does offer them a better deal.

To a great extent this holds true also in this country. You remain a stranger to your business colleagues if, for instance, you refuse to engage in small talk or voice your opinions on various

**136**

nonbusiness topics. Read the newspaper daily and keep informed of current events. Upwardly mobile people are invariably well rounded and exude confidence and poise in all circumstances.

When lunching with a business associate, it is customary to discuss nonbusiness matters initially. The person who is hosting the meal generally indicates when the small talk ends and serious discussion begins.

**Faux Pas #9: Inviting Your Boss or Other Superiors Out Socially Before They Have Issued Such an Invitation to You** Although it is perfectly acceptable for a boss to invite a staff member and her/his spouse to dinner, the reverse situation is tricky. Many bosses do not like to be indebted in any way to staff members because such indebtedness makes it harder for them to treat their employees objectively. Thus, you should not extend a social invitation to your boss unless she/he has entertained you first—or at least made it abundantly clear that you are friends in addition to being business colleagues.

If you do socialize with your superiors, business subjects are verboten unless the person with the highest corporate rank initiates the conversation. If the talk turns to business, make sure your husband or partner doesn't sound off about your company's problems, which will indicate to your superiors that you are indiscreet. Nor should a spouse or partner use a social occasion to try to promote your business advancement.

If you have entertained or been entertained by your boss, never try to take advantage of the situation by acting unduly familiar in the office the next day.

**Faux Pas #10: Failing to Say Thank You in Writing** People who fail to show proper appreciation for acts of kindness on the part of their colleagues are generally people who feel the world owes them a living. They are careless people who are incapable of seeing things from another person's point of view. It never occurs to them that another person's time is valuable. They do not realize that an executive who has granted them an interview to discuss general employment prospects in her/his industry has done them a big favor. Thus, they don't bother to acknowledge the favor with a thank you note.

Since the advent of the telephone as the principal form of business communication, the use of written thank you notes has waned. This is a pity. In our opinion, a written expression of thanks is far superior to a two-sentence aside during a telephone conversation. A letter is concrete; a spoken thank you is more easily forgotten.

Thank you notes are the one form of business correspondence that can be handwritten, if that is your preference. If you do write in longhand, 8½-by-11-sized stationery is the most appropriate. Again, it is imperative that you use the highest-quality stationery.

When is it appropriate to send a business thank you note? Whenever a business associate has done you even the smallest favor or extended you her/his hospitality. You cannot err on the side of too many thank you notes. You are making a great mistake, however, if you don't pen enough of them.

## Salary Skills: How to Get Paid What You're Worth

☐ ☐ ☐ ☐ You may think it's unusual to include a section on negotiating salary in a chapter about management skills. But negotiating a salary increase *is* a skill. And you can bet that your boss, and your boss's boss, and everyone else up the line has developed this skill to perfection. And since salary is generally an indication of upward progression through management ranks, it's the wise woman who learns the fine art of salary negotiation and practices it successfully.

If you deserve a raise for a job well done, you should definitely ask for it. But it is not enough to march into your boss's office and demand more money. There are effective and ineffective ways to ask for a raise. The effective way requires that, as a first step, you do your homework.

You should prepare for salary negotiations with the same diligent preparation you would give to a formal presentation in front of a group of people. In fact, talking to your boss about a raise *is* a presentation. You are trying to sell your boss on the idea that you deserve a raise for specific, objective reasons. We will discuss what those reasons may be in a moment, but first you must research three factors: (1) what a person with your skills and experience can command in salary at other companies; (2) your own employer's pay policies and practices; and (3) your boss's paycheck.

In general, salary offers are made and accepted based on the employer's and employee's calculations of their respective alternatives. From your employer's point of view, the question is will it be less expensive in the long run to keep this person and pay her more than it would be to replace her? If you convince your boss with a well-researched and well-reasoned argument that, in terms of the time and money involved in replacing you, keeping you is the best strategy, you'll get your raise.

How do you prepare for such an argument? By finding out what you are worth, in dollars and cents, in the marketplace. The following sources will give you an accurate picture of what you can expect to earn according to your current level of experience:

- employment ads in your local newspaper, trade publication, or the *Wall Street Journal* if you have achieved at least middle-management rank;

- reputable personnel agencies, or for a manager, executive recruiting firms;

- various U.S. Department of Labor publications—call the local office;

- your personal network of friends and business acquaintances;

- various salary surveys—available at public libraries—that have been conducted by magazines, trade and professional publications, or the Chamber of Commerce.

If you have plenty of nerve, you might even call the personnel departments of a representative group of companies, say you are conducting a survey of pay ranges in your field, and ask what the company pays its employees for doing such-and-such a job.

Be aware that what you *think* you should earn—based on the cost and extent of your education and your work experience—may differ considerably from what employers are willing to offer you in the real world. Also, keep in mind that salaries vary depending on the geographic area in which you live and the industry in which you are employed. Says Dudley V. I. Darling, a recruiter for the executive search firm Ward Howell Associates, "The pay scales of people from lower middle managers up through officers are usually pegged to the salary that the chief collects." In other words, middle managers are better paid in industries that are generous to their senior-level people. So when the business magazines publish their annual spring surveys of the salaries of America's business chieftains, pay attention.

Before you start working for any employer, you should find out as much as possible about the company's compensation policies and practices. Does the company have a formal salary review system? If so, what is the time interval between reviews? How flexible is the system? How much clout does your boss have when it comes to increasing the compensation of her/his staff?

If you do not already know this information about your present company, find out now. Generally, companies use four basic approaches in determining individual pay raises within an occupational classification: (1) the single-rate approach, (2) the automatic approach, (3) the informal approach, and (4) the merit approach. Frequently, a company combines elements of several of these approaches.

In factory jobs and in some lower-level clerical jobs, employees are paid according to a "single-rate" system. Because such jobs require little training and the standards of performance are fairly well prescribed, companies do not feel that singling out certain employees for merit increases is warranted.

The "automatic approach" is similar to the "single-rate approach." Jobs that fall into this category are routine, although they may require more training than the lower-level clerical jobs discussed above. Again, individual performance has no bearing on the increase. Employees are granted a fixed amount or percentage increase at regular intervals. Obviously, when this rigid system of pay increases is applied to jobs in which employee output can vary, it can have extremely deleterious consequences in terms of employee morale.

Small companies often adhere to the "informal approach." In short, bosses hand out raises and bonuses at their own discretion. Unless supervisors are extremely fair, this system—or lack of it—can be just as detrimental to employee morale as the two others we just described. On the other hand, if you follow the advice we are about to give you concerning how to conduct salary negotiations with your boss, you stand a better chance of winning under this very flexible, informal approach.

From an employee's point of view, the "merit pay approach" is obviously the most desirable. Here, raises are geared to the work accomplished. Usually, the company has a formal performance-appraisal system to help managers decide which of their subordinates deserve the highest raises. On the other hand, this system does not give managers carte blanche in handing out increases. More often than not, merit pay increases really mean increases granted within a certain pay range.

Personnel administrators agree that the frequency of raises depends on two factors: the level of an employee's job and the length of time the employee has worked for the organization. Employees in higher-level positions should undergo salary reviews *less* frequently than employees further down the ladder. Why? Because it takes longer to observe performance improvement in higher-level jobs. Length of employment is important because performance progress generally follows a learning curve. An employee tends to learn rapidly during her/his first months on the job, but then the rate of improvement usually slows down, and eventually levels off.

Keep all this in mind when structuring your case for a salary increase. Be familiar with company policy and don't ask for the impossible. However, do be aware that company *policy*—what is written down in the personnel manual—may differ from company *practice*. If your boss's immediate reaction is "What you are asking for is against company policy," be ready with several examples where company policy was waived. You will find out about such examples by establishing a network of contacts within the organization. A friend inside the personnel department is invaluable.

The last piece of homework concerns your boss's paycheck. A research study at Carnegie-Mellon University revealed that bosses adjust their staff's pay to coincide with the way they feel *they* are being treated financially. Expect very little sympathy—or generosity—from a high-performing boss who feels she/he is being shortchanged in her/his own paycheck. Her/his feeling, whether on a conscious or subconscious level, is: "If the company is going to be tight with me, I'm going to be tight with my staff."

**The Mechanics of Salary Negotiations**   Good timing is one of the keys to a successful salary interview. If possible, arrange to speak to your boss about an increase after you have scored a triumph. At such a time, your value to the company will be apparent and in the forefront of your boss's mind. It should be just as obvious to you that you *should not* arrange a salary discussion at a time when your boss is in a negative frame of mind, whether the reasons are business or personal.

Begin the meeting by telling your boss that you feel you deserve a raise at this time for a number of compelling reasons that you will outline. Those reasons may include any or all of the following:

- *A rise in the cost of living.*   Your argument is that the cost of living has gone up but your salary hasn't. Stop there. *Do not* cry poverty. *Do not* launch into a sob story about your sick mother or your little brother, Tiny Tim. It won't hurt if your boss knows about such problems either from you or other sources. But do not bring up these personal matters to justify a salary increase. To do so would be extremely unprofessional and make you look bad. You are not the only one with problems. Furthermore, do not say, "My husband agrees that I'm worth more money." The reply is likely to be, "If your husband thinks you're worth more money, then I advise you to work for your husband."

- *An outstanding attendance record.* This is an important consideration if you happen to be in a very visible position and complicated arrangements have to be made to cover for you every time you are out sick.

- *An outstanding on-time record.* Again, this is more important in some jobs than others.

- *An outstanding performance appraisal that has yet to be translated into dollars and cents.* A short discussion of your morale is in order here. Explain to your boss that two things motivate you to excel in your work: (1) a personal sense of accomplishment at the end of each day, and (2) a salary commensurate with your performance and experience level. Lately, you have been asking yourself, "Why am I working so hard when all I have to show for it is a pat on the back?" Stress that money is a great motivator to you—just in case there is any doubt in your boss's mind about that. There are still Neanderthal bosses around who believe that the only reason women work is to have some way to occupy themselves between nine and five each day while their husbands are out tracking down the big bacon.

If your performance appraisal is good, but points out several weaknesses, bring them up before your boss does. Make those weaknesses—and what you are doing to correct them—part of your argument for why you deserve more money. Point out any self-development plan you may have formulated and show your boss how this has improved your job performance.

If your company operates under a management-by-objectives system and you have met all or most of the objectives set out for you, that's what you should talk about during your meeting. If your company does not have such a system, then it is up to you to point out what you have done to help your company. Have you increased sales? Brought in new accounts? Instituted more efficient procedures in your department? Saved the company money? Earned the company praise from its clients? Have you taken on new responsibilities? Take the maximum amount of credit for any good things that have been happening in your department. Let your boss know that *you* know you are a valuable employee. Once your boss realizes that you know your worth in the marketplace, it will not take her/him long to figure out that you will also have the self-confidence to successfully sell your expertise elsewhere. In short, she/he had better take care of you financially or you will leave. Don't come right out and say so, however. Let your boss form her/his own conclusions.

When you get through stating the reasons why your boss should *want* to give you a raise, name a specific figure. Ask for a little more than you really think you deserve and be willing to negotiate down. Also, be willing to take your raise in nonmonetary form. For example, instead of getting a raise of $2,000 annually, consider an increase in your fringe benefits, a bonus in company stock, a longer vacation each year, a company car, or a larger expense account. If your boss seems sympathetic to your salary demands but sticks to the excuse that the company's profits are down, try to get her/him to agree—in writing—to give you a retroactive raise of a specific amount once the company's profits are back up. Name specific figures or your boss may "forget" your agreement even after earnings do improve.

In a middle-management or higher position, it is bad form to expect or to ask for a raise more than once a year. So try to get the full amount you want all at once. If you fail, then ask for another review in six months. You might say, "Mr. Jones, thank you for the raise, but as you know, it's considerably less than I requested. Since you feel the company can give me only an eight percent increase now, why don't we agree to review the matter again in six months?" What has your boss got to lose? At least it will get you off her/his back for a while, so she/he will probably say yes.

It is very likely that your boss will not have the final say in whether or not you do get your raise. She/he may have to sell the idea to a superior, so make this sales job as easy as possible. Summarize your case in a memo that you give to your boss at the close of your meeting. Attach to the memo any proof of your worth—for instance, congratulatory letters from clients, commendations from superiors, minutes of productive meetings, awards, or progress reports.

**How to React if the Answer Is No** Before you quit in a huff, ask yourself these questions:

- Is the reason for the rejection valid?

- Was careful deliberation given to my request before a decision was made?

- If I had made a more compelling case for myself, what is the likelihood that the answer would have been yes? (In other words, is the negative reaction my own fault?)

- Is my job satisfying in all other areas except salary?

- Do I really *need* a regular paycheck right now, even if I do wish it were more? (In short, can you afford to quit?)

If you answered these questions in the affirmative, calm down and stay put. Channel the negative energy you are feeling into a discreet job search. Don't let your boss or colleagues know you are looking, however. Should you eventually get a higher-paying job offer, either take it or use it as leverage to reopen negotiations concerning your less-than-adequate salary.

One final word of advice: If you do get your raise, by all means say thank you. A boss who has done battle for you deserves this courtesy.

# 5

# Tallying Up the Score: Your Personal Balance Sheet of Assets and Liabilities

In the previous chapter we described the various skills necessary to progress up the ladder into supervisory and management positions in an organization. Now it is time to find out which of those skills you already possess—and which ones you still need to develop.

There are various methods for evaluating your skills. You might, for example, use your company's performance-appraisal form, filling it in yourself. Eli Djeddah, a career counselor and author of the book *Moving Up*, suggests that you draw a line down the middle of a sheet of paper and on the left side, list all the functions that your employer expected you to perform as part of the job at the time you were

**146**

hired or promoted. On the right side, list all the functions, tasks, and procedures that were not necessarily part of the job when you took it, but are things you contributed on your own. Thus, the list on the right will indicate how you do the job *in practice* and the list on the left will indicate how it should be done *in theory*. The right-hand list will highlight your strengths—those special skills and talents you automatically bring to a job.

You can also review all your former jobs—or any of your achievements in the home or as a volunteer worker—in terms of the skills you used in each. The trick here is to attach the correct label to those skills. Perhaps you were a whiz at raising funds for a company charity, successfully lobbied to change a local ordinance, held an office in a volunteer organization, or helped your husband run his business. Translate such experiences into specific business skills. For instance, the ability to raise money demonstrates fund-raising and salesmanship skills. The ability to direct a team effort to accomplish a goal demonstrates problem-solving and communication skills. Serving as president of a volunteer organization shows leadership and management skills. Helping your husband may mean you acted as the office manager of a small business—taking phone orders, keeping the books, ordering supplies, processing sales reports, and acting as a general troubleshooter. In short, think in terms of the tasks you performed and the problems you solved.

Catalyst has designed a checklist to help you assess your present skills as well as your management skills potential. After reading each statement, put a check in the "yes" or "no" column on the right.

## How Do Your Management Skills Stack Up?

### Are You a Good Problem-Solver?

**1.** When asked to comment on business reports, proposals, and so on, I feel confi-

|  | Yes | No |
|---|---|---|
| dent about my analytical abilities—my ability to separate the major points from the secondary points, the facts from the opinions. | ☐ | ☐ |
| **2.** I am good at getting to the heart of a problem and dealing with that rather than just tackling its symptoms. | ☐ | ☐ |
| **3.** I know how to brainstorm solutions to a problem and can put aside any prejudices or preconceived notions I may have during this process. | ☐ | ☐ |
| **4.** I am creative when brainstorming, using the full power of my imagination as I formulate possible solutions. | ☐ | ☐ |
| **5.** When others are proposing solutions, I listen with an open mind and withhold criticism until I've heard everything the other person has to say. No matter how outrageous the idea seems, I consider it seriously before expressing any opinion. | ☐ | ☐ |
| **6.** I generally know how and where to go to research problems thoroughly. | ☐ | ☐ |
| **7.** I make sure I have done my homework on a problem before I attempt to decide which solution would be the best one. | ☐ | ☐ |
| **8.** In addition to considering the pros and cons of a solution, I take into account my "gut feeling" on a particular course of action. | ☐ | ☐ |
| **9.** When I am solving problems, I write myself notes, knowing I might forget important points if I rely solely on memory. | ☐ | ☐ |

## Are You a Good Decision-Maker?

|  | Yes | No |
|---|---|---|
| **10.** I don't rush into decisions. I consider all pertinent facts and opinions before making up my mind. | ☐ | ☐ |

Yes No

**11.** I come to a decision within a reasonable period of time. I don't put off decisions indefinitely, hoping that the problem will resolve itself without my input. ☐ ☐

**12.** I realize that indefinite procrastination—in short, not deciding—is in itself a decision, albeit a passive one. ☐ ☐

**13.** Once I make a decision, I am willing to accept responsibility for it.

## Are You a Good Planner?

**14.** In my daily activities, I am goal-oriented. In other words, I realize that all the seemingly disparate tasks I undertake have a common goal or objective, and I don't let the details of the tasks obscure that objective. ☐ ☐

**15.** I know how to break down long-range policy objectives into shorter-range goals. ☐ ☐

**16.** When assigned a short-range operational goal, I find out how that goal—in tandem with other short-range goals—will help the organization fulfill its long-range policy objectives. ☐ ☐

**17.** When I get bogged down in trivia, I stop and ask myself, "Is this necessary? What am I really trying to accomplish?" ☐ ☐

## Are You a Good Organizer?

**18.** When I am given an assignment, I stop to consider the various ways I could proceed. I analyze all alternatives before making a decision. ☐ ☐

**19.** I break down complicated projects into their component parts and perform each task in sequence. Big projects seem less overwhelming this way. ☐ ☐

|  | Yes | No |
|---|---|---|

**20.** If an assignment is complicated, I map out a detailed plan *on paper* before proceeding.  ☐ ☐

**21.** When working out a detailed plan, I always consider contingency measures should circumstances change at the last minute. That way, I am anticipating possible problems and obstacles.  ☐ ☐

## Are You Efficient?

**22.** At the beginning of most workdays, I formulate a list (either in my head or on paper) of the goals I want to accomplish by the end of the day and arrange them in order of their importance.  ☐ ☐

**23.** I know what time(s) of day my energy peaks and I save my most demanding tasks for those times.  ☐ ☐

**24.** I am very conscientious about meeting deadlines.  ☐ ☐

**25.** I allocate my time efficiently and am seldom guilty of wasting it.  ☐ ☐

**26.** I have learned not to be a perfectionist about small, unimportant details. Instead, I channel this conscientious streak into important visible projects that will earn me respect and recognition.  ☐ ☐

**27.** I feel time is precious and assert myself when I feel other people are wasting my time.  ☐ ☐

**28.** When I have spare time at work, I use it to learn more about important aspects of the business, information that will help me advance in my career.  ☐ ☐

**29.** I try to quit work at a high point, with a sense of accomplishment for that day.  ☐ ☐

**150**

Yes   No

**30.** I make it a point not to bring work home with me unless it's an emergency.   ☐  ☐

## Are You a Good Communicator?

**31.** I am a good listener and observer of others.   ☐  ☐

**32.** When trying to influence someone, I look at my proposition from the other person's point of view and discuss it in terms of how it will benefit her or him—*not* how it will benefit me.   ☐  ☐

**33.** I am aware of the nonverbal messages I emit (through gestures, facial expressions, and posture) and the effects these messages have on others.   ☐  ☐

**34.** Precision and clarity are always my primary goals in both my verbal and written communications.   ☐  ☐

**35.** I try to achieve a businesslike tone in my letters and memos without becoming pompous or resorting to jargon.   ☐  ☐

**36.** I keep my sentences and paragraphs—indeed, the whole letter, memo, or report—as short and concise as possible.   ☐  ☐

**37.** I make a conscious effort to use the active rather than the passive voice in my written communications.   ☐  ☐

**38.** I have evaluated my speech habits and tone of voice and I am making, or have made, an effort to improve them where necessary.   ☐  ☐

**39.** I realize that public-speaking skills are important and I have taken steps to educate myself in this area.   ☐  ☐

|  | Yes | No |
|---|---|---|
| **40.** If possible, I never leave a meeting without making a constructive contribution. | ☐ | ☐ |
| **41.** I resist the temptation to project myself as an authority on any subject during meetings or other group decision-making efforts, especially if the group is composed primarily of my peers. | ☐ | ☐ |
| **42.** I feel I have a good attitude about taking and giving constructive criticism. | ☐ | ☐ |
| **43.** I am articulate in explaining my point of view when introducing a new plan, policy, or system. | ☐ | ☐ |
| **44.** During unsettling altercations with colleagues, I keep my emotions in check. I focus on our common job objective rather than allowing myself to become rattled over highly charged words or discriminatory remarks. | ☐ | ☐ |

The following statements focus on management skills. Unless you have already attained a supervisory or middle-management post, you won't know how you would react in the situations described. However, try to envision yourself in a supervisory/management job and fill in the checklist. Put a check mark in the appropriate column based on how you think you would react.

## Are You a Good Delegator?

| | | |
|---|---|---|
| **45.** I work about the same number of hours as my staff. My work week is about average for people doing my job. | ☐ | ☐ |
| **46.** My staff members know how to take initiative and don't bring petty problems to me for solutions. | ☐ | ☐ |
| **47.** I no longer feel the compulsion to keep my finger in every single thing that is going on in my department. | ☐ | ☐ |

**152**

| | Yes | No |
|---|---|---|

**48.** I have gotten over the feeling that "If I want something done right, I have to do it myself." ☐ ☐

**49.** I try to focus on the larger picture and don't allow myself to get bogged down in small details that my staff can handle. ☐ ☐

**50.** I consult my staff during the formative stage of a project so that they can contribute ideas and feel more like part of a team. ☐ ☐

**51.** When I return from vacations, I find work has progressed on schedule and any crises have been handled competently by my staff. ☐ ☐

## Are You an Effective Manager?

**52.** Once I have communicated my objectives to my staff, I stand firm in seeing that those objectives are met. ☐ ☐

**53.** When assigning a project to someone, I tell her/him at what specific point(s) I want progress reports. ☐ ☐

**54.** I try to inspire my staff members to do their best by being optimistic and supportive and by encouraging them to demonstrate initiative. ☐ ☐

**55.** I realize that routine work day after day is demoralizing, so I provide opportunities for staff members to have a variety of experiences designed to challenge their capabilities, broaden their knowledge, and sharpen their skills. ☐ ☐

**56.** I am constantly grooming my staff members for more responsibility, recommending them for promotions when I feel they are ready. ☐ ☐

**153**

|  | Yes | No |
|---|---|---|
| **57.** I demonstrate a genuine concern for my staff members. I balance their individual needs against the collective needs of the organization. | ☐ | ☐ |
| **58.** I encourage teamwork and try to create an open, creative work environment. | ☐ | ☐ |
| **59.** I have the respect of my staff. | ☐ | ☐ |
| **60.** I relate well to my colleagues at all levels within the organization. | ☐ | ☐ |
| **61.** I listen with an open mind to feedback from both superiors and other staff members about my managerial shortcomings. | ☐ | ☐ |

## Assessment Centers: What Are They?

☐ ☐ ☐ ☐

If you work for a large and progressive company, your boss may one day inform you that you are scheduled to attend the firm's assessment center for several days in the near future. Should this happen, do not panic. Actually, it's a good sign. It indicates that your superiors think you may have management potential and want to find out for sure.

Assessment centers are just what the name implies. At assessment centers, small groups of employees are put through a series of exercises that simulate the kinds of situations managers face daily. Most assessment centers use six exercises devised by Douglas Bray, an industrial psychologist who pioneered the concept when he was hired by AT&T in 1956 to evaluate the management potential of 422 telephone company employees. Bray's exercises test for such employee skills as problem-analysis ability, judgment, decisiveness, leadership, interpersonal sensitivity, initiative, and organizational planning ability. As used in the Bell System, the results of the assessment indicate management potential, although people are not necessarily promoted

**Yes    No**

**62.** I have a questioning attitude. I keep abreast of developments in my field and industry, as well as of events in general. I believe that the well-rounded manager is the best manager.

☐      ☐

**Scoring**   How do your skills add up?

Every check in the "yes" column represents a skill you have mastered. Every check in the "no" column represents a skill you need to develop.

If you have a limited amount of money to spend on education, chapter 6 ("Skills Attainment via the Do-It-Yourself Plan") will tell you what you can do on your own to strengthen weak skills or develop new ones.

---

because of a good assessment. The results merely become part of an employee's permanent personnel record to be considered in conjunction with other more conventional evaluation methods, such as on-the-job performance and personal appraisal.

A typical assessment exercise calls for the candidate to tackle a full in-basket. It might contain interoffice memos, letters from clients, a union contract, and the rough draft of a story for the company newsletter. The candidate may spend several hours reading and analyzing the contents of the in-basket before taking any action. The decisions that the candidate makes and the subsequent action taken will reveal a lot about her/his ability to set priorities, solve problems, make judgments, and delegate authority.

By 1979, about 2,000 companies and government agencies were routinely putting selected employees through assessment centers in an effort to identify managerial talent among rank-and-file employees. Today, assessment centers are growing in popularity because they are one of the few personnel evaluation methods accepted by the Equal Employment Opportunity Commission as fair and unbiased.

**155**

# 6

# Skills Attainment via the Do-It-Yourself Plan: How to Prepare for a Better Job on a Shoestring Budget

Don't expect to acquire by osmosis the business skills we discussed in the two preceding chapters. It will never happen that way. There is only one way to do it—through diligent effort.

Every career goal a woman sets for herself involves learning of one sort or another. Secretaries who have moved up to department heads, salesclerks who have become buyers, assembly-line workers who have become foremen—all advanced because they knew how to acquire vital knowledge and skills faster and better than the next person. If you examine closely the careers of upwardly mobile people, you will find that continuing education—often the informal, do-it-yourself variety—played a large part in their success. In short, there is no way to succeed in business without really studying.

But the kind of studying you do need not be of the onerous, textbook variety. If you are creative about it, you should be able to incorporate the process of learning new business skills into your daily life. By following the program we are about to describe, you can acquire a number of valuable skills without setting foot in a classroom—or spending the money for tuition that classroom study entails. Our program will cost you no more than the price of some reading material or the cost of transportation to and from your local library or lecture hall.

**Step #1: Form a Daily Reading Habit** As an aspiring businesswoman, you cannot afford to ignore the news. Not only do current events give you something to talk about at business luncheons and other business/social occasions, but current events may also determine if you have a job from one day to the next. Consider, for a moment, how much your company's well-being depends on outside events—technological changes in the marketplace, the fluctuations of the stock market, natural disasters, the peaks and valleys of the national economy, world business conditions, political changes. How can you afford to be uninformed?

Gloria Emerson, the ex-*New York Times* Vietnam War correspondent and National Book Award–winner, posed the same question in *Savvy* magazine (February 1980): "Too many women," she contends, "decide not to read the news in their newspapers or news magazines, claiming they are too busy . . . or because it is 'too depressing' . . . or because it makes their hands dirty . . . or because they don't know what to do about the things they learn which disturb them . . . or because they can't believe what they read. None of these are acceptable reasons. I don't quite understand why women, understandably eager to prove themselves in the world of work, find it too much trouble to have an opinion on, say, the Panama Canal Treaty or the Israeli settlements on the West Bank."

If you don't have the time to read your local newspaper thoroughly every day, at least buy one and scan it. Reading the headlines and the first few paragraphs of the major news stories is better than not reading the newspaper at all.

The *Wall Street Journal* is another invaluable source of information. Any woman who is serious about her career should also read cover-to-cover the trade or professional journals in her field as well as several of the following periodicals: *Fortune* and *Business Week* for general-interest business news; *Forbes*, *Barron's*, or *Financial World* for investor, stock-market-oriented news; the *Harvard Business Review* for a more in-depth picture of what's happening in the business world; and *Time*, *Newsweek*, or *U.S. News and World Report* for every type and variety of current events.

In addition to absorbing information from published sources, you should also read attentively your incoming mail, company financial statements, annual reports, and contracts—anything that will expand your knowledge of your own company and improve your job performance. If you don't understand something, such as a technical term or an accounting procedure, go to the source and ask to have it explained. Asking questions is the only way to learn.

**Step #2: Research Your Specific Problem Areas** You know you waste a lot of time every day and you are not systematic in your approach to a project. Your boss knows it also and has reprimanded you about it on a number of occasions. What can you do to improve? You can go to the library or a bookstore and secure appropriate reading material.

"All my life when I did not know how," writes Dr. Joyce Brothers in her book *How to Get Whatever You Want Out of Life*, "I have looked for a book that told me how. A how-to book can make all the difference." But passively reading through every how-to book that exists is not quite enough. The analytical skills you bring to the book are what count. It is your ability to "absorb the information the book contains and make those facts, those insights, yours. If you know how to absorb information, you can do just about everything—start your own business, build a happy marriage, even shingle a roof."

Even Bobby Morse, portraying the hero in the Broadway musical *How to Succeed in Business Without Really Trying*, didn't move up by his wits alone. He made it from the mail room into the executive suite with a how-to book clutched in his fist.

When it comes to crash learning, Dr. Brothers may just be the all-time expert. Back in the 1950s when "The $64,000 Question" was one of the most popular programs on television, Dr. Brothers and her husband had a newborn baby, fledgling careers in the fields of psychology and medicine respectively, and very little money. In addition, Dr. Brothers had an image problem. An attractive blonde, she did not look the part of the serious psychologist. Her appearance and her profession were incongruous to many people. After mulling over all her problems, she finally hit on a novel solution: become a contestant on "The $64,000 Question." But to get on the show, she had to invent an exotic area of expertise. She chose boxing. She was asked to appear on the show.

To bone up on her supposed area of expertise, Dr. Brothers, coached by her husband, studied around the clock. She even borrowed films of the great fights of the century and ran them at home while her husband shot questions at her. The crash course in boxing paid off. Not only did she win "The $64,000 Question," but overnight she became a television celebrity. The short, attractive blonde psychologist who was having a hard time being taken seriously in her profession suddenly didn't have to worry about that anymore. She was taken seriously by a TV audience and she's practiced her profession in front of television cameras ever since.

Dr. Brothers has dubbed her cramming method the "Five-Step Learning Technique." She advises would-be students to first accumulate all the research pertaining to the subject about which they want to learn. Then they should sit down at a desk in a cool, quiet room, preferably at the time of day when their energy is at its peak. Next they should . . .

1. *Get an overview of the subject by skimming all the information they've gathered.* The objective here is to estimate how long it is going to take to absorb the material and how to go

about it. If you decide it's going to take a week to mentally digest the material, look for seven logical breaking points and place the material in seven piles.

2. *At the beginning of each study session, divide that day's pile into three parts.* Plan to spend the majority of your allotted time on part two because the easiest learning takes place at the beginning of a study session and the second easiest learning comes at the end. The hardest-to-grasp material is what's sandwiched in between. Emphasize it.

3. *Read through the material in part one, trying to retain as much information as possible.*

4. *Close the book or cover up the material you just read.*

5. *Recite the major points in the material you just read.* Recite it out loud if there's no one else around, repeating it several times. This will reinforce the points in your mind.

Use the same method with parts two and three of the day's study session. And follow the same system in succeeding study sessions. Says Dr. Brothers, "If you are already relatively successful or think you are so close to attaining your goal that none of this information on how to learn applies to you, think again. Top executives never stop learning. Learning is a lifelong process."

**Step #3: Attend Lectures** During the nineteenth century, lectures were a major source of entertainment for the American populace. For a time, Mark Twain made his living on the lecture circuit, as did such visiting Englishmen as Charles Dickens and Oscar Wilde. Perhaps the most famous gathering place of all for lecturers was the annual summer educational/recreational rite known as the Chautauqua Assembly in the town bearing that name in southwestern New York State.

Lecturing is by no means a dead form. There is probably at least one lecture held every night of the week in your town. You just have to learn to seek them out. Museums, libraries, and other cultural institutions are often the sites of free lectures. The subjects can range from "African Art in the Fourth Century B.C." to

"How to Get a Job When You've Just Been Fired and the Economy Is Depressed." The lecturers are frequently people with ulterior motives. They are plugging their new book or a new product or service, for example. That's all right. Let them plug away as long as they are also teaching you something.

Find out where lectures are given in your town. There may be a section of the local newspaper where community events such as lectures are announced, or a community bulletin board that you can scan for such announcements. Local YWCAs and church and women's groups often sponsor lecture programs. Large corporations also put on free educational programs. These programs are usually heavily advertised, since the programs are intended as a public relations gesture and getting the company's name in print is part of the strategy. Merrill Lynch runs periodic lectures on "How to Invest," for instance; and Clairol sponsored a nationwide series of workshops called "Entering the Job Market: A Workshop for Women Over Thirty." Colleges and universities also often sponsor free or inexpensive lectures on a variety of topics.

If you belong to a club or trade or professional organization, you will probably be invited to monthly meetings featuring a speaker. If the topic is interesting to you, by all means attend. And take paper and pencil with you. Just because a talk isn't being given in a classroom setting doesn't mean you shouldn't take notes. If the information is pragmatic and will help you in some way, write it down.

### Step #4: To Hone Your Teamwork Skills, Become Active in a Civic or Professional Organization

If you have a job that requires very little interaction with other people, you may not be able to practice the crucial interpersonal skills that managers must possess. Since you won't gain these skills between nine and five weekdays, plan on acquiring them after business hours—at night or on weekends.

To do this, you may not have to leave your neighborhood, for the kind of organization you join is not as important as how active you become in that organization. Since your goal is to learn to manage and supervise people, it hardly matters if you are the chairwoman of the fund-raising committee for the street fair or of a local businesswomen's organization. You can learn to be an effective committee chairwoman—in short, learn how to delegate authority and get results without having everyone hate you by the time your mission is accomplished—in almost any group setting.

These are just four ways you can acquire specific information and skills without spending much money. By using your imagination you can probably think of more innovative ways to acquire knowledge on a shoestring budget.

In your quest for a continuing education, keep in mind a saying of Epictetus: "It is impossible for anyone to begin to learn what he thinks he already knows." So be humble and admit it when there is something you do not know.

# 7

# Formal Training: A Big-Ticket Item with No Built-in Guarantees

Formal education can be costly and time-consuming. Should you decide that going back to school is the best way for you to pick up the skills you need for advancement, make sure you've asked and answered the following questions first:

*Why am I returning to the classroom?* In *What Color Is Your Parachute?*, Richard Nelson Bolles claims there are five reasons why most people go back to school: (1) they want to acquire more knowledge about a subject, for intellectual rather than vocational reasons; (2) they want to pick up additional marketable skills to help them advance in their present field; (3) they want to change fields and acquire the requisite skills to do so; (4) they want to

**163**

stretch their mental capacity by undertaking an intellectually rigorous course of study; and (5) they want a break from the world of work. Before you matriculate anywhere, make sure you are clear about your goals.

*What school will provide me with the best training and/or credentials?* Schools vary markedly in the quality of their educational programs and in the reputations they have among employers. This is particularly true of graduate business schools and law schools. Thus, a degree from a nonaccredited institution with a mediocre reputation may at the worst be a liability or a black mark on your résumé as well as a waste of time and money. Investigate schools thoroughly before you make a decision.

*How am I going to finance my education?* While it is rare for an employer to help underwrite the costs of returning to school to finish up an undergraduate degree, many large corporations will send promising employees to short-term "management programs" and pay the full bill. Typically, such programs are offered by the country's prestigious graduate business schools (for example, Stanford, Harvard, Columbia, Simmons), and cost anywhere from $4,000 to $10,000 for a four- to thirteen-week course of study. In most cases, you don't suggest one of these programs to your employer. You have to be one of the company's rising stars to qualify and your employer comes to you with the idea.

Some companies also have tuition-reimbursement programs. The requirements for participation in these programs vary, but most companies specify that the courses an employee takes must be job-related. In addition, if the employee is taking the course for credit, she must complete it with a satisfactory grade. Some companies will underwrite the full tuition, while other companies will pay only a percentage of the tuition.

The directories listed at the end of this chapter may also give you ideas about sources of loans and scholarships to finance your education.

# Degrees and Their Market Value

□   □   □   □

Unfortunately, an undergraduate degree is no longer a mark of distinction guaranteeing the recipient special treatment in the job market. In fact, an undergraduate degree is now a basic requirement for mere *entry* into the job market. As a result, in today's competitive marketplace, many graduates with a BA in humanities are finding it difficult to compete with graduates holding technical or science degrees. Often they find themselves overqualified for clerical and blue-collar work and they lack the necessary training for the skilled trades.

What is the solution to this vocational quandary? If you are a college student who has yet to choose her major, your most marketable choice might be a technical or scientific discipline—math, accounting, engineering, or computer science, for instance. If you do choose to major in the liberal arts, it would be wise to include some business, accounting, or economics courses as electives or, better yet, as a minor. If you already have a BA in a subject like English literature or history, and feel completely stymied in your efforts to advance in your career, consider returning to graduate school—full-time or at night—to get a master's degree in a specific field. Select that field carefully, however, since even such promising fields as law and business administration are now becoming overcrowded.

In 1980, the College Placement Council reported that graduates with an MBA degree were offered salaries averaging $22,000. Recent liberal arts graduates with BA degrees were offered slightly less than $13,000.

In its May 1980 issue, *Money* magazine assessed the market for newly minted attorneys and MBAs and concluded that three factors have the most significant influence on hiring: the applicant's school, experience, and the geographic location of the potential employer. In both professions, the graduates of the top twenty or so schools got the most and the highest-paying offers, and graduates with previous work experience commanded even higher salaries.

For the working woman who doesn't want to interrupt her career to go back to school full-time, there is another option: life-experience credits offered by the off-campus branches of a select group of colleges. These schools allow students to claim up to two years' worth of class credits for experiences accumulated on the job, in their family lives, or through volunteer work. The credit-for-life-experience concept was pioneered by Brooklyn College in New York back in 1954, but only recently, with the influx of women into the work force, has the movement gained momentum. By 1979, life-experience programs had been adopted at more than 400 schools in the United States with upwards of 10,000 students participating.

Other options to consider are: nonresidence college degree programs such as the University Without Walls, where a student may carry out an independent study program under the aegis of about thirty colleges across the country; and external degree programs such as the Regents External Degree Program of the University of the State of New York, which enables the student to enroll and earn a college degree from the university regardless of where she/he lives. Programs like these generally grant credit based upon a combination of factors, such as examinations, independent study, conventional college courses, work internships, and field research.

Finally, you should also look into college credit by examination programs such as CLEP (College Level Examination Program). Administered by the College Entrance Examination Board in Princeton, New Jersey, CLEP tests a person's proficiency in college-level academic subjects. Appropriate credit is awarded to those whose scores are above a certain cutoff point. CLEP test scores are accepted in lieu of classroom attendance at about 1,500 colleges and universities. Other schools don't accept CLEP scores at all, or only translate them into credits for certain subjects. (For more information about CLEP and the participating schools write: College Board Publication Orders, Box 2815, Princeton, N.J. 08540.)

If you decide to participate in a nontraditional learning program, do keep in mind that credits earned in this way may not be transferable from one college to another. So plan to stay in the same program until you earn your degree. (For more information on nontraditional educational programs, consult the resource bibliography at the end of this chapter.)

You should be aware, however, that there is some controversy surrounding these nontraditional educational programs. On one side of the debate are people like John Sawhill, former president of New York University, who has charged that many schools are "approaching the territory of lifelong learning with standards, forethought, and a sense of dignity reminiscent of the California Gold Rush."

Norman H. Sam, the director of Lehigh University's Continuing Education School, adds: "There is a flimflam scheme going on in academia, a merchandising of meaningless credit, providing degree candidates with little new learning at exorbitant cost. It is a prostitution of American educational values to take tuition money without offering instruction in return."

Proponents of nontraditional programs claim such criticism typically emanates from the larger, established colleges that are concerned about the branch schools draining adult students from their more traditional, campus courses. They point out that their programs offer specially tailored courses given at flexible hours in convenient locations for working adults who need a degree for career advancement. Says Morris Keeton, the director of the Council for the Advancement of Experiential Learning in Columbia, Maryland, "There is nothing wrong with giving academic credit to people who have spent their lives in jobs or pastimes that have equipped them with a wealth of practical and important knowledge."

While degrees are certainly important for the aspiring career woman, don't overestimate what they can do for you. Mary Mericle, assistant professor of business at Duke University's graduate business school, believes that educational credentials are definitely more important for women than for men, but warns that too many women assume that their academic rewards will continue in the corporate world. "A college degree is almost essential for women, more so than for men. Unfortunately, I think there's a greater probability that a woman's job will underutilize her education. . . . The degree doesn't have that much to do with corporate success. A credential doesn't hurt; it always has some impact. But it won't help as much as women tend to think. It's not a magic key."

# Workshops and Seminars: Short-Term Confidence Builders

□     □     □     □

A workshop generally can be defined as a one-day crash course usually involving a relatively small group of people with a great deal of interaction between the workshop leader and the participants. A seminar is of similar format only longer—often three to five days. Workshops and seminars are used extensively these days by a number of professional training organizations to attract ambitious businessmen and women who feel in need of self-improvement.

Most short-term courses fall into one of two categories: personal development or professional skills development. Under personal development are such course offerings as: assertiveness training, dressing for success, corporate politics, and group career counseling. Typical skills development programs cover such subjects as: accounting for the nonfinancial executive, data processing for the manager, time management, organization theory, and supervisory skills for managers. Generally, personal development courses do not offer credit while the successful completion of a skills development course will yield a "certificate of participation." A skills development course can result in academic credit if you take a full semester course at a university or community college.

One other factor distinguishes most personal development from skills development courses: the gender of the participants. Because of the subject matter of personal development courses, women are the primary participants. Indeed, how could anyone design an effective how-to-dress-for-business course aimed at both men and women? Skills development courses, on the other hand, are seldom gender-typed.

If your company has a tuition-reimbursement program, it will probably pick up the tab for a skills development course. Personal development courses are another matter. You may be hard pressed to convince your boss that an assertiveness training program is truly relevant to your job. Thus, some salesmanship on your part may be in order.

Before you approach your superior for permission to attend a workshop or seminar under your company's tuition benefit plan, make sure you have checked out the course and the sponsoring institution thoroughly. Here are some do's and don'ts for choosing a seminar:

- *Do* check out the reputation of the school or organization. Continuing education programs are given by university extensions, community colleges, high school adult education programs, museums, professional and trade associations, YWCAs, and by private training companies such as Executive Enterprises Inc. and the American Management Association. The educational quality of these programs can range from exceptional to poor. Your company's training director or personnel manager would be an excellent person to ask for leads to the best programs. Also, ask friends or work colleagues who have participated in such programs for their recommendations.

- *Do* find out everything you can about the curriculum of any course you are considering. For example, is the description of the course in the sales brochure detailed and an accurate depiction of what you will learn? Was the course designed by the speaker, or is it an "off-the-shelf" program purchased from an educational design firm? Is the course material new or is it a rehash of ideas contained in the speaker's books? (If so, you can just read the books.)

- *Do* ascertain the format of the course ahead of time. Is it a lecture program before a large group? Or a small workshop with a lot of group interaction? Such questions will tell you how much personal attention you can expect.

- *Do* ask about the backgrounds of the participants who typically register for the course. What percentage are men and what percentage are women? For what companies or organizations do they work? What is their general level of proficiency or experience? If you are a newly promoted supervisor, consider how you'd feel if you found yourself in a course aimed at middle managers of Fortune 500 corporations.

- *Do* inquire about the background of the seminar leader. Never take a course when the leader is "to be announced." That indicates that the course will probably be patched together at the last minute. Make sure the teacher's credentials are relevant to the subject matter of the course. People involved with the subject on a day-to-day basis are your best bet. If the course leader is well known, make sure that person will conduct the whole course and not turn most of it over to her or his assistants. If possible, talk to the person conducting the course before you sign up.

- *Do* get an itemized list of exactly what expenses the fee covers. Does it cover tuition only? Or does it also include meals, travel, and hotel accommodations? What about books or any other necessary course materials? If you do have to purchase materials, are they available through the organization or school or will you have to purchase them independently?

- *Do* get the names of several people who have taken the course already. Call them and ask how they liked the program.

- *Don't* sign up for a course with a "hidden agenda." Such a course has one primary purpose—to sell you even more services. Say you take a course in assertiveness training given by a psychologist with a private practice. That psychologist may subtly design the course so that participants come away feeling as if some individual therapy is in order. And who is quick to offer her/his services? The psychologist, of course. In short, avoid courses that incorporate a sales pitch for further training or counseling.

- *Don't* sign up for wide-ranging, all-purpose programs that promise to teach you everything there is to know about a

**170**

broad subject in a short period of time. Don't expect to learn in one day all there is to know about being a manager, for instance. Covering a single aspect of a manager's job—delegating authority or conducting a performance appraisal—in one day is more realistic.

If you've followed the advice outlined above, you should be able to put together a persuasive memo explaining why you believe a particular course qualifies for your company's tuition-reimbursement program—and why that course is important enough to justify your missing anywhere from one to three days of work. Your case will be even more convincing if the course covers an area that was considered one of your weaknesses during your last performance appraisal.

If you are not granted formal permission to take the course, consider taking it anyway if it is given on a weekend or at night. You can deduct the costs from your income tax, assuming that the course or courses have a "direct and proximate" relationship to your job. Do not try to stretch that relationship too far, however. In 1980, the Tax Court ruled on one such case: A lawyer tried to deduct $1,822 for the expenses (parking, gas, books, tuition) of attending an English literature course at Georgetown University. He argued that the course—which covered Blake, Keats, Coleridge, and other Victorian writers—was necessary to improve his writing, speaking, and analytical skills. The Tax Court disagreed: "We are unwilling to declare that the study of English literature in its best forms—prose, poetry or drama—bears the sort of proximate relationship to the improvement of an appellate attorney's legal skills to justify the deduction."

## Corporate Educational Offerings

☐ ☐ ☐ ☐ If your request to attend an outside training seminar under your employer's tuition-reimbursement program has been denied, make sure it isn't because your company offers a similar seminar to its employees, free of charge, as part of its internal training program. If this is the case, ask to attend the company-sponsored program instead.

Internal training has become big business. In 1978 alone, AT&T spent $700 million on internal education programs, more than three times the annual budget of M.I.T. The Conference Board, a business research organization, estimates that U.S. corporations now employ more than 45,000 people to run internal training and education programs.

Strictly speaking, there is a difference between corporate *education* and *training*. The purpose of education is to develop in an individual the capacity for analyzing and solving problems. In contrast, the purpose of training is to develop very practical skills.

Corporate training is usually conducted on the company's premises and the courses are usually designed to teach employees either the skills they will need for promotion or the skills they need to help the company solve specific problems. At AT&T, for example, curriculum designers receive lengthy memos from line managers about their problems. Curriculum designers then formulate programs that help managers solve these problems. Of course, at a high-technology company like AT&T, training serves one other function: to teach workers how to handle the latest piece of sophisticated electronic equipment on the market. AT&T trainers claim engineering and science courses at universities tend to be several years behind industry in incorporating into their curricula the material that telephone company technicians need to know to do their jobs.

On the other hand, universities are often active participants in these corporate training programs. Corporate training directors often retain university professors as consultants or as guest lecturers. Companies have also been known to contract with nearby universities and colleges to design as well as teach a series of corporate programs.

If your company has a training department, find out what courses are offered and the requirements for participation.

# The Nine Most Frequently Asked Questions About MBA Degrees

☐ ☐ ☐ ☐

For most ambitious women, the mere mention of masters in business administration degrees stimulates an immediate barrage of questions. Following are some of the most commonly asked questions:

1. *What are the advantages of getting an MBA?* A business school degree can bestow upon you the four corporate Cs: confidence, credibility, credentials, and camaraderie. The successful completion of a difficult graduate program can add tangibly to your sense of professionalism and skills confidence. The MBA can also add to your credibility as good management material; people willing to undergo the rigors of graduate business school programs are generally viewed as individuals with a serious career commitment. Your credentials will get a boost as you sharpen previously acquired skills and develop new analytical and problem-solving skills. Finally, learning to participate in classroom team study is a good foundation for the requisite teamwork of the corporate environment. In short, the MBA certifies that you've acquired an invaluable set of skills.

2. *Are there any limitations that accompany an MBA?* Although increased salary is one reason for getting an MBA, some aspiring women MBA candidates may be in for a disappointment. In its October/November 1978 issue, *MBA* magazine published a comprehensive "1978 MBA Salary Survey" with data provided by 7,006 working MBAs. The survey revealed that while female MBAs under twenty-six years old were offered approximately $1,000 more in starting salary than their white male counterparts, the males surpassed them in pay after only a few years on the job—and usually stayed ahead in the salary race from then on. The fact that male MBAs pull in higher salaries than fe-

males has been documented in a number of other studies as well. Anne Harlan, an assistant professor of organizational behavior at the Harvard Business School, has studied this phenomenon among Harvard graduates and gives this as the reason: More of Harvard's male graduates pursue jobs with line responsibility, particularly with manufacturing firms. The women graduates are more likely to accept staff jobs, in research or consulting, for example.

MBAs encounter other disappointments. Not all business school graduates get job offers, even if they've attended one of the better schools. If an individual cannot add to her/his educational credentials by presenting a credible business "image" during employment interviews, the job offers just will not be made.

Other reasons why some MBAs are hard to place include: (a) they are too arrogant and play the I'm-the-cream-of-the-crop-so-woo-me game with recruiters; (b) they appear unfocused in their career goals; or (c) they are considered "too old" (forty plus) to give large "training ground" companies the proper return on their investment.

3. *Are undergraduates with nonbusiness or nonquantitative majors at a disadvantage in an MBA program?* Various studies of business school students' performance indicate that an undergraduate business major does not earn any higher grades than, say, an undergraduate English major. The significant factor in predicting grades is whether the student is bright and conscientious. In short, a good student is a good student regardless of her undergraduate background.

4. *Is it better to pursue an MBA immediately after graduating from college or is it better to work a few years first?* In a 1974 *MBA* magazine article, "Experience vs. Innocence: Who Makes the Better Student?," a survey of twenty business school deans revealed that a graduate business school's preference for one type of student over the other depends chiefly on the school's curriculum.

Those schools which teach by the case method—having the students solve broad-based, real-life corporate problems from a teamwork approach—believe their method demands a high proportion of experienced students, with a median age of twenty-five to twenty-six. "It's awfully hard to have a good case discussion if everyone in the class is about the same age and has the same intellectual, emotional, and financial experience," says Lawrence E. Fouraker, former dean of the Harvard Business School, which pioneered the case-study method. "On the other hand, if you tried to lecture to some of our students who have first-hand knowledge of the business world, they would simply tune you out."

In contrast, quantitatively oriented schools—schools that rely heavily on an analytic, problem-solving approach in their teaching methods—are perfectly happy to accept bright "greenhorns." "No, I do not think that the world of work is better preparation for graduate study than the world of intellectual activity," says Jeff Metcalf, former dean of students at the University of Chicago Graduate School of Business. "After all, whoever heard of telling a guy who wanted to go to medical school that he ought to work as an assistant in a mortuary for a few years first? Or a prospective lawyer that he should work for two years as a police reporter before going to law school? Why should business school students be any different?"

The deans at the business schools with a mixed curriculum—part case-study method, part textbook and lecture method—tend to dispute the conventional wisdom that the case method needs experienced students to be effective. Thus, these schools usually have close to a fifty-fifty ratio of experienced students to recent college graduates.

All the business school deans agreed, however, that graduating MBAs with previous work experience command higher salaries than their inexperienced counterparts. On the other hand, studies have also shown that five to seven years after graduation, there is no difference in the level of responsibility and salaries of students who had had previous work experience and those who had not.

5. *How important is it to get your MBA from one of the country's prestigious business schools?* Very important. The proliferation of new MBA programs and of new degree holders in the 1970s has tended to lessen the degree's value and caused forecasters to predict a glut on the market by 1983. The number of people awarded MBAs has risen from 4,643 per year in 1960 to over 54,000 per year by 1981. Today, there are about 670 different schools awarding MBAs, of which only 217—about 32 percent— are accredited by the American Assembly of Collegiate Schools of Business (AACSB). To make matters worse, many Fortune 500 employers will not even recruit at the "second-tier" schools.

Which are the top-ranked schools? The Cartter Report, prepared as part of a research study commissioned by the California Board of Regents, lists the following "top ten" private and public business schools:

**Private**

Stanford University
Harvard University
Massachusetts Institute of
  Technology
University of Chicago
Carnegie-Mellon University
University of Pennsylvania
Northwestern University
Cornell University
Columbia University
New York University

**Public**

University of California,
  Berkeley
University of California, Los
  Angeles
University of Washington
Purdue University
University of Michigan
Indiana University
University of Wisconsin
University of North Carolina
  at Chapel Hill
University of Texas
University of Illinois

6. *Does a part-time or night-school MBA carry as much weight as one earned in a full-time program?* It is the

prestige of the business school you attend, rather than the full- or part-time nature of your study, that makes the difference. A study done by Steven Langer, Ph.D., in 1976 revealed that the median incomes of MBAs who had gone to school full-time and those who had gone part-time were almost identical.

Today, there are twice as many MBA candidates studying for the degree on a part-time basis as there are full-time candidates. In 1971, the ratio was closer to fifty-fifty. One reason for the increasing popularity of night-school programs is that more and more employers are willing to subsidize employees' efforts to get their degrees.

There are disadvantages associated with these part-time programs, however. Many of the top business schools do not admit students on a part-time basis. Secondly, the two-year submersion method of study gives you a chance to form close friendships with America's future business leaders—contacts that can be invaluable throughout your career. Part-time programs make it harder to form such lasting ties.

7. *Is it important to have a strong specialty rather than trying to market yourself as a business generalist?* Business school placement officers claim that although company presidents may say they want MBAs who are generalists, the personnel directors who actually do the hiring want specialists. They counsel MBA candidates to take a large number of courses in their majors, so there can be no doubt about their specialties when it comes to graduation.

All business schools require their students to take a group of basic courses during the first semester. In succeeding semesters, students are encouraged to specialize. Different schools have strengths in different specialties. The most common majors are accounting, finance, banking/investments, economics, general management, computer science, marketing, and international finance. Beyond these broad categories, there are even narrower subspecialties such as taxation (usually under the aegis of the accounting department) and advertising (a division of marketing).

8. *What industries or companies are the biggest employers of MBAs?* Traditionally, banks have been the largest employers of MBAs, but in recent years other industries have started to recruit heavily. Today, the biggest recruiters are: banks and other financial institutions, management consulting firms, advertising agencies, retailers and other merchandising-oriented companies, real estate firms (excluding construction), petroleum and chemicals producers, publishing companies, and conglomerates. The nonprofit and public sectors of the economy also try to hire MBAs, but salaries are usually lower there.

9. *To advance in business, which is better—an MBA or law degree?* According to conventional business wisdom, a law degree was the best ticket into the executive suite. While it is true that many company presidents hold law degrees, currently more and more MBA degree holders are capturing the top spots in the corporate hierarchy. Although a law degree is still considered more prestigious than an MBA, it is no longer considered a better advancement tool for the person who aspires to climb the corporate ladder.

## For Additional Information

## Continuing Education Resources

*Bricker's International Directory of University Sponsored Executive Development Programs* by George W. Bricker and Samuel A. Pond.

*College Degrees for Adults* by Wayne Blaze and John Nero.

*College Learning Anytime, Anywhere* by Ewald B. Nyquist, Jack N. Arbolino, and Gene R. Hawes.

*Continuing Education: A Guide to Career Development Programs.*

*The Future of Adult Education* by Fred Harvey Harrington.

*Getting College Course Credits by Examination to Save $$$* by Gene R. Hawes.

*Guide to Career Education* by Muriel Lederer.

*Happier by Degrees: A College Reentry Guide for Women* by Pamela Mendelsohn.

*The Life Long Learner* by Ronald Gross.

*The MBA Degree* by G. D. Eppen et al.

*Weekend Education Source Book* by Wilbur Cross.

## Financial Aid Resources

*College Blue Book: Scholarships, Fellowships, Grants and Loans.*

**179**

*The Directory of Financial Aids for Women* by Gail Ann Schlachter.

*Educational Financial Aid Sources for Women.*

*Financial Aids for Higher Education: 1978–1979 Catalogue* by Oreon Keeslar.

*Guide to Graduate and Professional Study, 1977–79.*

*The Harvard Guide to Grants.*

*Scholarships, Fellowships and Loans* by S. Norman Feingold and Marie Feingold.

*A Woman's Guide to Career Preparation: Scholarships, Grants, and Loans* by Ann J. Jawin.

# 8

# What High Visibility Can Do for You

Margaret Hennig and Anne Jardim, co-authors of *The Managerial Woman*, claim that one of the perceptual handicaps holding women back in business is their failure to recognize the power of personal publicity. Compared to the average male executive, women don't promote themselves effectively and underestimate the importance of gaining the attention of influential superiors.

Hennig and Jardim cite the example of a businessman who wanted to speed up the issuance of a report because he saw that circumstances had changed and management was now receptive to the proposed project. However, his female co-worker balked at the revised time schedule because she

**181**

wanted ample time to make sure every detail in the report was letter perfect.

Moral: The woman was so involved in the minutiae of the task that she failed to see that her work, no matter how excellent, would have little impact at a later date. Her co-worker, on the other hand, knew how to seize an opportunity and capture maximum attention, both for himself and the proposed project.

## High Visibility Is Vital

☐ ☐ ☐ ☐ Is a perceptional handicap causing you to overlook opportunities? Do you think that merit always wins out in the end and that if you do your job well—and a good bit of everybody else's job in your department as well— your superiors couldn't possibly turn you down for a promotion? They could—especially if you've been excelling very quietly in your corner of the company and your superiors in the executive suite don't know you exist. Consider this scenario.

One of your company's vice-presidents has read about you in the in-house magazine. He's heard good things about you from others and he's filed you in his mind under the heading "up-and-comer." One day during a company social function, this vice-president says to your boss, "Why haven't you ever recommended that assistant of yours for a promotion? She strikes me as ambitious and she's certainly qualified enough. Or are you trying to keep a super assistant all to yourself?" Coming from a V.P., a gentle rebuke like this can be enough to make your boss think twice about rejecting your request for a promotion the next time a better position opens up. But how do you get top management's attention without being so obvious that you appear to be a scheming operator to your boss and co-workers?

You do it by promoting yourself just the same way publicists promote new products—not only through good word-of-mouth reviews, but also through written publicity in company newsletters, magazines, and local newspapers.

As one woman manager told us, "You have to be identified as the person who gets the job done. If you're behind the scenes, then the job gets done 'mysteriously.' Once you become known as the person who does that job well and is willing to do more and grow, then you pretty much have won that battle. Then *you* are sought out."

## Hire an Expert

☐ ☐ ☐ ☐ Now that we've established the importance of high visibility, you are probably asking yourself, "How do I go about accomplishing this goal?"

One way is to hire, secretly, a personal public relations consultant to work her or his "magic" on your behalf. From the outset, professional PR people hold several aces. They have extensive media contacts and writing ability. They can act as your advance staff and do your boasting for you while you stand back and smile modestly. And they can give you feedback on your appearance and demeanor and explain the best techniques for dealing with the press. They should also be able to keep you from displaying any symptoms of the dread "foot-in-mouth" disease that plagues so many inexperienced people when they get within earshot of a reporter.

However, public relations expertise is expensive. Although there is a small but growing industry of these personal marketing specialists, most gear their fees to the executive in the $50,000-plus salary category, placing their services out of reach of the average ambitious businesswoman. Their monthly retainers generally range from $500 to $3,000.

Of course, if you are a company's director of consumer affairs and you have some clout, you may be able to get your company to foot the bill on the premise that the company's reputation will be enhanced by having an articulate, personable spokeswoman specially trained to handle probing press questions. It is also a good defense should the harsh spotlight of public controversy be cast in your employer's direction.

Of course, from the corporate point of view, there are hidden disadvantages. A female director of consumer affairs who turns out to be another Bess Myerson will probably be spirited away by an executive recruiter in no time and the ambushed employer will be left with a gaping, high-level vacancy to fill and a whopping PR bill to pay. This is one reason why some company presidents expressly forbid their senior managers to seize the limelight. "Personal public relations is like mainlining dope for ambitious executives," says Thomas McCann, former vice-president in charge of PR for United Brands. "They can never get enough to be satisfied."

Besides possibly transforming you into an unbearable egomaniac, personal publicity has other risks. Public relations, like any sub-rosa service business, has its share of fast talkers. For three years, one particular roving PR man made a handsome living by conning gullible, publicity-mad American and Canadian business people who believed his claim that he could literally "buy" them publicity in respectable magazines. For $6,000 he would deliver a *Fortune* feature; for $1,000, a *People* profile; for $350, a *Business Week* item. In Los Angeles alone, thirty unfortunates paid him some $33,000 with the understanding that their money was going to pay off editors. It is the rare editor who takes bribes, so head for the nearest Better Business Bureau if you ever get this low-life pitch from a publicist.

Finally, beware of the brand of publicist derisively known as a flack, who has long beat the drum for show-biz personalities, and more recently for political aspirants. A flack's techniques—which include the staging of publicity stunts and the simulation of romances between clients and big-name flashbulb-popping celebrities—are far too flamboyant. Such antics could destroy a staid business pro's credibility. Remember, your goal is recognition, not notoriety; career advancement, not personal aggrandizement.

If you are a rising professional woman and want to hire a personal marketing advisor, your best bets are former corporate PR people and speech writers turned free-lance practitioners, or small public relations firms that handle dignified corporate-image accounts. Their contacts with the business, financial, and trade press will be first-rate and their services dependable.

## Do-It-Yourself PR

□　　□　　□　　□

Your other option is to quietly mount your own PR campaign. Before you do, however, take stock of yourself. As David Ogilvy, the advertising whiz, once pointed out: The quickest way to kill a mediocre product is to call attention to it. The slickest ad campaign in the world can't combat bad word-of-mouth reviews. Ask yourself, "Do I really have the basic intelligence, skills, and temperament for that dream job at the end of the rainbow?" Be honest with yourself, for there's no humiliation worse than a brash public failure.

On the other hand, you may, indeed, have all the raw materials for success in your field but suffer from the Uncut-Diamond Syndrome. In short, your assets have never been integrated into a salable commodity. You need packaging. Maybe your dress is inappropriate for the magnitude of the job or your speech lacks refinement. The advice contained in chapter 3 of this book is designed to help you eliminate these exterior red lights. Do so *before* you start seeking media exposure.

The following guidelines should help you launch your own low-key, surreptitious (that means even your best friends don't know) personal promotion campaign:

**Step 1: Cultivate Editors, Writers, and Radio-TV Reporters** For your purposes, the ideal media targets are newspapers, both in the community where you live and the city where you work; trade, professional, and civic organizations' publications; alumnae journals; company house organs; and local radio and TV news and talk shows. The people in decision-making jobs with these outlets are who you want to meet.

Ideally, try to meet journalists socially and keep your relationship on that level. If no such opportunities present themselves, think of an excuse to call and introduce yourself or invite an editor to lunch. Maybe you have just become head of a charity fundraising drive or the membership chairperson of the League of Women Voters. (Incidentally, in small towns, civic and service organizations are usually a good place to meet local media people.)

Once you have made the initial contact with a few journalists, don't have an ulterior motive every time you talk to them. If they call you for a favor—and to a reporter, a favor means information—tell them what you know and ask that your comments remain "off the record," if you think a mention in the story would be damaging. If not, by all means suggest, "You may quote me by name." Once you become one of a reporter's regular "sources," you are in a position to ask for a few favors of your own. But don't overdo it.

*Warning: Never* lie to journalists or give them the impression they are being used. One overly ambitious supervisor in a large advertising agency was so anxious to appear in her company's in-house magazine that she supplied the editor with a photo of her family gathered around the Christmas tree for a feature on the way employees celebrate the holidays. Of course, she failed to mention that she had been separated from her husband for six months. When the editor discovered the truth—just as the magazine was going to press—he had to work until midnight to make the necessary editorial changes and vowed to blackball the double-dealer from any future publicity.

### Step 2: Become Newsworthy, If You Aren't Already

No editor will give you exposure, no matter how many favors you have delivered, if you are not newsworthy. What is "newsworthy"? Roughly, anything that is first, best, worst, a breakthrough, unusual, offbeat, amusing, timely, or of special interest to the audience. That last point is key—reader or viewer interest. The readers of the *Journal of Accountancy* do not expect to read about a person who developed a new method for refining oil. Nor do the readers of the *Oil & Gas Journal* expect to see an article about a change in GAAP (generally accepted account principles) in their publication. In short, "news" has as many definitions as there are audiences.

This is where a pro has the edge over you. A good PR expert, like a journalist, instinctively knows what constitutes a compelling story. Most amateurs, however, mistakenly assume anything *they* find fascinating has universal appeal. (Unfortunately, the thing they find most fascinating is often themselves!)

Here are a few characteristics that might qualify you as newsworthy:

- You have an offbeat job or hobby.

- You are a recognized authority on a subject.

- You have done something highly unusual: for instance, you were one of the first U.S. citizens to visit Red China; or you and your husband built a southwestern, Spanish-style hacienda in the middle of a development of split-level homes in Maine; or you started a women's "network" within your company or industry long before it became the "in" thing to do.

- You have won a contest or prestigious award. In publicity terms, you've hit the jackpot if you can capture a statewide or national award, particularly one in your field. On the other hand, if you have won your country club's tennis tournament, expect top billing in the club newsletter, nothing more.

- You witnessed or participated in an important event. You will probably be one step ahead in the "interesting" category if you accidentally tripped a bank robber making his getaway and saved the day!

- You can link yourself with a major celebrity. Suppose you hosted a party for a well-known actress or had the governor of your state as a houseguest. Get photos! "Running with powerful people, social people, and important people is a way to get visibility for yourself," says advertising ace Jane Trahey.

Let good taste be your guide when selecting those aspects of your life that you want publicized. It may indeed be newsworthy that you accepted a dare on the Fourth of July and scrambled up the fifty-foot flagpole at the end of your block. But do you really want to see a photograph of yourself, perched up there, on the front page of your local newspaper?

**Step 3: Prepare Appropriate "Sales Promotion" Materials** As a general rule, reporters are overworked and they are most appreciative if you can make their job easier by having handouts available. This is why new products are always introduced with press kits jammed with press releases and glossy photographs. It is also one way to make sure the information that gets into print is accurate and what you wanted.

Unfortunately, you are not a PR person, so you can't prepare a formal press release about yourself and send it around to the media without causing considerable negative comment. Tipping your hand and making it obvious you want coverage is the surest way *not* to get it.

What you can have ready for an inquiring reporter—*when he or she approaches you*—are:

- a one-page biography (an up-to-date résumé will do);
- reprints of any significant publicity you have already received;
- copies of any important speeches you have given;
- a formal head shot;
- a selection of 35mm *black-and-white* candid, human-interest photos that capture you at your newsworthy best.

Keep in mind that a good photo with a snappy caption can stand by itself as a newsworthy item. Also remember that editors *like* action shots and *dislike* stiff, smiling-at-the-camera portraits except to accompany straightforward announcements. "Candid" means you are caught up in what you are doing—welcoming a visiting dignitary, accepting an important award, recruiting for your employer at your alma mater, gesturing forcefully during a speech—and not in the fact that you are having your picture taken. And remember to dress appropriately for the particular situation.

**Step 4: If You Can Write or Have a Knack for Smelling Out News, Get Your By-line in Print** Be realistic about your talent, however. The ability to compose business memos is not the same thing as a flair for journalistic prose. If you have talent, there are various possibilities. If your company's house organ editor appoints employees as field reporters or assistant editors to cover a specific topic or "beat," take the assignment. It will heighten your visibility—you will be circulating among your colleagues to gather news—and increase your control over what is printed. Remember, personal publicity is not your only goal. Favorable publicity about the department you supervise is just as good.

Your community newspaper is another outlet. The editor might welcome a column written by an "expert" provided it is entertaining and informative. For instance, a corporation lawyer might write a "Legal Briefs" column, answering readers' questions about their legal problems.

Writing a column in your industry's trade paper is even more effective because it gives you exposure among your peers. For three years, Jane Trahey penned a column in *Advertising Age*, the bible of that industry. Trahey says, "I was able to get an enormous amount of recognition in the advertising field as an expert because the best trade paper in the industry was using my material."

Finally, exploit any opportunities to get your by-lined technical articles published in the trade journals. Another good bet is to publicize any original research, such as a master's degree thesis on a hot topic in your field. If you cannot write well, all is not lost, since most large companies will do everything possible to help you achieve this goal, including provide you with a professional ghost-writer (many PR departments have them on staff). Why? Because it reflects well on a company if it employs industry spokespeople. And such articles can grace you with the imprimatur of an authority.

**Step 5: Give Speeches** Sure the idea scares you to death. It also strikes terror in the hearts of millions of other Americans. When *The Book of Lists* identified the "Fourteen Worst Human Fears," "Speaking before a group" came out number one, ahead of sickness, death, financial problems, and flying.

Carl Terzian, the Los Angeles–based personal marketing consultant, claims that "the career of more than one business leader has been enriched, or even substantially altered, by her performance at the podium." Besides giving you the chance to establish authority and credibility, he believes public speaking helps you gain self-confidence and poise—two important assets for anyone who wants to get ahead.

In addition, public speaking helps you build what Terzian refers to as "inside and outside visibility." To gain greater exposure *within* your company, speak up at meetings, ask questions at conferences, spearhead discussions at staff workshops, and host customer-relations seminars. To gain greater exposure *outside* your company, get a list of local organizations and offer to address them on a catchy topic pertaining to your field. The Kiwanis, Rotary, Lions, Federated Women's Club, and Optimists are always looking for speakers. Approach the program chairperson with a cover letter, photo of you, bio sheet, and suggested introduction.

Public-speaking skills can be acquired; it pays to read a few books on the subject or take a speaking course before you venture forth. You will improve with practice and may even find that you enjoy it.

Once you have your act together and have boosted your confidence level, go after more prestigious speaking engagements. Shoot for keynote speaker at your industry's convention or luncheon speaker before a nationally recognized association or well-known club, for example. Remember, the bigger the soapbox, the greater the chance your talk will be publicized. Go in with a prepared text but have a boiled-down version available as a press handout. If the organization is publicity-conscious, its PR functionary will hawk your appearance with the press. In lieu of that, alert your company's PR staff to your activities.

### Step 6: Become an Active Member of Your Industry or Professional Association

This strategy is virtually guaranteed to move you up swiftly via the job-hopping route. In essence, it is the ticket, not necessarily to the top of your present company, but to the top of your field. If your peers know who you are, it is only a matter of time before the rest of the business world—including executive recruiters—will take notice.

For this to happen, you must become more than just another name on a long membership list. Accept an officership in your local chapter. Get mentioned in the industry newsletter. Attend the national conventions and trade shows and *circulate*. And by all means, join panel discussions and give those speeches!

At this point, you may be asking yourself, "Is all this work worth it?" That depends on the intensity of your ambition. Perhaps a more pertinent question is: "Is it all necessary?" There are always flukes—people who remain in the shadows and, by sheer luck, manage to get discovered. But these instances are rare. Power, position, and money accrue to those who learn how to exude power, position, and affluence—and who can get other people to accept this perception as reality.

### For Additional Reading

If you need further convincing, these books explain and outline the execution of a personal publicity program:

*Establish Yourself as an Authority* by Sol H. Marshall.

*How to Write a Book About Your Specialty* by Thomas F. Doyle, Jr.

*Your Personal Column Will Help You Win Recognition, Enhance Your Status and Influence in the Community and Your Profession* by J. B. Hunter.

*How To Advertise Yourself* by Maxwell Sackheim.

*How to Create Your Own Publicity for Names, Products or Services and Get It for Free!* by Steve Berman.

*How to Get Happily Published: A Complete and Candid Guide* by Judith Appelbaum and Nancy Evans.

*How to Handle Your Own Public Relations* by H. Gordon Lewis.

*How to Make News and Influence People* by Morgan Harris and Patti Karp.

*Publicity: How to Get It* by Richard O'Brien.

# 9

# Hitch a Ride on a Coattail!

Aside from merit, a path that men have traditionally followed in order to advance in business was to cultivate a mentor—a person who is older (hence the term "old boy"), wiser, in the same field, and willing to groom his "wards" for bigger and better things. Men have also relied heavily on their "old boy" contacts to tell them when and where jobs were opening up and what to do to get them.

Now, astute career women also are exploring the benefits of the buddy system and learning how it can work to *their* advantage as they attempt to scale the corporate heights. Ambitious working women are enlisting the aid of other women—and, in some cases, men—in two ways: by forming a one-to-one, selective relationship with a highly placed female executive who is willing to assume the role of "godmother" and lend a professional helping hand; and by banding together with their female peers in groups called "networks."

The first type of support system is vertical, a kind of mutual admiration society between two people at different hierarchical levels in the same organization. "Networking," on the other hand, involves a more broad-based, horizontal pattern of relationships that usually cuts across both company and industry lines.

## Making the Right Connection

☐　　☐　　☐　　☐　　How can a mentor further your career?

A well-intentioned sponsor, believing you merit advancement (and perhaps that you can be an asset to her or his career as well), facilitates your promotions. Besides advising you of openings you would never have heard about otherwise, she or he can: act as your personal publicist, praising you to those influential people higher up; advise you about career moves, for example, whether to make that lateral move from a staff job into sales; open your eyes to company politics and explain how you can be helped or hindered; and alert you to information, rumors, and just plain gossip making the rounds of the executive suite.

On a more elementary level, a patron might advise you about appropriate dress, when to speak up at meetings and what to say, whom to contradict and whom to agree with. She or he might even advise you on such personal matters as where to live and what friendships to make. After all, your life-style can affect your advancement, especially if entertaining clients is an integral part of your job.

The importance of close patron-protégé relationships to the success of male business leaders has been amply documented in sociological studies. Gerard R. Roche, president and chief executive officer of Heidrick and Struggles, Inc., an international management consulting firm, writes in the January–February 1979 issue of the *Harvard Business Review* that mentor relationships have become more prevalent in the last twenty years. While not every executive has had a mentor, mentor and protégé(e) relationships are fairly extensive in the business world, and executives who have had a sponsor "earn more money at a younger age, are better educated, are more likely to follow a career plan, and, in turn, sponsor more protégés than executives who have not had a mentor."

The majority of mentor relationships start when the protégé(e) is young—in her or his twenties or thirties; they are on the wane or over completely by the time a person reaches age forty. How do these relationships develop? Most patronage ties develop informally and naturally after the two parties have worked together for a while and gained each other's professional respect.

The ideal mentor adopts the role willingly without regard to the gender of the "ward." Talent is the only criterion. Such sponsors are usually exceptionally secure professionals, ambitious, willing to take risks, relatively young, and may see themselves as mavericks. They choose their protégé(e)s carefully and do not make a habit of singling out women. And if the sponsor is male, he will not try to take advantage of the relationship sexually.

It is more difficult for women than men to find mentors because of the scarcity of top-level female executives. Younger women who ally themselves with "the sisterhood" have not risen  to influential posts as yet, while older women who have are often subject to the "queen bee syndrome." A "queen bee" likes being the lone female in a male world and remains unmoved by feminist causes. After all, she reasons, if she could progress without benefit of equal employment opportunity legislation, why can't other women?

Not only do some female managers who have made it to the top shrink from helping their more lowly female counterparts, but also these dynamos actually often stand as negative role models. As one female observer put it, "The majority of the women who have gained entry to the men's club we call 'business' are still unique. Many are twice as talented as their male peers. They had to be to buck the opposition. They've got some special drive, talent, quirk, or neurosis that got them where they are and they've usually sacrificed their personal lives to do it. I don't think today's average, upwardly mobile, young career woman cares to emulate them in terms of type."

Because god*mothers* are in such short supply, many young women are forced to rely on god*fathers.* But sexual tensions, different interests and hobbies, and even jealous wives conspire to keep more of these male-female mentor relationships from developing. Meanwhile, ambitious young men are busy cultivating easy friendships with their superiors on the golf course, over drinks, or at sporting events.

Ironically, women need the psychological and tactical support of patrons more than men do. The average woman has not been inculcated with the same determination to succeed as her male colleagues, so she can be diverted from her career objectives more easily. But a mentor can change all that and encourage a woman to replace her small, timid steps with bold strides.

But don't be naïve. Whether male or female, mentors generally have very pragmatic reasons for playing Pygmalion to a subordinate's Galatea. It's an arduous task at best, and it's the rare patron who is interested in identifying talent merely for the sake of identifying talent. Mentors want to strengthen *your* career so you'll strengthen *theirs.*

For a woman manager, mentoring can have additional benefits. "Mentoring is both a proof of the executive woman's power and a means of impressing it upon others," observes Carol J. Beeman, performance analyst for the Chrysler Institute of Detroit. "Not only does the mentor role show that the woman is not a token, but it is also a way to secure her own future."

## How to Attract a Mentor

☐    ☐    ☐    ☐

Any superior in a position to influence your career within your company is a potential sponsor. However, the methods you use to locate one must be suited to the size and style of your organization.

In a large company, where superiors may not even know who you are, let alone what you can do, a patron is de rigueur. But be careful. An aggressive search for a mentor among male managers can easily be misconstrued and trigger a sexual rather than a professional response. In a smaller company, where colleagues are fully aware of one another's capabilities, a patron may not be necessary. If sponsorship is required—to break through a discriminatory roadblock, for instance—the close proximity of management to subordinates works in your favor. Here, in the more informal atmosphere of a smaller organization, a woman can more actively solicit aid without fear of misinterpretation.

Before you read any further, implant one idea firmly in your head: fairy godmothers—or fathers—don't materialize out of nowhere. Nor do they grant your fondest wishes with the easy stroke of a pen. If you want the Cinderella treatment, *you* have to be worth the effort and your *godparent* clearly has to realize some professional benefit from your advancement.

Generally, it is better to let a mentor think she or he has discovered you, although there are circumstances when the straightforward approach works best. The following suggestions are designed to help you locate and enlist the aid of a professional helpmate within your organization:

- *Publicize your goals.* Whether your goal is to rise quickly within your department or learn a new skill in another corner of the company, let people know. The day has not yet arrived when people automatically assume a woman wants to move ahead. They are more likely to assume that a woman wants a secure, routine job and to dismiss any extra effort on her part as normal, supportive female behavior. Women rarely get promotions they haven't asked for.

- *Excel.* Lobbying for a better job won't work if you aren't competent in the one you've got—even if you do dislike it and consider it demeaning. Playing politics is not a substitute for hard work and solid accomplishment. Remember, if your company is well managed, it is a meritocracy. However, if it is large with a rigid, hierarchical structure, watch out for the unscrupulous boss or co-worker who may attempt to take credit for your ideas. To guard against this . . .

- *Seek high visibility.* In a small company, a high profile is built into your job. In a large one, you must create it. Take on projects that will widen your circle of acquaintances and introduce you to important people both inside and outside the firm; a compliment from a client never hurt anyone's career. Where no such opportunities exist, make them. Organize a "network" of women in your industry or start a company fund drive or bowling league or arrange a theater outing with proceeds donated to a favorite charity. Another way to gain exposure is to . . .

- *Take risks.* Women are often weak in this area, but ambitious ones are learning that playing it safe is a surefire way to bring a career to a standstill. Security breeds more security. It will not win you kudos. So screw up your courage and maneuver yourself into a responsible position where you can make decisions. Your objective is to save the day. Accept the challenge of starting a new department, for example. Clean up the mess left by a predecessor. Experiment in a small, unstructured situation where people work as a team and jobs are not gender-typed. Once you have triumphed in one of these spots, become a heroine and . . .

- *Publicize your achievements.* Women have been raised to minimize their intellectual abilities, so, if necessary, force yourself to advertise your successes, preferably in print. Your company's house organ is a perfect vehicle.

  Linda Howes, who has progressed from saleswoman to sales manager in a small, worldwide corporation within two years, says: "It's hard for a woman to toot her own horn, but essential. If you keep quiet like a little mouse, they'll bury you. If you call attention to what you've accomplished and outline what you deserve as a reward, they label you 'pushy.' Since there's no way to win, a woman might as well err in a forward direction."

So sing your own praises until you've identified a patron. To know when you have, you must:

- *Read the signals correctly.* Contrary to your fantasies, a potential sponsor—who will probably be a man, consider-

**198**

ing the scarcity of executive-level women—will not just turn up one day wearing a lapel button with your name printed on it. In fact, the lucky candidate may not even realize he is assuming a mentor role. All he knows is he likes your work and has told you so. Silent admirers who can't manage a compliment are not mentor material! On the other hand, don't discount the person who thinks you're great and spreads the word to everyone—except *you*.

"When a patron appears, it's usually obvious," claims David King, director of Careers for Women, which specializes in training and placing women in sales jobs. "The potential mentor is the one who says, 'I like what you're doing. Keep up the good work!' "

However, King warns that a woman's actions at this point can make or break the relationship. "A woman who tries too hard to cultivate a male patron is creating a problem for herself. Every time a woman becomes too solicitous, she falls into the traditional female enchantress role. The guy will either get scared and disappear or zero in. He might figure, why not take advantage of the situation, since I probably won't be held responsible for the outcome anyway? So the horny devil decides to masquerade as casting director and see where that gets him. The worst thing a woman can do is sleep with a prospective patron. The second worst thing she can do is encourage him and then turn him down."

Once a patron has clearly demonstrated his *professional* interest in you:

- *Ask for guidance.* Think of your mentor as a guidance counselor. Let him help you formulate your career plans. Don't give him the impression that his only use is to implement them, however. With that attitude, he won't.

- *Be loyal.* Return your sponsor's favors. Be his press agent, corporate eavesdropper; give him feedback and cover for him when necessary. But . . .

- *Beware.* Since your prestige to a large extent depends on your patron's success, his fall from corporate grace will also reflect negatively on you. If you see a nose dive coming, self-interest demands that you bail out before the crash. Loyalty is one thing. Survival is quite another.

- *Be above reproach.* An overly chummy patron-protégée relationship is a joy to experience—and a target for gossip. It's not enough that *you* know you're innocent. A vicious rumor can destroy your chances for success in your organization. Jealous wives can be another problem. If you cultivate anyone, cultivate them. Turn them into allies, not enemies. Keep in mind that a sexual liaison may get you a fatter paycheck, extra days off, and a few trips. But it won't necessarily propel you skyward within your company.

Establishing a relationship with a mentor can be invaluable to your career. But keep sight of the fact that working your way up the corporate ladder depends as much on your own skill and accomplishments as it does on your mentor's influence. So heed our advice: *excel, take risks, publicize your achievements, learn to read the signals correctly, be loyal, and be above reproach!*

## Networking

☐ ☐ ☐ ☐ When women executives began to realize in recent years that clout is partially a function of the prestige of one's subordinates, the concept of networking sprouted roots. In short, you can't just hitch your own wagon. You've got to have some mule teams behind you as backup.

According to Brenda Broz Eddy, a Georgetown University professor and management specialist, there are six "support" needs we all have: intimacy, sharing, self-worth, assistance, guidance, and challenge. For women trying to advance in business, it is crucial that these last five needs be met. An emerging "old girl network" is doing just that.

The "old girl network"—or more accurately, the "new woman network"—takes up where the consciousness raising of the early 1970s left off. Instead of rehashing the abuses heaped on the female sex by selfish husbands, insensitive lovers, and discriminatory bosses, the women who congregate at networking meetings discuss more positive, career-oriented issues—how to deal with a sticky political situation in the office, how to find a good day-care center, how to get your boss to give you the title and money that match the job you are doing.

Although the individual groups that comprise this new female alliance may be highly structured with, in some cases, restrictive membership, the whole constellation of groups forms a very loose unorganized web of interconnections. Any woman affiliated with a working woman's group is generally assumed to be willing to help other women similarly inclined. Referrals are the name of the game. In effect, the network provides a way for women to multiply their contacts many times over. Where once a woman might have had only one close friend to consult for career advice, she now has hundreds of acquaintances located throughout the country and in many different industries and occupations.

Networking is a form of female bonding that didn't exist before. In the past, women seldom organized themselves into groups unless the purpose was strictly feminine—to provide for the needs of the poor or less fortunate (mothering role); to act as an auxiliary to men's civic and fraternal organizations (helpmate role); to increase their appeal to the opposite sex (seductress role).

Now women want money and power themselves and are taking their cues from the male of the species about how to get it. For women, lesson number one is: The whole is more powerful than its individual parts, to paraphrase an old cliché. In short, teamwork works. Men, who generally spend their formative years battling it out on baseball teams, hockey teams, and every other conceivable type of team, seem to know this instinctively. "To a boy, it doesn't matter whether the other eight players on his baseball team are his friends," a prominent sociologist remarked, "so long as they want to play ball and are reasonably good at it." Women, in contrast, are less willing to "play ball" with people they don't like personally. For a business professional, that attitude is counterproductive to say the least.

Team sports and military training teach men something else

that most women have had to learn the hard way—respect for authority. As anthropologist Lionel Tiger points out, women left to their own devices will generally organize themselves in a latticework pattern and interact with each other in a freewheeling fashion with little regard for the relative status of the other women. Men will organize themselves into a hierarchy, or pyramid, with each member of the group assigned a fairly clear-cut role. In this setup, those on the bottom seldom seek out those at the top for counsel, confining themselves instead to other men whose status more closely resembles their own. Since the structure of corporations, associations, and other business organizations is hierarchical, it makes sense that the average man understands the unwritten rules of business etiquette better than the average woman.

The existence of the "new woman network" does not mean, however, that a female vice-president with feminist leanings is, by definition, willing to join just any women's group to show her solidarity with "the cause," particularly if the group in question is composed primarily of secretaries and low-level supervisors trying desperately to boost themselves up to the next rung on the corporate ladder. A busy female executive, like her male counterpart, does not have excess time to waste in meetings that aren't going to advance her own career. Such a woman would probably be delighted to address a group of ambitious young women and give them the benefit of her hard-won wisdom. She might even single out several exceptionally gifted members and offer to meet with them informally to discuss their specific career problems. But you can hardly expect this woman to join the group at a peer level and attend meetings regularly.

For this reason, most women's groups are organized along either hierarchical or professional lines, although a few large corporations have internal women's networks whose meetings are open to any interested female employee, from file clerk through senior vice-president. More common, however, are extra-company groups that restrict their membership to middle- and/or top-management-ranked women.

Generally, the larger the city, the more elite the women's group. While the New Girl's Network of Winston-Salem, North

Carolina, welcomes almost any interested woman to its weekly meeting in the Salem College cafeteria, Philadelphia's Forum for Executive Women is open only to women who have management jobs paying at least $25,000 a year—or jobs that, in the club's view, are worth that figure. Furthermore, prospective members must undergo a selection process akin to a sorority rush, have three sponsors, and receive approval of a membership committee. If they surmount all those hurdles, they become eligible to join, for an annual membership fee of $50.

Women's professional dinner and luncheon clubs are now established enough that many employers are underwriting the dues, just as companies have historically done for men who belong to country clubs and exclusive luncheon groups.

Like businessmen's groups, the women's career clubs often have formal programs with invited speakers and panel discussions. But the real networking takes place during the cocktail hour, just as the real value of men's clubs lies in the opportunity for members to converse informally over cigars and brandy.

The value of both mentors and networks to striving young career women cannot be underestimated. Working together, these two types of support systems create a skyrocket effect and cannot fail to advance a woman faster than her less fortunate colleagues.

Dr. Judith Stiehm, a professor of political science at the University of Southern California, claims that "for a woman to get really incorporated in a company, as opposed to being merely hired, she definitely needs a sponsor. Then she needs colleagues who will recommend her, who understand the difference between normal rivalry and destructive competition. Beyond this there are tremendous dividends if you are known to be admired outside your company. This is where you get your 'legitimization,' and this is where horizontal networks of women across different professions and businesses can be so valuable."

But once a woman has a sponsor, is recommended by colleagues, gets some external legitimization, and begins to move up in an organization, the need for other women's help does not end. At this point, a woman needs boosters, according to Dr.

Stiehm, "Women following her who will act like a wedge, pushing her up so that they can occupy the ranks immediately be-
neath her."

The most successful male executives tend to be those who are
organizers of winning teams. And the same is true of successful
female managers.

## Case Histories: Women Who Have Advanced in Their Careers with the Help of Mentors

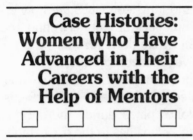

**Case History A**    Paula Brown is something of a
legend at AT&T. She's probably broken through more anti-
female job barriers faster than any woman in the company's history. Even before the giant public service company signed the
1973 consent decree pledging to reform its hiring and promotion policies for women, Paula had pushed and shoved her way
into such traditionally male preserves as the plant department, a
unit that maintains the huge electromechanical switching ma-
chine for long-distance calls. There she supervised three hundred
men and did it *without* being raped, as the man who helped her
get the job had "jokingly" predicted.

Yet that man was one of two whom Paula refers to as her
"sponsors," men who helped guide and promote her advancement. She maintains that her case is not unusual; behind every
successful woman at AT&T, there is a mentor. "You can't be
naïve politically and succeed in a company as large as this unless
you happen to fall into the affirmative-action numbers game.
And that will only take you so far."

Ms. Brown describes her "godfathers" as men "who were receptive to looking objectively at what I was accomplishing de-

spite the fact I am female." How did she get their attention? "By astounding them with such productivity that they didn't know what to make of it. It violated everything they'd been taught to believe that a woman should be doing."

One of her sponsors was her first boss, who hired her after she admitted her goal was to become an AT&T vice-president one day. "Why not president?" he had asked in a state of shock. "Because a woman won't be given that opportunity in my lifetime," she'd answered matter-of-factly.

Ms. Brown concedes her mentors bucked strong head winds to help her. Why did they bother? Because they, untypically, found her talent and ambition stimulating.

"The difference between my sponsors and the majority of men in the corporate world was not that they could identify 'male' qualities in me which would make me successful in business, but that they could accept them," she says. "Most men feel threatened and think: 'My god! Aggressiveness is one thing in a man, but I don't want to see it in a woman.' They immediately relate it to their wives and think, 'I don't want my wife to be like that. I might have to compete with her.'"

Eventually Paula Brown's patrons left the company and she experienced an immediate loss of power. "I knew why it was happening," she says, "but I couldn't believe it. It was so subliminal. I had a new boss who seemed to want me to fail."

Ms. Brown has continued to advance, but her halcyon days with sponsorship are over.

**Case History B** Barbara Massey came to the stock brokerage firm of Donaldson Lufkin & Jenrette fourteen years ago when it still had only seventy employees. In the intervening years, she got married, had a child, took a leave of absence, returned, was promoted to head of administrative services, and gradually grew dissatisfied.

"There I was—den mother to six hundred and fifty people. I suppose I should have been ecstatically happy. But the closer I got to serving all the needs of all the men in the firm, the less satisfying I found the whole experience. I kept asking myself,

'Why do I always have to be the cost center while they're the profit center?' "

She finally confided her feelings to her boss, who made a deal with her: he'd lay the groundwork for her to move elsewhere within the firm if she'd guarantee a smooth transition with her replacement. Thus, after conferences with various department heads—all arranged by her boss—Barbara eventually accepted a job as a retail sales trainee. She suspects the outcome would have been far different without her boss as advance man.

"If I had approached the head of retail sales directly, he probably would have said, 'Gee, Barbara, I'm sure you would be a great salesperson someday, but I am hiring guys who are already producing over five hundred thousand dollars in commissions per year and I just don't want to bother training a novice.' "

**Case History C**   The rigid hierarchical structure of large corporations can work against high-level executives extending a helping hand down into the ranks of middle management. And when it does happen, the sponsor-apprentice relationship is generally more tenuous—although it can still be helpful.

IBM programmer Jackie Hussey and her patron, a member of the top management team, met briefly once but have communicated via an intermediary ever since. In her case, the mentor-protégée relationship was sparked when the senior manager observed her conducting a class for the company's community-fund-drive volunteers. He was so impressed that he offered to help her advance within the organization.

Ms. Hussey is careful not to abuse the privilege, however, and does not complain to him at every turn. She knows his usefulness and has waited until the propitious moment to call for his assistance. She is currently bucking for a promotion and "going through the proper channels to get it. But if I don't get it within the time frame I've worked out, I'll get a message to him for help. There are rules to this game, and I try to abide by them."

# How to Infiltrate
# Your Local Network

☐  ☐  ☐  ☐

Since new groups of working women are emerging every day, the associations, clubs, and societies listed below are by no means the only ones available to those seeking to plug into the country's "new woman network" at the local level.

Don't be discouraged if you don't see on the list a group located in your area or specializing in your discipline. Instead, consult the most recent edition of the *Encyclopedia of Associations*, a staple in any public library, for a women's organization suited to your needs and level of achievement.

Because most women's organizations are structured along geographic, professional (functional), political, industry, or company lines, they have been grouped that way here.

## Local Women's Groups

Majority Money (New York)
Albany Women's Forum
Working on Working (Washington, D.C.)
Washington Women's Network
Women in Business in Washington
Advocates for Women (San Francisco)
Women's Lunch Group (Boston)
Women in Business, Inc. (Los Angeles)
Women's Forum (Denver and New York)
Forum for Executive Women (Philadelphia)
Executive Women's Council of Greater Pittsburgh
New Girls' Network of Winston-Salem, North Carolina

## Women's Professional Organizations (job function)

Society of Women Engineers
Financial Women's Association of New York

National Association of Women Deans, Administrators, and Counselors
Counterparts (corporate affirmative action officers)
Women's Bar Associations
Women in Wisconsin Apprenticeship (skilled trades)
Association of Women Business Owners
National Association of Black Professional Women
Women in Communications
Women's National Book Association

## Women's Political Groups

National Organization for Women (NOW)
Women's Political Caucus
Network for Economic Rights
Ad Hoc Coalition for Women's Appointments
Loose Umbrella Network Association (LUNA)

## Women's Industry Groups

Advertising Women of New York
Women's Media Group
American Association of University Women
American Women in Radio and Television, Inc.
National Association of Bank Women
Women in Construction
International Association of Personnel Women

## Women's Groups Within Companies

Alliance for Women (AT&T)
Networks (Equitable Life Assurance Society)

## Women's Information Clearinghouses

Catalyst, Inc. (New York)
Barnard College Women's Center (New York)

Women's Bureau—U.S. Department of Labor

Schlesinger Library on the History of Women in America (Radcliffe College)

Women's Action Alliance (New York)

YWCA Resource Center for Women (New York)

Women's History Library (Berkeley)

Higher Education Resource Services—HERS (Wellesley College)

Business and Professional Women's Foundation Library (Washington, D.C.)

Thomas F. Holgate Library, Afro-American Women's Collection (Bennett College, Greensboro, North Carolina)

## Some Views on the Importance of Mentors

☐   ☐   ☐   ☐

"Before my mentor appeared, I didn't realize the political implications of things I was saying or friends I might make."

—Evelyn Anderson, production manager with a Fortune 500 corporation

"Pick the people who can most strongly determine your success and stay in direct, personal, continuous touch with them."

—Richard R. Conarroe, President, Walden Public Relations

"The coach can be an intellectual mentor who helps you set the standard of professional performance, meet it, and set the next standard. Or [the coach can be] a cultural mentor who introduces you to the environment and provides a sort of interpretation."

—Lynn H. Cullum, faculty member, General Electric Management Development Institute, *Business Week*, October 23, 1978

"A mentor has to be secure enough to help a woman who may turn out to have more talent than he or she does. And he or she should be able to adapt to change. If a mentor has these two key elements, gender is unimportant."

—Natalie Lang, Vice-President, Booz, Allen & Hamilton

"Patrons, Rabbis, Mentors—Whatever You Call Them, Women Need Them, Too."

—*MBA* magazine article, February 1976

## Some Views on Networking

☐ ☐ ☐ ☐

"What constitutes an individual's network? Well, it is a combination of formal and informal clusterings of people and organizations, both personal and professional. Keep in mind, too, that one is always plugged into several networks of varying sizes at any given time.

"What is the purpose of networking? To extend one's range of contacts and connections, to exchange ideas and information, to trade names and resources, to provide oneself with support groups, and to share common concerns. The reverse is isolation, operating in a vacuum and missing out on information personally and professionally significant."

—Anita Lands, Director, East Coast Office, National Association of Bank Women, Inc.

"I would tend to view this whole network-building issue as a necessary phase in developing an identity for women in corporations. . . . However, as the pendulum begins to swing, I would not view a new girls' network as an end in itself. Once we have our own network and it's operating well for us, we all should begin working toward a 'human network,' where both men and women will share with each other for the good of the entire company."

—Nancy Wilson Nollen, faculty member, American University, "Women Together: It Works," *The NABW Journal*, July–August 1978

"I'm most comfortable getting information in situations where I can *trade*—which means I go to women. With men it's usually a *favor* for which you're supposed to feel grateful. Men are raised in a different environment, almost a different culture, where they learn to form alliances easily and naturally. That's fine—but the trouble is that I can't be a part of it. So I need parallel arrangements. Women must have trading networks of their own, and there's nothing sinister, implying the exclusion of men, in that."

—Virginia Carter, Vice-President, Tandem Productions, "The New Girl Network: A Power System for the Future," *New York* magazine, April 4, 1977

"In seeking professional positions, women know they can't just go to the personnel office. They need the kind of contacts men have."

—Martha Fleer, Director of Continuing Education, Salem College, "An 'Old Girl Network' Is Born," *Business Week*, November 20, 1978

"Networking is the next step after consciousness-raising. A lot of women have gone through that. Now many want to discuss careers rather than personal issues. A number are already on the road to the jobs they want, or the careers they have planned, but moving along is tough, which is why women need some kind of support system."

—Aline Novak, executive assistant and founder of a women's network at Equitable Life Assurance Society, "How Can Business Women Combat the 'Old Boy' Network?" *New York Daily News*, December 15, 1978

# 10

# The Lucky Break: How to Recognize It and Exploit It

Max Gunther, an authority on luck, defines the phenomenon as "events that influence your life and are seemingly beyond your control." For his book *The Luck Factor*, Gunther made an exhaustive study of the subject and came away absolutely convinced that lucky people aren't necessarily born that way. Lucky people share certain characteristics that anyone can learn. By the same token, chronic losers share certain traits that they could *un*learn if they set their minds to it.

John Gibson, another writer on the subject, concurs. He claims that luck is largely self-generated. "If you want to change your luck, change your attitude," he writes. "All psychological studies indicate that a person's 'luck,' the good or bad fortune which comes to him, is influenced to a very large extent by his state of mind."

In this chapter, we are going to break down the phenomenon of luck into its component parts. The following generalizations describe the most salient characteristics of so-called lucky people.

---

## Ten Things Lucky People Have in Common

☐　　☐　　☐　　☐

---

**Generalization #1: Lucky People Are Extroverts** Many ambitious career women would consider a telephone call out of the blue from an executive recruiter a stroke of luck. But is such a call really a matter of luck or the result of many people knowing you personally or having heard good reports about you from others? Recruiters themselves admit that the candidates they find are all people who, in some way or another, maintain high visibility in their fields. They join professional and trade associations and become active participants. They make sure they meet as many people as possible at work. They also have active social lives, possibly as members of several clubs. In short, they get to know a vast number of people, if not intimately, then at least on a casual first-name basis.

Says recruiter O. William Battalia of the firm Battalia, Lotz and Associates: "The majority of people I find have never given much thought to the possibility of being tapped by a recruiter. A lot of them are simply people who have somehow made themselves *known* to many other people, usually without thinking about it. It's their style. They are gregarious. They go out of their way to be friendly. They talk to strangers. They are joiners, meeters, greeters. If they sit next to somebody on an airplane, they start a conversation. The guy who sells them their morning newspaper is more than just a face. They know his name and how many kids he has and where he went on his vacation. This is the kind of person I can find."

Unfortunately, plenty of highly qualified people are never wooed by recruiters because they are introverts. They avoid meeting other people, thus never building the chains of relationships that make some form of pleasant surprise—concerning either one's business or social life—almost inevitable.

"There's always a feeling of frustration when we begin a search," Battalia claims. "There's always the feeling that hundreds of potential candidates are scattered around the country somewhere, but out of those hundreds we'll only find a fraction. In fact, it's more than a feeling, it's a certainty. Some very talented people just aren't visible."

### Generalization #2: Lucky People Have Magnetic Personalities

Being outgoing is not enough, however. You may want to mingle with other people, but if they don't want to mingle with you, you have a problem. Your personal chemistry may be turning other people off, rather than on.

Dr. Stephen Barrett, a psychiatrist based in Allentown, Pennsylvania, refers to this personal chemistry as a "communication field." He claims a positive communication field makes strangers want to initiate contact with you. "In general, people who are considered lucky—people who get lucky breaks handed to them by other people—are those whose communication field is inviting and comfortable."

Your communication field is made up of many elements: your voice, speech, choice of words, dress and grooming, body language, facial expressions, eye contact, poise, and manners, to list a few. If you have a negative communication field, you can do something about it. As discussed in previous chapters, recently a whole new industry of "image consultants" has appeared on the business scene, ready to give clients advice about everything from what to wear to what to say and how to say it.

Barbara Blaes, president and founder of Barbara Blaes & Associates, an image consulting firm in Washington, D.C., offers this advice about how to analyze your personal communication field; she calls it "An Exercise in Self-Discovery":

"This exercise relies heavily on visualization techniques. Pretend you are starring in an imaginary play. You are the only character. The play concerns the external aspects of your image—past and present.

"Figuratively speaking, I want you to step outside yourself and sit in the audience watching yourself. As the lights dim, keep your eyes on the stage. The play begins with a historical monologue tracing your image development. Listen carefully as you hear yourself discuss how you arrived at your present image. Laugh, cry, clap—whatever comes naturally.

"Next, take your play on the road and watch yourself perform in real-life situations for three days. Every day, step outside yourself and watch that other person cross the street, ask directions, accept a compliment, enter a room, chair a meeting. Listen to her on the telephone. Note how she communicates with her friends, colleagues, and her boss. Compare her voice with that of the female anchor women on the TV news. Typecast her. Is she the fresh outdoorsy type? Ultrasophisticated? Conservative and classic? Approachable and cute?

"When your play finally closes, write a review. Analyze the star. What are her strengths? What are her weaknesses?"

Blaes contends that a woman who does this exercise conscientiously for three days will come away with a good grasp of her personal style.

## Generalization #3: Lucky People Are in Touch with Their Feelings

According to Dr. Eugene Gendlin, a New York City psychologist, lucky people have developed an ability to "feel" their way through life. By trusting their gut feelings, they manage to make the right personal decisions most of the time.

In essence, Dr. Gendlin believes that at a subconscious level of awareness, most of us know the answers to our problems. But unless we are plugged into this subconscious well of knowledge, we will flounder and possibly make wrong decisions. While Dr. Gendlin calls probing this subsurface storehouse of data "focusing," other experts call it everything from "programming the subconscious" to "relying on intuition" and "hunching."

**Generalization #4: Lucky People Know the Difference Between a Hunch and a Hope**    Max Gunther defines a hunch as "a conclusion that is based on perfectly real data—on objective facts that have been accurately observed, efficiently stored, logically processed in your mind. The facts on which the hunch is based, however, are *facts you don't consciously know*. This is why a hunch comes with that peculiar feeling of almost-but-not-quite-knowing. It is something that you think you know, but you don't know how you know it."

A hope is something quite different. According to the *Random House Dictionary of the English Language*, a hope is "the feeling that what is desired is also possible, or that events may turn out for the best." Hopes are not based on facts. Hopes are composed of dreams, of illusions, of pleasant whimsy. There is no objective basis for assuming that a hope will come true.

Always distrust a hunch that corresponds with what you *want* to happen, rather than with what you rationally sense *might* happen. "A lot of bad hunches are just strong wishes in disguise," says Dr. Natalie Shainess, a New York psychiatrist.

To distinguish a hunch from a hope, ask yourself if this strong feeling you are experiencing stands on a solid base of homework. "You can trust a hunch only if you've had experience in the situation it deals with," says Dr. Shainess. "I often do intuitive things in treating patients, for instance. I trust these hunches because I've had long experience in the field. But if I had a hunch about some field I didn't know—let's say a hunch about making a killing in soybean futures—I wouldn't trust it. It couldn't be a true perception." In other words, don't fall back on supposed hunches to avoid doing your homework.

**Generalization #5: Lucky People Do Their Homework**    Lucky people are anything but lazy. They steep themselves in the subject at hand. Once they have gathered all the facts, they try to reach a decision based on consciously known data. When that fails—because there is a piece of the factual puzzle missing and they can't locate it—they rely on *rational* hunching.

Cautions Max Gunther, "Anytime you want to act on what you fondly think is a hunch, ask yourself earnestly whether you are merely inventing an excuse for avoiding honest study—or for avoiding people who might answer your questions."

### Generalization #6: Lucky People Recognize an Opportunity When It Comes Along

An opportunity is a favorable or advantageous set of circumstances that can be exploited to your, or somebody else's, benefit. Unfortunately, most opportunities do not come into view with a sign attached that reads OPPORTUNITY in bold print. It is up to you to be alert enough to recognize an opportunity for what it is—hopefully before the next person does. Opportunities probably drift by you every day, but do you see them? And even if you do, are you prepared to take advantage of them?

Say you are stuck in a dead-end job, but it pays fairly well and offers you maximum security. You know you can drift in this job for years, getting cost-of-living raises and periodic bonuses, and that you will never get fired. Unfortunately, you are bored. One day a friend tells you about a ground-floor opportunity in a fledgling company in a young and very promising industry. However, you dismiss what your friend says as idle lunchtime conversation. You don't give it a second thought.

Well, you may have just passed up a golden opportunity. If you have on blinders and believe in proceeding in a straight line to retirement, with no zigzag career moves, you will continue to ignore every piece of luck—every possible opportunity—that comes your way. And you will probably be the first to wonder why "Some people have all the luck!"

"You hear it said that people make their own luck," comments Dr. Charles Cardwell, a philosophy professor at the Virginia Polytechnic Institute. "But if you take 'luck' to mean chance events, happenstance, then the statement isn't true. Luck happens to everybody. You don't make your own luck. It comes and goes on its own. But you *can* make your own fortune, by staying alert and using luck wisely."

**Generalization #7: Lucky People Are Prepared to Take Risks** It will not do you much good to be able to recognize opportunities unless you are prepared to do something about them. There's an old Latin proverb: "Audentes fortuna juvat," or "Fortune favors the bold." As a group, lucky people tend to be bold people. They are willing to deviate from a career or life plan should an unexpected opportunity come their way. They are willing to do something a little unorthodox if the probability of success is there.

Note we used the word *probability*, not *possibility*. Lucky people may be risk-takers, but they are not foolhardy. They are not rash in their decision making. When faced with an opportunity, they weigh the odds of its success. They figure out what they stand to lose should the venture fail, and whether they would be able to recoup their losses. Which brings us to . . .

**Generalization #8: Lucky People Are Skeptics** Lucky people always consider the fact that a venture could fail. After all, nothing in this world is foolproof, although *unlucky* people often seem to think so. They are the people who go around saying "It can't miss! I'm sure of it." Lucky people, on the other hand, are never one-hundred-percent sure of anything.

J. Paul Getty, the oil billionaire who died in 1976, used to say, "When I go into any business deal, my chief thoughts are on how I'm going to save myself if things go wrong." Gerald M. Loeb, the successful stock market speculator and author of the book *The Battle for Investment Survival*, stated flatly: "On the stock market, optimism can kill you."

If you want fortune to favor you, always have a fallback solution worked out way in advance.

### Generalization #9: Lucky People Know When to Quit—While They Are Still Ahead

Should a venture with a sunny forecast start giving off storm warnings, pay heed. Stubborn people are often *unlucky* people for just the opposite reason: They refuse to give up. They carry perseverance too far. Frequently, they can't bring themselves to accept a small loss and so end up with a major disaster on their hands instead.

We do not want to give you the impression that lucky people are fickle, however—that they bounce from one situation to the next capriciously. On the contrary, lucky people do not embrace change for the mere sake of change. They are not aimless job-hoppers, believers that the grass is always greener elsewhere. Rather, they seize opportunities only when the odds are in their favor and stick with their decision only as long as the situation continues to produce the desired results.

### Generalization #10: Lucky People Can Admit Their Mistakes

Can you look other people straight in the eye and say, "I was wrong," and then proceed to rectify your error? Generalization #10 is actually a corollary of #9, for people who can't admit their mistakes do not get out of deteriorating situations soon enough. They hang on, determined to keep their precious reputations for invincibility intact.

The stock market is a good place to look for examples to illustrate this point. In a 1973 book *Psyche, Sex and Stocks*, psychiatrist Stanley Block and psychologist Samuel Correnti examined the phenomenon of stock market losers. Their study revealed that these *unlucky* men and women had "an overwhelming need to prove their brilliance." They were almost constitutionally incapable of admitting they were ever wrong.

**220**

# How Lucky Can You Get?

☐ ☐ ☐ ☐

Now that we have explored the phenomenon of luck in greater depth, the following simple quiz can help you decide if *you* have a "lucky" attitude:

|  | Yes | No |
|---|---|---|
| **1.** I am an outgoing person and have a vast network of friends and acquaintances. | ☐ | ☐ |
| **2.** A number of my friends are influential people or in a higher social or career bracket than myself. | ☐ | ☐ |
| **3.** I always try to meet new people at the social functions and activities I attend regularly. | ☐ | ☐ |
| **4.** I keep up my relationships with old friends even though I am making new friends. | ☐ | ☐ |
| **5.** I maintain high visibility in my career field. | ☐ | ☐ |
| **6.** I am intuitive. I do not strictly approach problems and decisions in an analytical way; I think impressions of a situation are as important to weigh as the hard facts. | ☐ | ☐ |
| **7.** I know how to "surface" and analyze my subconscious thoughts to help me reach a decision that *feels* right—and, more frequently than not, *is* right. | ☐ | ☐ |
| **8.** I realize there is a vast difference between a hunch and a hope and I don't confuse the two. | ☐ | ☐ |
| **9.** I do my homework. I am a conscientious, hard-working person and do not habitually resort to rash decision making to avoid thoroughly investigating a problem. | ☐ | ☐ |

**221**

Yes    No

**10.** I generally view change as a prelude to new opportunities rather than a prelude to all that is negative and evil. ☐ ☐

**11.** Even though I have mapped out a career/life plan, I am willing to deviate from it should some unforeseen opportunity intervene. ☐ ☐

**12.** I generally have a good sense of timing when it comes to making major changes in my life. ☐ ☐

**13.** I have a knack for seeing the opportunity that is embedded in a chance event. ☐ ☐

**14.** I am a bold person, I am willing to take risks. On the other hand, I am not so bold as to be foolhardy; I look before I leap. ☐ ☐

**15.** Although seizing an opportunity for which I am not entirely prepared scares me, I usually do it anyway. I do not insist on having total advance knowledge of every situation I enter. ☐ ☐

**16.** I am an initiator. I don't wait for things to happen; I make them happen. ☐ ☐

**17.** I maintain a healthy skepticism at all times. To me, skepticism means anticipating what can go wrong if I take a certain course of action. But I do not confuse skepticism with pessimism, the assumption that nothing will ever go right, no matter what action I take. ☐ ☐

**18.** Disorder created by unforeseeable events beyond my control displeases me, but it doesn't surprise or frustrate me. I accept the disorder as a fact that I must deal with, whether I like it or not. ☐ ☐

**19.** While I am not a pessimist, I realize that no one is totally immune from a case of bad luck now and then. ☐ ☐

|  | Yes | No |
|---|---|---|
| **20.** When bad luck strikes, I am not totally demoralized. My attitude is: "That's life. Tomorrow is another day." | ☐ | ☐ |
| **21.** If good luck strikes, on the other hand, I don't question whether I deserve this "freebie." I embrace it. | ☐ | ☐ |
| **22.** I feel good luck is rare. I do not treat it cavalierly, assuming there is plenty more where that came from. | ☐ | ☐ |
| **23.** I enter most situations with contingency plans, or at least with some sketchy idea of what I will do should ensuing events go badly. | ☐ | ☐ |
| **24.** I know the difference between perseverance and foolish stubbornness. When a situation turns sour, I know when to cut my losses, when to quit while I am still ahead. | ☐ | ☐ |
| **25.** I am willing to accept a string of small losses while waiting for the big gain. | ☐ | ☐ |
| **26.** I can admit to myself and other people when I have made a mistake. I don't dwell on mistakes—I learn from them. | ☐ | ☐ |

The more check marks you have in the "Yes" column, the more likely you are to be receptive to Destiny's smile. The opposite is true if your check marks are clustered in the "No" column; bad luck—in the form of lack of control over your own career—may be holding you back.

In a career sense, luck and skill are two sides of the same coin. When you have a particular skill or set of skills, you have a measure of control over your career destiny. But if you are ambitious and shooting for the top, that kind of control will take you only so far. Even if you are incredibly good at what you do, you still need a lucky break every now and then—and the foresight to recognize and seize the opportunity when luck does come your way.

# Case Histories of Lucky Women

☐　☐　☐　☐

## Case History A

During her twenty-six-year career, Joan Manley has had several brushes with that phenomenon called luck. "Timing and luck played a great part in my good fortune," admits Manley, today the chairwoman of the board of Time-Life Books.

Like most people who seem to lead "charmed" lives, Manley has a pretty flexible definition of luck. In an interview for *Working Woman* (February 1979), she explained, for instance, why she never experienced sex discrimination: "I think that was really a matter of lucky timing. If I were ten years older [she turned forty-eight in 1981], I probably would have run into discrimination and wouldn't have this job. If I were ten years younger, the competition would have been too tough. There'd be plenty of good women around to promote. As it turned out, I was the right answer at the right time when the company felt compelled to move women along."

Fresh from the University of California at Berkeley with a BA in English and history, Manley moved east and took a secretarial job at Doubleday, the publishing firm, in 1954. At the time, Manley was disappointed in the job because she was working in the sales rather than the more glamorous editorial department. In retrospect, she considers that exposure to sales her first lucky break.

"I was totally unaware of my native talent and inclination for marketing," she says. "I simply had no idea I could be good at that." She had mistakenly assumed her abilities lay strictly in the editorial end of the business.

Once she realized the opportunities that a career in sales afforded her, Manley wasted no time in learning the necessary skills. Under her first boss's tutelage, she picked up the knack for writing ads that worked, ads that *sold* books. From her second

**224**

boss, she learned the ins and outs of budgeting. Indeed, her exposure to her second boss was another stroke of luck. He left Doubleday in 1960 to build Time, Inc.'s fledgling book publishing business and took Manley with him. At Time, her career took off like a skyrocket. She became circulation director of Time's book division in 1966; director of sales in 1968; publisher in 1970; a Time, Inc., vice-president in 1971; a group vice-president in 1975; and a member of the board of directors in 1978.

While Manley credits luck with much of her good fortune, she does not downplay the role of hard work in her career. "Certainly, the work ethic is deeply ingrained in me. That work is a duty and a good thing is certainly part of my understanding of what life is all about." But, to Manley, so is taking advantage of a lucky opportunity. "Everyone I have ever worked for was perfectly willing to give me more responsibility when I was ready to take it. I never asked for a more important job"—but she never turned one down when it was offered either.

## Case History B

If a lucky person can be defined as an individual who recognizes and seizes opportunities, Betsy Ancker-Johnson certainly qualifies. But while some people may think that a phone call out of the blue from a prospective employer represents luck, in Betsy Ancker-Johnson's case there is a more rational explanation. She has switched employers eight times during her career, most often because the new employer sought *her* out, seldom the other way around.

At her fifth job as a research scientist at the Boeing Corporation in Seattle, by her own admission, Ancker-Johnson gained an international reputation in her field. She was prolific in turning out scholarly papers, particularly on semiconductor electronics, and her name became well known in professional scientific circles. The result was a call from the White House in 1973 offering her the job of assistant secretary for science and technology in the U.S. Department of Commerce.

"I've often wondered how I fell out of the White House computer to get that job," says Johnson in an interview with *Working Woman* (February 1980). But she wasted little time trying to figure it out. She accepted. "I have always believed you should take a job because it is challenging and because you want to do it." Clearly, Ancker-Johnson does not agonize too long over career decisions. If she is offered a job with "a new mountain to climb," she takes it.

When her government tenure was up, Ancker-Johnson moved on to the post of associate laboratory director for physical research at the Argonne National Laboratory near Chicago. Then another one of those "surprise" phone calls came, as she puts it, "out of the blue." At the other end of the line was a General Motors vice-president, now her boss.

"He started out by saying that GM practically never goes outside the ranks to hire someone," she recalls, "and we went from there." Needless to say, it didn't take much convincing to get Ancker-Johnson to accept the job being offered: vice-president in charge of the environmental activities department at the General Motors Corporation. By accepting that post, Ancker-Johnson had the singular distinction of becoming the first woman vice-president in the history of the U.S. automobile industry.

While her frequent career moves surely would have made a shambles of any well-mapped-out career plan, look how far Ancker-Johnson has progressed by following her instincts and taking these risks. Where other women would have hesitated in the face of such challenges, Ancker-Johnson seized upon them as opportunities. "I like to win," she explains, "especially if there is a competition. And if there isn't, I like to make it into one."

## Some Views on Luck

☐　☐　☐　☐

"Lucky breaks don't just happen; they're made. Lucky breaks are usually made up of common sense, planning, resolve—raw materials that are available to everyone."

—R. V. Price, "Success Is As Easy As ABC,"
*Success Unlimited*, November 1974

"To attract lucky chances, you must put yourself in a position to receive them—'expose yourself as fully as possible to the fluid circumstances of life.' To boil this down to its essentials, this means simply to get into contact with as many people as possible."

—Max Gunther, *The Very, Very Rich and How They Got That Way*

"One thing leads to another. You see an opportunity, and everything after that falls in place."

—Armand Hammer, Chairman, Occidental Petroleum Company, *Time*, January 28, 1966

"I'd rather be lucky than smart, 'cause a lot of smart people ain't eatin' regular."

—Sid Richardson, Texas oil wildcatter, *Fort Worth Star-Telegram*, November 17, 1954

"All our earnest efforts at self-improvement become virtually futile unless accompanied by the right breaks. You can have courage and perseverance and every other trait admired by the Protestant Ethic, and you can have love and humility and all the traits admired by the poets, but unless you also have good luck, none of it does you much good."

—Max Gunther, *The Luck Factor*

"All evidence is that 'luck' is to a large extent self-generated. If you want to change your luck, change your attitude."

—John E. Gibson, *How to Size Up People*

## For Additional Reading

"Are You Inviting or Avoiding Luck?" by Paul B. Chance, Ph.D., *Self* magazine, February 1979.

*How to Attract Good Luck* by A. H. Z. Carr.

*The Luck Factor* by Max Gunther.

"What It Takes to Be Lucky: A Self-Generated Syndrome," in *How to Size Up People* by John E. Gibson.

# 11

# Getting the Salary, Title, and Status to Match the Job You're Already Doing

If you are a man, it is pretty easy to tell how your career is progressing. A man on the way up in a company is steadily given more responsibility and, in line with his new duties, his title is automatically upgraded and his paycheck fattened—often without his having to utter a "reminder" to his boss. Between white-collar males it is understood: More work means more money and a better title.

Unfortunately, that axiom does not hold true for women. When a woman is given more work—work that may or may not entail more actual responsibility—it should be taken at face value. She has simply been given more work to do. Period. A woman shouldn't assume that her new duties will

**229**

net her a better title or more money—at least not without her bringing it to the boss's attention. Even then there is no guarantee.

Many ambitious women gratefully accept more and more work thinking it will ensure an automatic boost up the ladder. They assume that once they prove they can shoulder additional duties, a promotion will magically follow. They fail to consider the wisdom of the Working Woman's Law: If unchecked, work will flow to the most competent woman in every office until she drops dead of overwork.

Why are women taken advantage of while men who take on more work reap almost immediate rewards? Dee Estelle Alpert, a NOW affirmative-action counselor, claims it is because men are permitted to assume two distinct roles in our society while women, even businesswomen, can never escape the overlapping roles of wife, mother, and lover.

"We have an entirely different set of expectations for men at home and at work, with respect both to the work they do and to the behavior they are supposed to exhibit while doing that work," says Alpert. "Men are handy at home; male managers are not expected to be handy at the work place—they don't fix the plumbing or paint walls. Woman's work, in contrast, is commonly transferred from home to the office and added on to the job function for which she was hired. In effect, we transfer women's roles from home to the office while permitting men the luxury of leaving one set of expectations and activities at their front door, not to be reassumed until they return again at night."

## Extra Work—Should I Accept It?

☐   ☐   ☐   ☐   What should you do if your boss comes to you with extra work, but with no mention of any tangible reward for taking on the extra load? Your response will depend on several variables:

- the size of your company;

- the clout that your boss or the person assigning you the work has;

- the nature of the extra work (i.e., is the work dull and self-contained or exciting and highly visible? will you pick up new information or another marketable skill from doing the work?).

If you work for a small organization, any extra work on your part will be noticed. Ideally, you want as many people as possible to notice your efforts, particularly influential executives in a position to advance your career. In a large company, it is harder to get recognition for work done beyond the call of duty or behind the scenes. Think long and hard before you agree to take on more work for the same amount of pay in such a situation. In other words, ask yourself, "What's in it for me?"

Give some thought to the personality of the person assigning you extra work. If it is the boss, ask yourself if she or he is a person who appreciates and rewards loyal and hardworking staff members. Or is your boss a person who takes advantage of others with no sense of obligation about repaying extra effort—particularly that of women employees?

If the extra-work directive comes from the executive suite, by all means do it. It is your chance to prove your worth to the top brass. Jacqueline Brandwynne, who now heads her own advertising agency, began her career working for the Helena Rubinstein cosmetics firm. Brandwynne didn't wait to be assigned work. She was constantly dreaming up new projects and volunteering to implement them. Madame Rubinstein herself finally suggested that Brandwynne come and talk to her at home early in the morning. Those early-morning chats gave Brandwynne an opportunity to learn a great deal about the beauty business while also giving her a chance to demonstrate her ability to Madame Rubinstein, perhaps the foremost woman in the industry.

This example, from Caroline Bird's *Everything a Woman Needs to Know to Get Paid What She's Worth*, underlines the third consideration: the nature of the extra work. Obviously extra work that will enrich your work experience or help you develop

**231**

new skills is preferable to extra work that is task-oriented, solitary, and routine. For an assistant buyer in a retail clothing store, for example, it would be the difference between being asked to coordinate a videotape of a season's fashions to send around to branch stores and being asked to write up 25 percent more orders every week. The videotape project would give the assistant buyer an opportunity to work in a new medium and to demonstrate her creative and organizational skills. Writing up extra orders every week would be just more of the same routine she did anyway.

By the same token, you probably should accept any extra work that will add a new skill to your repertoire of abilities. Skills are marketable commodities. They bolster your bargaining position both within your company and with potential employers. With a new skill, you can say to an interviewer: "By the way, in addition to my regular duties as an office manager, I wrote some advertising copy for Mr. Winston. He used it in his last presentation to a prospective client and he got the account. Mr. Winston and others have encouraged me to go after a copy-writing job. I would like to show you examples of my work."

## Definite Don'ts

□     □     □     □

No matter who assigns you more work or what the nature of that work is, there are two sentences you must never utter: "I'm too busy" and "That's not my job." While one or both reactions may be justified, bosses universally hate to hear those words. Either of those replies, or any variations of them, is a surefire way to win your boss's enmity and thwart your chances for an eventual promotion. Those words reflect a poor attitude. They imply that you believe your boss or company is out to exploit its employees—and that is a serious accusation even if it is only implied.

If you feel that you are being unduly burdened with extra work, there are more diplomatic ways to signal your discontent.

First of all, don't assume that your boss realizes that she/he is giving you "extra" work. She/he may think it is just part of your job. "I'm not a mind reader," says William Hussey, the head of his own marketing consulting firm. "If an employee of mine feels she is being overtaxed, she has to speak up. She has to tell me if she needs extra help, better equipment, or overtime pay because she can't complete her work between nine and five every day. Then we can discuss it and come to some equitable agreement."

In such cases, Mr. Hussey is always pleased if an overworked employee not only brings it to his attention, but also has a solution thought out. "That demonstrates constructive, problem-solving-type thinking," he says. "It shows initiative. An employee who comes to me with a plan for redistributing the work load will definitely get a hearing and may eventually get a promotion. In my opinion, any employee who can see a problem from management's point of view as well as her own is worth her weight in gold."

When your boss or a superior comes to you with extra work, respond positively and cheerfully whether or not you actually intend to do the work. Say: "It's wonderful we have gotten all this new business. Do you want me to put this new work at the top of my list of priorities? I do have a full work schedule already, so if you want me to do this first, I'm afraid something else is going to have to wait." In short, kill your boss with kindness while making sure you are not overworked.

A definition of "overwork" is probably in order here. You are not being overworked if you are employed as a CPA, for example, and your work load doubles between January 1 and April 15 every year. When you were offered the job, you were probably told that work flow in the office was seasonal and that the tax season required that all office personnel work at a faster pace. In contrast, there are also slow seasons in a CPA's practice when the work slows to a trickle. When you take a job, you should ask about the pace of daily activity and whether it is constant all year or ebbs and flows. Be fair to your employer. Your definition of a normal work load should not be based on the activity level at the slowest time of the year.

You can often save yourself from haggling over what is and is not a part of your job if you insist on a written job description *before* you accept any new position. Then you can discuss how you feel about working overtime without receiving any overtime pay, or doing everyone else's work in the office because you happen to be extremely efficient—before it all drops into your lap. Seeing it on paper can also help you to negotiate *out* of a job description any catchall phrases such as "... and any other duties as may be required." A phrase like that opens the door to exploitation and leaves you little bargaining strength should your boss or anyone else in the office try to foist off work on you.

One final "don't": If after giving your employer the benefit of the doubt, you are convinced that your work load is growing with no tangible reward—i.e., an upgrading of your title *and* salary—in sight, by all means speak up. But don't approach your boss with a hostile or accusatory attitude or you will only end up in an angry confrontation. Be constructive in thought, work, and deed while getting across the message that: (1) you are ambitious and want to move up; and (2) hard work is fine as long as it is rewarded by an increase in status and salary.

## The Showdown: How to Keep It from Becoming a Shoot-out

☐    ☐    ☐    ☐    It is preferable to have a serious talk with your boss precisely at the point when you feel your new responsibilities make you a candidate for a promotion—that is, a better title and more money. A word of caution here: An increase in the routine tasks you perform *every day* may entitle you to overtime pay or a bonus, but does not entitle you to a promotion. Don't make a pitch for a better title unless you have been asked to make more decisions and assume more responsibility in your department.

The timing of your interview with your boss is extremely im-

portant. It should occur either when your boss has just compli-
mented you on your exceptional performance or at a critical time
when your boss really needs your extra help. For example: Your
company has just landed an important new account and your
boss wants you to help service that account. She/he is effusive
about the new business and tries to elicit the same enthusiastic
response from you, yet says nothing about elevating your job in
line with the authority she/he is about to delegate to you. The
time to speak up is *before* you start staying until nine o'clock every night in order to keep abreast of the new work load. In fact,
the time to speak up is usually just *before* you accept more responsibilities.

Bad timing is one reason why women fail to get the promotions they deserve. They take on the new project, perform trium-
phantly, and then wait to be rewarded. They mistakenly assume
their employer is just dying to increase the payroll by immediately rewarding every good worker who puts in some extra effort. It
is the rare employer who does not have to be prodded when it
comes to merit raises.

But you don't want just a raise. If you are smart, you also want
a better title—and the status symbols that accompany that title.
Thus, your showdown with your boss has a triple-pronged objective: (1) a better title, (2) a raise in line with that title, and (3) the
accoutrements that normally accompany that title. You haven't
really won the battle if you win only one or two of these objectives.

Suppose, for example, that you work for an organization with
a poor record of promoting women. You are the assistant to the
personnel director, a man. The personnel department is about to
undertake a major project—the computerization of all its records—when your boss announces his resignation, effective one
month hence. You are delighted when he recommends you as
his replacement. You want the job. Although the vice-president
in charge of operations, your boss's superior, expresses some reservations, he says he will consider you for the job. The vice-president calls you into his office two weeks later with this
proposition: You will assume the title "acting personnel director"
for a six-month trial period. During that time you will get an in-

crease in pay "commensurate with that title." The vice-president does not give a dollar figure. If after the trial period, it is clear you can do the work, you will get the full title and another raise. Again, no mention of the exact amount. How should you respond to this proposition?

First of all, you should say you will think it over. The longer you stall, the closer it gets to your boss's last day. Your employer needs somebody to fill your boss's shoes, especially with the mammoth computerization project about to begin.

Secondly, you should be savvy enough to realize that this offer is heavily weighted in the company's favor, not yours. They need you right now because of the computerization project—you have already spent eight months preparing for it, which makes you a keystone to its success. You have the company over a barrel rather than the other way around. Still, the vice-president is acting like she/he is doing you a favor.

Don't fall for it. The word *acting* in the proposed job title spells the difference between genuine management responsibility and being set up as an interim solution. To the outside world, the word *acting* in your title means your job is still open; all qualified applicants should send in their résumés to the company president at once. Inside the company, your position is even shakier. Why should your subordinate follow your orders when you do not even have enough clout to lay secure claim to your new job? You were their equal last month, and with the title "acting personnel director," they will probably continue to treat you that way. With everybody undermining your new authority, think what will happen to your self-esteem—a hard-won promotion is supposed to make it rise, not hit the floor.

The *acting* in the title is insulting enough, but refusing to discuss money with you is a dead giveaway that you have no power in the eyes of the company higher-ups. They see you as a pawn they can manipulate to serve their own ends, and unless you prove otherwise, they will continue to treat you that way.

What can you do? Here is one tactic: Wait until the very last minute—your hesitation alone signifies your severe reservations—and then ask for another hearing with the vice-president. Don't reject her/his offer; that would be a negative approach to

**236**

the situation. Instead, tell her/him you have a counterproposal: You will be happy to accept the post of "personnel director"— that title and no other. If you fall down on the job, you expect to be fired like anyone else. But you don't want to be set up for failure by being saddled with the title "acting personnel director." Next, cite the salary increase and fringe benefits that you feel should accompany the promotion (but be willing to negotiate on this score). If your former boss has a company membership in a luncheon club, ask for the same. After all, there is no harm in trying. Finally, point out to the vice-president that should the company turn down your proposition, you cannot assume any responsibility for the computerization project. That burden will have to rest with whomever becomes personnel director.

If the company ignores that last implied threat on the assumption that you are too conscientious a worker to make good on it, you must do exactly what you told them: assume no responsibility whatsoever for the computerization project. At that point, it is the company's headache, not yours. In light of the company's behavior, however, you will have to reevaluate your chances for advancement if you remain with that employer. It might be easier to upgrade both your salary and title by looking for a better opportunity with another company.

Obviously, it takes guts to negotiate a big promotion and perhaps you will lose a few nights' sleep during the negotiation process. But even if you don't win (in the above case, there's a good chance you would), the experience will be valuable. You will have to negotiate more than once in your career. The more you negotiate, the better you will become at it and the less nervous you will be. With experience, you will instinctively know when you are negotiating from a position of strength. You will learn to spot the advantages and disadvantages of a situation— on both sides. You will know when to try bluffing and when it pays to lay all your cards on the table. Who knows? In time, you may even come to enjoy it!

# Success Stories of Women Who Have Learned the Art of Negotiation

☐     ☐     ☐     ☐

## Success Story A

Although Dena Skalka had a rather routine job as a salary administrator at Bell Laboratories in New Jersey, she was the one person in the personnel department to whom other women employees went with their problems. Dena used that fact as leverage to gain a promotion into a more exciting job.

How did she do it? As she explained in an interview with *Working Woman* (March 1980), "I made no secret of the fact that women were flocking to me with their problems. There were ten levels of management; women never had risen above the second. Bell's federal contracts required that it institute a strong affirmative-action program. The company was seeking sensible solutions and I had some. Within a year after I began my campaign, the company named me affirmative-action officer. My salary was upped to $29,000, tripling my entry wages."

Not only was her new position better paying, it was also a challenge, an opportunity for her to advance a cause she really believed in. Through her work, Dena feels she helped make Bell Laboratories more responsive to the needs and aspirations of its female employees. She established special sessions for middle management to sensitize participants to the women's issues. She persuaded management to agree to let women travel more frequently. She recruited talented women science graduates from the top colleges and founded a scholarship program for women that provided each winner with a summer job at Bell.

But most exciting of all, Dena identified women in lower-middle-management ranks who deserved promotions up to fifth-level management. In many cases, such women were already producing work entitling them to much better jobs. Dena reevaluated their jobs and saw to it that they were given the appropriate salaries and titles.

**238**

## Success Story B

Lawyer Joan Kilcone still remembers the day the senior partner called her into his office to tell her she had just been elected into the firm's partnership. It had taken a long ten years to achieve that honor. She remembers even more vividly what happened next.

"He walked me down the hallowed halls of the law firm and stopped in front of a tiny isolated inner office sandwiched between the library and the ladies' room. Although I'd never given much thought to business power symbols, I instinctively knew I would never be treated like an equal by the other partners—all male—if I accepted this office. It was a slap in the face. I recall smiling sheepishly and shaking my head. Finally, I managed to blurt out a firm refusal to move my things into that cubbyhole."

Joan walked through the firm, studying who had what office. By five o'clock, she had decided she wanted the office of an associate attorney who had been with the firm for only two years. She told the senior partner that money and titles meant nothing unless they were accompanied by the appropriate status symbols, one of which was a centrally located office. She wanted X's office and said she would work at home until that office was ready for her to move into.

"I must have sounded convincing enough, although my stomach was churning," she recalls. "After one day biting my nails by the telephone at home, the senior partner's secretary called to tell me my office was ready for me. I felt like the female liberation front had just won an important battle in the war against the chauvinists."

Nine months later, one of Joan's male colleagues took his wife on a tour around the offices. They stopped into Joan's office and he introduced her as "the only female partner in the firm," which by that time was no longer true. When Joan corrected him, he said, "Technically, you may be right. There is another woman partner. But what kind of partner allows herself to be hidden off in a two-by-four office with no windows next to the ladies' room?"

## Some Views on Job Titles, Promotions, and Salary Increases

☐   ☐   ☐   ☐

"It used to be that it wasn't *nice* for a woman to talk about money. But that's changing. You'd better believe it's nice to talk about money or you're not going to have any!"

—Venita VanCaspel, President, VanCaspel
& Company, Houston, *Working Woman*,
January 1980

"Find out what men are earning at your job level. Expect to earn as much and proceed as rapidly as a man might."

—Maxine Wineapple, career counselor,
*Women Who Work*, vol. 5, no. 5

"There's a simple way to define a woman's job. Whatever the duties are, and they vary from place to place and time to time, a woman's job is anything that pays less than a man will do it for."

—Caroline Bird, *Everything a Woman
Needs to Know to Get Paid What She's
Worth*

"You have a duty to yourself and to your employer to have ideas about how the work can be better done and an obligation to discuss these ideas. If you aren't talking to your employers openly and frankly about growth where you are now, that's a clear indication that you are not giving your company an opportunity to take advantage of your full potential. And you are throwing away opportunities that are readily within reach."

—Richard Lathrop, *Who's Hiring Who*

"Progress can be made in any organization—in one as highly structured as the country's largest companies, which always seem to go by the rule book. Take positive action and make sure your contributions are known and recognized by your superior. Know your boss, know how he operates, and work at your very best level to help him. . . . In this area of creating positions, you

**240**

cannot make progress by killing off your superiors in the hope of occupying their chairs. It is only in a growing situation that you can grow. It is by pushing someone who is ahead of you along by assisting him that you can fill his seat when he is promoted."
—Eli Djeddah, *Moving Up*

"Take a look at the frequency of your promotions. Generally you can learn about eighty percent of any job in one year. In the next half year, you probably assimilate the remaining twenty percent. So if you're not promoted every eighteen months to two years, you may be right to question your superior about your advancement."

—Carl Menk, President, Boyden Associates

## For Additional Reading

*The Negotiator: A Manual for Winners* by Royce A. Coffin.

*Fundamentals of Negotiating* by Gerard I. Nierenberg.

*How to Negotiate a Raise* by John J. Tarrant.

*Winning by Negotiation* by Tessa Albert Warshaw.

*The Negotiation Process* William Zartman, ed.

*Winning the Salary Game* by Sherry Chastain.

*Successful Negotiating Skills for Women* by John Ilich and Barbara S. Jones.

# 12

# The Rules of the Game: Office Politics

The game is office politics and it is played in one form or another in every organization. While there are companies that are relatively nonpolitical, where competence largely determines whether employees gain promotions, these "meritocracies" are the exception rather than the rule. There are far more organizations in the work world where who you know and how well you deal with people are as important, if not more important, than what you know. Regardless of the environment in which you work you will need to develop your interpersonal or "people" skills in order to move ahead. First, however, you need to learn the "rules" of the game for your particular company.

243

If you have read this book carefully you should already have an accurate picture of your employer. Turn back to the "Checklists for Diagnosing a Company's Health" on pages 42–46 and fill them in if you haven't done so already. Next, reread "Hierarchies and Power: What the Organizational Chart Won't Tell You" (pages 46–50). Draw up an informal organization chart, first for your department and division and then for the whole company. This will tell you who the people of influence really are. By listening to and observing these people you will develop a sense for the type of behavior and attitudes that lead to success in your company. These are what you are going to have to develop if you want to play the "game."

## Making the Team

☐    ☐    ☐    ☐    To be good at the game of office politics, you must possess the following characteristics and abilities. Ask yourself:

- *Do I have a strong self-image and sense of purpose?* If you are a person who is indecisive and easily intimidated by others, you will easily fall prey to the truly Machiavellian office politician. "You have to understand your own inner resources," says Matina Horner, psychologist and president of Radcliffe College. Know and acknowledge your own strengths. You cannot allow yourself to be put down either by deliberate attempts to undermine your self-esteem or by unintended slights. A thick skin and confidence in yourself and your abilities are definite assets.

- *Can I keep my own counsel?* In other words, do you know when to keep your mouth shut or must you always confide all your intentions to your best friend? The wise player keeps her tactics to herself. While it is a good idea to make your superiors and colleagues aware of your higher aspirations, you don't have to disclose all your career plans in full detail. Then, if things don't work out the way you planned, you are spared the embarrassment of looking foolish. Besides, it is always better to keep a few options up your sleeve.

- *Am I an initiator?* You tested yourself for this trait back in chapter 1 ("What Personality Type Are You?" page 16). To be good at office politics, you have to be a self-motivated, assertive person. Successful executives are those who can act without the constant supervision or reassurance of others. They have a streak of independence that always keeps them one step ahead of the crowd.

- *Do I have a good sense of timing?* The timing of any move is extremely important, whether it is asking for a promotion or presenting a new idea to your superiors. Common sense dictates that you always make your move when the other party is most disposed to listen—for instance, when you've just pulled off a coup or when you've maneuvered yourself into a position of power vis-à-vis the other person.

- *Do I remain cool under pressure?* The ability to maintain your equilibrium when you find yourself in the eye of an office hurricane is a vital asset. If you let yourself be overcome by your emotions every time you find yourself in the hot seat, you won't stand a chance against a calculating competitor. In order to analyze the behind-the-scenes maneuvering in your office, you have to have a clear head. Figuring out what's going on around you is hard enough, but if you have emotional blinders on, it is impossible.

  People with a sense of humor often make excellent power strategists. Why? Because the ability to see the humorous side of a tense situation indicates an ability to distance oneself emotionally. It indicates a flexible perspective—an ability to view events from more than one vantage point.

- *Can I see office events in a broad context, or am I determined to win all the small everyday skirmishes while losing the war?* If Pyrrhic victories are your forte, then you are failing to see the overall picture. The smart office politician does *not* try to win every battle. She saves her strength for the important confrontations, the ones that are going to determine who gets the promotion.

  Look at it this way: It is clever strategy to lose now and

then to a competitor, especially if you retain control of the situation and consciously *allow* your competitor to win. It is clever because it puts you in an excellent position to surprise your competitor when you eventually lock horns over a really important matter.

- *Do I try to fulfill my boss's concept of the way my job should be done?* Dr. Margaret Hennig and Dr. Anne Jardim claim this is one area where ambitious men and ambitious women sometimes part company. "Men tend to focus on their bosses' expectations of them, while women tend to concentrate on their own concept of themselves," they write. "The difference can be critical. It means that men will necessarily be more alert to cues and signals from their superiors. The signals may concern very small things such as how one speaks or dresses; whether one appears quick and clever, or slow and reflective. Most men ask themselves, 'What does this boss want?' since they reason that the boss can probably make or break them for the next job up."

  In contrast, women often stubbornly refuse to bow to the expectations of others. Their attitude is "This is who I am—take it or leave it." According to Hennig and Jardim, "They generally have little sense of playing the game, little willingness to temporarily adopt a different style for reasons of self-interest." You can't afford to get caught in this trap if you want to excel at political gameswomanship.

- *Do I give the appearance of being a good team player?* The good gamester recognizes the importance of team play. She knows how to cooperate with others to accomplish a common objective. She understands that she has to support others on issues important to them in order to get them to support her on her favorite causes. But she also knows that no one—male or female—ever gets ahead in a large organization by simply going along with the will of the majority. The time comes in every ambitious person's career when she or he has to move ahead of the crowd, has to open her or his mouth and speak up and get noticed. The trick is knowing *when* to do it.

- *Can I size people up quickly and accurately?* In order to work effectively with a person, you have to understand that person's point of view, background, and biases. And in today's fast-paced business environment, you often don't have time to get to know your associates slowly over a period of time. You must learn to make almost instantaneous judgments about them based on such clues as the way they dress, their speech (tone, inflection, accent, vocabulary), their body language, and their manners. Your instant evaluations must be accurate and perceptive.

Social psychologists claim that whenever we meet someone new, all of us make these judgments, even if it is only on a subconscious level. Our first impression of any stranger is usually visual and crystallized before she or he says a word. Our second impression, on the other hand, is formed *after* the stranger utters her/his first sentence.

How do you develop the ability to assess people quickly and accurately? By keeping your eyes and ears open at all times. By staying alert to the seemingly inconsequential signals emitted by other human beings. It is a skill developed over time. The more you listen and observe, the more expert you will become at determining an individual's particular perspective and motivation and how you can best deal with her/him.

- *Do my colleagues find me congenial to work with?* Political skills, simply defined, are nothing more than people skills. The word *political*, in fact, is derived from the Greek word *polis*, which means citizen and implies dealing with other people on a face-to-face basis. Being able to deal with people and form useful friendships is an important element of business life and you would be wise to cultivate your human relations skills to their fullest.

- *For the sake of my career, am I willing to cooperate with people I do not like as individuals and would not choose as my friends?* Women are often shocked at the false camaraderie exhibited by male business associates who are known to dislike each other on a personal level. Women tend to view such behavior as hypocritical, if not downright immoral.

We can choose our friends but, unfortunately, we can't be as selective about our business associates, not if we want to get ahead in the work world. Women must learn to work cooperatively with people they don't necessarily

**247**

like if they are to succeed in their careers.

In business, whether or not you like someone is immaterial. Can this person you dislike be a useful ally? If the answer is yes, then suppress your negative feelings and channel your energy into figuring out how you two can be helpful to each other.

- *Am I fluent in the language of business?* In business, people tend to speak in euphemisms because saying what they really mean would make them appear too dictatorial or harsh. On the other hand, if you take this doublespeak communication at face value, you would be making a big mistake. When a new boss says to you, "No one punches a time clock around here. Just come in when you feel like it," you'd be making a grave mistake if you sauntered in at 10:30 every morning. The message your new boss meant to convey with that statement was that she/he is a reasonable person who doesn't check employees' comings and goings by the clock. She/he did not literally mean you should feel free to arrive at any odd hour of the day.

Here are some other examples of office code language that should not be taken literally:

"Please take care of this as soon as you get a minute." (translation: Do it immediately!)

"I'll look into the matter and get back to you." (translation: Maybe I'll look into the matter and maybe I won't. It is not high on my priority list.)

"Got a minute?" (translation: Got an hour?)

"I've got an interesting project for you." (translation: I hope you find it interesting because I'm going to stick you with it whether you find it interesting or not.)

While these comments represent universal office code language, most companies also develop their own special doublespeak phrases and terms. To an outsider, these phrases won't mean a thing. But as an insider—an ambitious employee in that company—you had better not only understand what the phrases mean, but also be able to speak the lingo yourself.

**248**

# Practice: A Hypothetical Office Situation

□   □   □   □

If you answered yes to six or more of the preceding questions, you have the makings of a good political strategist.

To test your political skills, we now present you with an example of a typical office power ploy. In the example, one of your associates is about to seize power from you. Your objective is to readjust the balance to your favor. After reading the description of your "competitor's ploy," decide how you would respond *before* reading what we suggest as a "possible counterstrategy." Remember, when it comes to power politics, it is not a matter of right and wrong ways to proceed, but which way will be the most effective in achieving your goal.

When figuring out your counterstrategy, always state your goal first. Next, assess carefully the personalities with whom you are dealing. An accurate analysis of your co-workers and their motivations is absolutely essential.

> You are at a meeting that unexpectedly turns into a brainstorming session about a sticky marketing problem. You have a reputation for being a good idea person, so you aren't surprised when those assembled start bombarding you with questions to get your creative juices flowing. You are flattered by the attention, and soon you are bursting with good ideas that you spew out in rapid succession.
>
> After one particularly brilliant flash of insight, one of your colleagues starts taking notes and querying you for more details. You begin to feel that your brain is being picked clean, but with all eyes upon you, you feel you can't suddenly refuse to answer your colleague's insistent questions.
>
> When the meeting is over, you corner your co-worker and ask him why he is so interested in your ideas. He responds, "I often run into the president of the company and I thought I'd try your idea out on him and see how he likes it."

*Possible Counterstrategy:* Your rival's big mistake is telling you his true intentions. A really smart idea thief would have said

**249**

something vague: "I thought I'd mull the idea over in my mind. I just took notes so I wouldn't forget any of the details." He would have left you guessing about what he intended to do.

In contrast, this man was very open about this thievery; you should be open, too. Now it's your turn to ask him a few questions: Why does he think it is such a good idea? Does he feel he's an especially good judge of ideas? Has he come up with any good ideas of his own lately that he'd like to share with you? Close the conversation with this remark: "You know, Bob, I wasn't so sure about that idea, but you've convinced me it is dynamite. I'm going back to my office right now and write my own memo to the president about it. Of course, I certainly would appreciate it if you would give my idea your backing the next time you see the president. That would be awfully nice of you." (You should, of course, be very cordial during this conversation.)

Whether or not you feel compelled to actually write your memo will depend on how you size up your rival. If he's a super-ambitious type who will stop at nothing to get ahead, by all means write the memo. You have probably headed him off at the pass already and no further action on your part will be necessary.

*Footnote*: In the future, don't sit in brainstorming meetings and allow your colleagues to swoop down on you like vultures. Throw out the germ of an idea. If it is well received, go back to your office and develop the idea in memo form before you discuss it any further. As advertising maven Jane Trahey puts it: "If you must dish out ideas for your pay, at least write them down and sign them before you dish them up for common consumption."

## Office Politics: A Historical Perspective

☐ ☐ ☐ ☐

There was a time not long ago when office politics was less in vogue than it is today. In his book *The Gamesman,* Michael Maccoby identifies four basic character types who work for large corporations. They are:

- *the company man* or institutional loyalist, whose identity comes from being a part of the protective corporate organization;

- *the craftsman,* whose only concern is in making a product or overseeing a specific process;

- *the jungle fighter* or entrepreneur, who founds a company almost single-handedly;

- *the gamesman* or unbridled opportunist, who views everything in terms of his or her own self-interest.

The jungle fighter is the prototype for men who built this country, particularly the late-nineteenth-century robber barons—Henry Ford, John D. Rockefeller, Henry Clay Frick, Cornelius Vanderbilt. The craftsmen worked for these jungle fighters; or they were independent inventors who came up with new technologies that other people exploited. (The craftsman channels his energies in ways that make other people rich.)

The company man emerged after World War II. In 1956, William Whyte, Jr., dubbed this type "The Organization Man" in his classic book of the same name. Maccoby, writing in the 1970s, sees President Eisenhower as the symbol of the organization man or company-man leader. "He was the guy who cooled things, solved problems by making sure that different competing interests were brought together. He stopped the extremists on Vietnam, for example, with budgetary questions. He could use the bureaucratic means to keep things from moving. That style was true of many large companies in the 1950s."

Enter a new breed, the gamesman, in the 1960s. Maccoby

**251**

sees President John F. Kennedy as the model for this type. The gamesman has the killer instincts of the jungle fighter combined with the slick, teamwork exterior of the company man. But inside, the gamesman remains loyal to only one being—himself.

According to Maccoby, increased business and political competition from abroad in the 1960s paved the way for the emergence of the gamesman. "In the 1950s, the gamesman was too independent and irreverent to reach the top of the largest corporations. As long as American business retained hegemony in the world, American business leaders could remain complacent, hardworking, and loyal to their companies. There was no need to take a lot of risks. But that changed in the 1960s. At that point, the modern climate of competition, innovation, interdependent teams, and fast-moving flexibility demanded the gamesman's skills. The gamesman is unlikely to go do something completely new, but he can react under fast scheduling. He is cool under a lot of pressure and tension."

But the gamesman's impact on American business has not been entirely benign in the last twenty years. Maccoby cites the example of the gamesman who gets himself transferred the moment a project she/he initiated appears to be in trouble. Of course, the smart gamesman gets out *before* anyone else sees that it is going to fail. "Now, an executive with real concern for the organization warns people that this is a bad project and that it must be stopped," says Maccoby. "No more money should be thrown into it. The gamesman only worries about rescuing his own reputation."

If the gamesman has a redeeming feature, it is his self-deprecating sense of humor. Maccoby thinks a gamesman without it is dead. "He can't get any emotional distance, he can't get back to reality by making fun of himself," Maccoby writes. "I think that's why people felt such affection for Kennedy. Despite his negative gamesman qualities, he always had a sense of humor. He could turn in on himself."

## Some Views on Office Politics

□     □     □     □

"Everyone who accepts a paid job tacitly announces that she is prepared to play on a certain team. It is assumed by everyone else that she will abide by that game's rules. Just accepting a job puts you in the game, like it or not. If you subsequently refuse to play, that is tantamount to coming to bat in a baseball game and suddenly insisting: 'I'm not going to swing that silly wooden stick! I brought my own tennis racket from home and I'll only hit with that.' "

—Betty Lehan Harragan, "Strategies and Tactics," *Savvy*, August 1980

"Human relations are important. You cannot improve your position if everyone dislikes you."

—Eli Djeddah, *Moving Up*

"Timing the presentation of a proposal or a plan is vital. Be intuitive enough to sense when it is premature, too late, or about the right moment."

—Nathaniel Stewart, *The Effective Woman Manager*

"If you know how to reflect an almost duplicate image of some unique aspects of your boss's way of doing things, you've got a good start toward presenting yourself in a way that will get your boss to like you and your work. The psychological explanation is simple. When bosses see some unique aspects of themselves reflected in your behavior, it has to lead to acceptance of you. Otherwise, they would be rejecting themselves, which is contrary to human nature."

—Dr. Ernest Dichter, Dichter Associates International, Ltd.

"When you are unable to have an effect on the plans and activities of those with whom you interact, they have more power than you. When you can affect their plans and activities and they can affect yours, power is then equal. But when you can affect the plans and activities of others and they can't affect yours, you have the greater power."

—Samuel Feinberg, "From Where I Sit" column, *Women's Wear Daily*, March 25, 1977

"If you let yourself get tangled in emotional responses such as defensiveness or anger, you don't stand a chance against a calculating power strategist."

—Dr. Ann Frisch and Dianne Partie, *Mademoiselle*, March 1977

"Seventy-five percent of the people who fail at a job fail not because they couldn't do the job, but because they failed politically."

—Marilyn Moats Kennedy, founder, Career Strategies

"Knowing politics is vital. Most women steer away from the terms 'politics' and 'power' but there is nothing wrong with power. It depends on how you use it."

—Anne Hyde, co-founder, Management Woman

THE RULES OF THE GAME: OFFICE POLITICS

**For Additional Reading**

*The Art of Conversation: Magic Key to Personal and Social Popularity* by James A. Morris, Jr.

*Boss Lady: An Executive Woman Talks About Making It* by Jo Foxworth.

*Games Mother Never Taught You: Corporate Gamesmanship for Women* by Betty Lehan Harragan.

*How to Expand Your S.I.Q. (Social Intelligence Quotient)* by Dane Archer, Ph.D.

*How to Talk with Practically Anybody About Practically Anything* by Barbara Walters.

*Jobmanship: How to Get Ahead by "Psyching Out" Your Boss and Co-Workers* by S. R. Redford.

*Making Contact: A Guide to Overcoming Shyness, Making New Relationships and Keeping Those You Already Have* by Dr. Arthur C. Wassmer.

*Office Politics: Seizing Power, Wielding Clout* by Marilyn Moats Kennedy.

*The Shyness Workbook* by Philip G. Zimbardo and Shirley Radl.

*Success! How Every Man and Woman Can Achieve It* by Michael Korda.

*Jane Trahey on Women and Power: Who's Got It, How to Get It* by Jane Trahey.

*Upward Nobility: How to Win the Rat Race Without Becoming a Rat* by Addison Steele.

*Winning: How to Make Yourself More Likeable* by Art Elphick.

**255**

# Making Tokenism Work for You

If discrimination means not being offered a job you are eminently qualified for, then tokenism means just the reverse: being pushed into a job for which you are underqualified. According to sociologist Rosabeth Moss Kanter, "Tokenism is supplanting segregation and discrimination as the fast track to stress and failure. Having jumped the first hurdle—getting hired—women and minorities find themselves faced with a new situation, tokenism."

Why would an employer encourage a woman to accept a job or a promotion that is beyond her capabilities? Because in this age of equal employment opportunity legislation, it is in the employer's interests to do so. After all, a smattering of token women can do wonders for a company in terms of public relations. Let's say a company has one female vice-president and thirty-seven male vice-presidents. All the company has to do is appoint two more women vice-presidents and, presto, it can send out a press release claiming the company has just increased the number of women in vice-presidential posts by 200 percent. Of course, feminists would immediately point out that still only 7.5 percent of this company's vice-presidents are women.

Unfortunately, such statistical sleight of hand is commonplace in all too many corporate personnel departments. There's a lot of rhetoric flying around about corporate affirmative action these days, but few honest efforts in that direction. In the opinion of Barbara Boyle Sullivan: "Only twenty percent to twenty-five percent of companies are serious about affirmative action, up from about ten percent in 1971. Five years ago, there was a lot of activity, a lot of flurry, but significant progress is not being made."

Tokenism is an example of a lot of seemingly constructive activity that signifies very little in terms of the average woman's advancement.

## Fast Tracking: The Flip Side of the Coin

□     □     □     □

Of course, not all ambitious women view tokenism as a trap. Rather, they see it as an opportunity, a chance to prove themselves. For them, tokenism goes hand in hand with "fast tracking."

Unfortunately, the management women who hold this opinion are not average achievers. Usually, they are quite the opposite—superconfident superstars. The fact that they are advancing rapidly *because* of their gender—rather than *in spite* of it—bothers them not one whit. Nothing intimidates them, not even the knowledge that their superiors expect them to fail. If anything, they are amused by this idea, since the word *failure* is not in their vocabulary. Failure is something that applies to other people, not to them.

As Rosabeth Moss Kanter has pointed out, there are two categories of women workers who are most frequently singled out for token status. There is the superstar, so extraordinary in her abilities that the average woman can't use her as a role model and the average man labels her an "exception." And there is the less qualified woman who flounders in her token job, giving her male colleagues the opportunity to lord it over her with the comment, "You're living proof that women can't really make it in the business world."

Note that it is the average woman who is left out of this equation. It is as if companies are either determined to make women look good by promoting only those women who will perform magnificently; or they are determined to make women look bad by promoting only the ones who they know can't possibly make it. The average woman, with her 50 percent chance of succeeding, is seemingly ignored.

## How to Spot the Token Job

☐　　☐　　☐　　☐　　Certain types of jobs are token by definition. We refer to those occupations that are gender-typed. Although about half of the adult female population in the United States is in paid employment, did you know that approximately 75 percent of them are concentrated in five predominately "female professions"? These vocations are: secretary-stenographer, household worker, bookkeeper, elementary school teacher, and waitress. Moreover, in business organizations, only 5.6 percent of all management or administrative jobs were held by women in 1976, and the situation has not improved appreciably since then. In contrast, half of all male workers are broadly distributed in over sixty-five occupations. And at the executive level, they outnumber women six hundred to one.

The problem with female-stereotyped jobs is that they are usually dead ends. Female career ladders (that is, occupational groups or series of jobs arranged along hierarchical lines) usually begin at lower entry levels than those traditionally held by men, and offer fewer possibilities for advancement.

"Even when women achieve higher-level administrative jobs," write George E. Biles, the director of American University's Personnel and Industrial Relations Program, and Holly A. Pryatel, employee relations specialist at the Communications Satellite Corporation, "the latter do not often lead to top management posts. Rather, they are ancillary positions from which women 'help' to attain organizational goals. The jump from such 'helping' roles into management is exceedingly difficult, even though these jobs are often good training for high-level positions."

Any middle-management or even executive-level *staff* position is potentially a token job. (Turn back to "Choice E: Line vs. Staff Jobs," page 91, to refresh your memory about the distinguishing characteristics of line and staff jobs.) However, don't assume that a line job is, by definition, free of the taint of tokenism. Any job—line or staff—can be turned into a token (i.e., powerless) job by superiors.

To decide whether a new job or promotion has the potential of transforming you into the "token woman," ask yourself these questions:

- Is this a line or staff job?

- Has this position been filled traditionally by women? If so, what kind of track record did they have? Where are these women now?

- In the past, was this job considered a powerful post within the company?

- Do you have the skills to handle this job? (Make a list of the skills required.) If you decide you do not have the necessary skills, ascertain whether the people offering you the job realize your shortcomings in this regard. This is crucial in deciding whether you are being set up for failure.

- If your superiors realize you do not have the skills to immediately perform effectively in the new job, are they willing to put you through an appropriate training program or pro-grams?

- What percentage of your new peer group will be male?

- Is the job a newly created position with a title that seems too grandiose for the salary and duties it entails?

- Have your superiors explained to you where this new post should lead in terms of your career advancement?

- Is your new boss a person with a reputation for evenhand-ed, unbiased treatment of her/his subordinates?

- Is this job one in which you will be highly visible to the com-pany's outside constituencies (i.e., public relations, consum-er relations, sales)?

- Does the company have a pattern of success in promoting women? In terms of discrimination against women, is the company part of the problem or part of the solution? (Use the "Checklists for Diagnosing a Company's Health," pages 42–46, to help you formulate answers to these questions.)

Answering these questions should give you a fix on what is going on in the minds of the people offering you, in their words, this "golden opportunity." Should you decide this "opportunity" is really a trap—a no-win situation—you should obviously decline. But, by all means, explain why this "golden opportunity" looks so bleak to you. Who knows. Your superiors may be well-mean-ing people after all. They may agree to make the concessions necessary to attract you.

On the other hand, after answering these questions, you may have no clear-cut idea of what's in store for you should you ac-cept the post. The job may have its token aspects, but it also looks like an incredible opportunity *provided* you perform up to or beyond expectations—which may mean being twice as good as your male counterparts.

Auren Uris and Jack Tarrant, the authors of *Getting to the Top Fast*, recommend that women facing this dilemma examine their career goals carefully to decide whether their ambition is strong enough to warrant stepping into such a pressure-cooker situation. "The question of how to handle [tokenism] will be easier to answer if you've thought your way through to clearly defined goals and strategies," they point out. "If you're going all out for a cause [feminism], and the acceptance of tokenism would demean you, then don't accept. But if your objectives lie elsewhere, consider with the utmost objectivity where you're going and whether this move takes you closer or farther away. . . . Given the realities, many women determine to take every advantage that comes their way—whether it stems from male guilt, fear of the law, or true recognition of merit."

Jane Pauley, Barbara Walter's successor as host of NBC's "Today" show, is one woman who would opt for taking the better job, whether or not it has the patina of tokenism. She claims she would rather endure the pressure and have a very good opportunity than not have it at all.

# The Dynamics of Tokenism

□   □   □   □

Before you make up your mind about a suspicious promotion or job offer, consider for a moment the possible consequences you can expect should you find yourself in a token job. While it is unlikely that all these consequences would converge on you, some combination of them is a strong possibility:

- *You will be given less responsibility and will thus have less power than your male peers.* Anne Harlan, Ph.D., and Carol L. Weiss, Ed.D., of the Wellesley College Center for Research on Women, recently completed a major two-year study of fifty men and fifty women middle managers in two large retail companies, divisions of the same corporation. Harlan and Weiss interviewed a number of men and women who were ostensibly equals. They held the same job titles and claimed they shouldered equal responsibility.

Under closer scrutiny, however, their equality turned out to be a myth. In an interview for *Working Woman* (August 1980) they explained their findings. "When we compared their statements with personnel records, we saw that across the board, the men wielded more power," said the researchers. "In one marketing team, for example, a man and woman had identical jobs—but the woman had a smaller operating budget." Men also managed greater numbers of people, generally had more freedom to hire and fire staff members, and had more direct control over the company's assets than their female peers. Over 70 percent of the men said they had some input in setting company policy. Less than 33 percent of the women made the same claim.

How do such inequities evolve? "Tokens are brought in for show," comments Elizabeth Janeway, an expert on power and author of *The Powers of the Weak.* "No one expects them to do or know much, and just to make sure, the regular ongoing processes are kept from them as much as possible."

Should a management woman discover she is being given less responsibility than her male counterparts, Harlan and Weiss advise her to call the fact to her superior's or personnel director's attention as soon as possible.

- *You will get inaccurate feedback on your performance.* Token women tend to get the kid-glove treatment from their male superiors when it comes to criticism. Ironically, they get just the opposite—overly harsh feedback—from their female superiors.

  In an article by Susan Seliger for the *Washingtonian* (December 1979), Lynne Finney, the first female director on the Federal Home Loan Bank Board in Washington, D.C., tells why women in management jobs are so hard on each other. "I went to a management training lab once, and there was only one other woman," she recalls. "I realized I was being much more critical of the one woman leading the group than all of the men when they led groups. It was because I wanted her to succeed. If she didn't, I felt it would reflect on me. And then I realized the women at the bank must look at me that way. I had known there was pressure, and suddenly I realized where it was coming from." Finney cautions women to support each other and offer *constructive* rather than destructive criticism.

A number of studies—the most recent from Cleveland State University—bear out the contention that male executives tend to be too forgiving of female managers when they aren't meeting the required standards. For this reason, women managers performing poorly are far more likely to think they are performing well than men who are performing poorly. An inaccurate performance appraisal puts an ambitious woman at a severe disadvantage in her attempts to scale the corporate ladder. Also, it makes male co-workers resentful that a woman is "getting away with something."

"A woman in any company should make certain that she is getting honest feedback from her supervisors—even if that means confronting her boss and explaining why it is important to her," advises Harlan.

- *You will be the victim of men's stereotypical thinking about women.* One of the reasons men don't like to criticize women is because they are members of the "weaker sex." In short, men assume women can't take it.

Rosabeth Moss Kanter, in *Men and Women of the Corporation*, theorizes that the average male executive tries to fit all the women in his purview—including professional businesswomen—into one of four distinct categories: (1) the mother, (2) the seductress, (3) the pet or amusing mascot, or (4) the iron maiden.

"These roles represent familiar categories that men can respond to and understand," says Kanter. "Each is formed around one behavioral tendency of the token, building this into an image of the token's place in the group and forcing her to continue to live up to that image." Kanter points out that each role represents a single male response to a woman's sexuality. "The first two roles make use of men's need to handle women's sexuality by envisioning them as either 'madonnas' or 'whores'—as either asexual mothers or overly sexual, debased seductresses, perhaps as a function of Victorian family patterns, which encourage separation of idealistic adoration toward the mother and animalistic eroticism. The others, termed the 'pet' and the 'iron maiden,' also have family counterparts in the kid sister and the virgin aunt."

Avoiding this typecasting is not easy. Indeed, in a really chauvinistic environment, it may be impossible. Knowing such stereotypical thinking exists should help you deal with it, however. Discussing the problem with a support group of other women also helps.

One top advertising woman has devised the following formula for working with, rather than against, the stereotypes. "I accept the fact that men in business have definite stereotyped ideas about me. Just because I'm female, they assume I'm perfectly capable of bursting into tears, fainting, or making petty, catty remarks. They also think I'm naturally helpful, considerate, and trustworthy. The trick is never to confirm their negative notions. For instance, no matter how many bitchy things I'd like to say about one particular woman colleague, I simply don't. Even when goaded. On the other hand, I play positive female virtues for all they're worth. I'm considerate of everyone. I remember birthdays. I thank people for things. And, above all, I'm a good listener."

- *You will be on constant display.* That high visibility we urged you to seek out in chapter 8 is the cross that token women bear every working day. Yes, high visibility can help you advance your career provided you know what to do with it. But chronic high visibility is something else again. With the spotlight on your every move, you can't afford to make even little mistakes. Says Warren Bennis, a U.S.C. professor of business management, commenting for the *Wall Street Journal* on Jane Cahill Pfeiffer's firing from the National Broadcasting Company chairmanship: "Being a woman at that level makes you unusual, a freak. Every error and victory is more marked, pronounced, and dramatized."

Not only are token women gossiped about constantly, but the gossip also often consists of distortions to the point of lies. For example, on a business trip to Washington, one token woman inadvertently swore in an elevator on the way to meet some business colleagues. In less than two days, word had gotten back to headquarters in Chicago that the woman was a "radical." Some token women are also used as public relations showpieces, paraded before the company's public in ways that may violate the woman's sense of personal dignity. Finally, because of the limelight conditions, tokens have less freedom of action and opinion than their male counterparts. While male managers are often quite open about their lack of corporate loyalty and dissatisfaction with their jobs, token female managers usually feel they shouldn't voice any negative feelings. They must maintain the split between their public image and private self.

- *You will have to prove yourself constantly.* This is a corollary of both the stereotyping and high-visibility problems. The male ego being what it is, a woman is automatically assumed to be less capable than a man in performing in any traditionally "male" job. Thus, you will have to prove to your male peers and superiors that you are an exception, a woman who can succeed against all obstacles—including, in their view, your sex.

  As a token, you will be on the receiving end of a hundred "tests" instigated by practically everyone—peers, superiors, subordinates, even older women subordinates who may be jealous. Furthermore, you will have to endure the speculation that you got the job only because of affirmative action, or because you threatened to sue the company, or because you're sleeping with the boss.

  But Robert Schrank, a management specialist at the Ford Foundation, thinks that the hardest tests to ignore are those that come from male contemporaries who perceive you as a triple threat to their egos and their chances for advancement. As women begin to scale the corporate pyramid—in the process squeezing out some of the competition as they approach the apex—the men around them will feel threatened because: (1) they feel they may be the next to be squeezed out; (2) the token women are their age and thus will be competitors for a long time to come; and (3) during the 1980s, there will be too few good jobs to accommodate all the well-educated baby-boom aspirants and they are desperate to end up in the winner's circle.

The token woman should be aware of one further aspect of this lack of peer acceptance. In most large organizations, peer acceptance is considered extremely important. The goodwill and

respect of your peers indicate that you possess leadership qualities. Indeed, the emphasis on peer acceptance indicates one way
that employees lower down in the managerial hierarchy retain
some control over who gets promoted, and exert pressure to
keep the system running equitably, at least equitably to their way
of thinking. One ambitious male manager summed up the view
of many supposedly liberated young businessmen today: "It's
okay for women to have these jobs—as long as they don't go
zooming by me."

On the other hand, whoever said that corporate ladder climbing was easy—whether you are a man or a woman. Just because
the going is rough, don't automatically assume it is because of
your token status. Anne Harlan maintains that too many women
are their own worst enemies in this regard. They are overly sensitive about their uniqueness in their organization and succumb to
self-pity.

"The women we interviewed frequently described themselves
as outsiders who had to struggle to be accepted," says Harlan.
"They complained about having to prove their credibility with
each new task or encounter—something the men we interviewed
never mentioned. In some cases women *were* treated as outsiders, but they were often pointing to situations that men simply
took for granted as part of the normal demands of the job. Wom-
en weren't necessarily being tested as women, but as managers."
You will have to learn to tell the difference.

## Being Forewarned Means Being Forearmed

☐   ☐   ☐   ☐   We have just enlightened you
about some of the unpleasant consequences that can result
should you forge ahead bravely in the role of pioneer, or token
woman. How you handle the uncomfortable situations that will
inevitably arise is largely a matter of personal chemistry. No two

women will handle these situations in quite the same way nor are we going to give you a set of rules to memorize that will solve all your problems. We do suggest, however, that you adhere to a few broad guidelines:

- *Don't* accept a token job that other people know full well you are not qualified for.

- *Don't* take every little slight or remark personally. After all, you are not the first woman to experience the slings and arrows of tokenism, although it may feel that way sometimes.

- *Don't* accept a token job if you are completely isolated, lacking the support of either those "significant others" in your life or a networking group of helpful women.

- Finally, once you have succeeded as a token woman, *don't* attribute it all to luck, the help of your wonderful male mentor, and the fact that you didn't act like a "typical" feminist. Says advertising ace and author Jane Trahey, "Whether or not successful, high-level women are sensitive enough to realize it (or whether they ever can admit it to themselves), they *didn't* succeed alone. It's taken twenty-five years of the female revolution—a single sex revolution at that—to have conditioned the corporate world into accepting females at the top and allowing them in more and more numbers into the middle role of management. The women's movement has been fought for at the grass-roots level by so many women who have yet to cash in on it all. It seems appalling to me that the few who have, go out of their way to knock it."

## Some Views on Tokenism

☐ ☐ ☐ ☐

"Tokens are thought of as 'other,' not quite human; you can't predict what they're going to do, since they aren't 'normal.' But as the number of tokens increases, you begin to get more of a political situation."

—Elizabeth Janeway, interview in *Working Woman*, August 1980

"Things are hardest when there is only one woman [in management], then get easier as the numbers increase—until the proportion nears the danger stage. This more difficult period, when tensions surface, probably lasts until women reach the 35 to 40 percent range. It's only a guess; there are no major corporations with that balance yet."

—Anne Harlan, Ph.D., and Carol L. Weiss, Ed.D., "What's Wrong with 'Success' Books," *Working Woman*, August 1980

"Self-repression and refraining from certain kinds of expressiveness are part of the culture in large organizations. But tokens especially are in a position where true disclosure to peers is not possible, and tokens may not even easily join peers in their characteristic modes of tension release—after-work drinks, for example."

—Rosabeth Moss Kanter, "Tokenism—Opportunity or Trap?" *MBA* magazine, January 1978

"A company may feel that it can get by with hiring 'token' women in executive jobs. You get a resounding title and you're placed near the door so that the government inspector can see you; but you don't have the responsibility given to men in equivalent positions, and you probably don't make the same money."

—Auren Uris and Jack Tarrant, *Getting to the Top Fast*

**268**

"This is the meaning of female tokenism: that power withheld from the vast majority of women is offered to a few, so that it may appear that any truly qualified woman can gain access to leadership, recognition, and reward; hence that justice based on merit actually prevails."

—Adrienne Rich, "Privilege, Power, and Tokenism," *Ms.*, September 1979

"The most painful experience was being a solo woman. It works the same if you're a token black, double if you're a black female. Men in groups tend to ignore a solo woman. You're not treated as an equal colleague."

—Elsa Porter, Assistant Secretary for Administration, U.S. Department of Commerce, *Washingtonian* magazine, December 1979

"You're different, so you get more attention paid to you. Of course, then the burden is on you to be just a little better than the average man."

—Joyce Stevens, auditor for the U.S. General Accounting Office, "On Being Black and Female and an Accountant," *MBA* magazine, February 1975

"Women executives are often hired as tokens. They come in with a big public relations blitz, and once they're in their job, they're given very little support. Women executives have to do twice as much as a man to get credit for half the work."

—Gloria Allred, President, Women's Equal Rights Legal Defense and Education Group, Los Angeles, *Wall Street Journal*, July 10, 1980

# 14

# The Road to Success: A Fable

Once upon a time, there was a woman named Persistence. Persistence wanted very much to be a Success. But she'd heard that success must be earned. This was not difficult for her, since by nature she was very hardworking. So Persistence volunteered for extra work, covered for lazy co-workers, and answered the office phone during lunch hours. Persistence accomplished a tremendous amount, but no one seemed to notice. So she worked even harder. Before long, she was doing four jobs, including two that should really have been handled by her subordinates. But still no one noticed. Desperate, Persistence decided to follow the advice in a newspaper article aimed at those women seeking career advancement.

The author of the article said that Persistence had to change her image—in order to be made a MANager, she had to look like a MANager. So Persistence wore a gray flannel suit and black pumps every day. She ate lunch at her desk with papers spread all about her; she lurked around the office after hours and she imitated her boss, carrying a bulging briefcase home over the weekend. Every day she wrote at least one memo that she circulated to the Higher-Ups. She cultivated her superiors and ate dinner only in the finest Executive Restaurants. Persistence followed strictly the Law of the Three Cs: Always be Calm, Cool, and Collected. What happened? Alas, nothing very good. Persistence spilled a soda all over the memo she had just typed, her boss thought she was making fun of him, and she was suspected of pilfering the office supplies. The Executive Dinners cleaned out her bank account, and her suppressed emotions made her a Nervous Wreck. But she got no raise, no promotion, not even a pat on the back.

Obviously, something was wrong. So Persistence tried another tack—"I'll *think* my way to a better job," she said. If she could change her mind, she could change the world! So she thought PROMOTION, she thought EXECUTIVE, she thought AMBITION. She smiled a lot, tried to be aggressive, and then tried to be less aggressive. She was going to make it to the TOP. But while Persistence was daydreaming about the future, Prudence, another woman on the staff, was doing something productive about getting ahead. Prudence was promoted over Persistence in no time at all. So Persistence resigned herself quietly to this turn of events and resolved to do her work diligently, hoping someone someday would take notice.

*Moral:* Some people are careerwise, some are otherwise; *or,* Prudence goeth before Persistence.

Persistence is the perfect example of style without substance. Her Strategies for Success were purely superficial. Persistence never stopped to determine where—if anywhere—all this extra work or maneuvering would lead her. She failed to see that while imitation may be the sincerest form of flattery, flattery would get

**271**

her nowhere, because Persistence had never really planned where she was going or how she would get there. For her, the TOP was some vague pinnacle that had to be reached. Persistence concentrated on conforming to an outward image of The Successful Woman without taking the time to recognize and develop the qualities *within herself* that would truly make her a success.

In short, single-minded persistence will not get you very far. However, make no mistake about it, persistence is a quality that can help you throughout your career. In fact, a better moral for the story might be: Prudence *and* Persistence are the better part of Success.

Not only will you have to overcome some internal obstacles on the road to success, but there will be many external ones to be dealt with as well. For one thing, it is still a man's world and you are a woman. Don't take it personally, but *do* recognize that because of your sex you will face special obstacles, from the trivial to the profound, from the sublime to the ridiculous. But while these obstacles affect you as an individual, they are really directed at an entire class of human beings: women.

Many job problems occur today because there are still relatively few women at high levels. Many problems have been alleviated and many more will disappear as more women move up through management ranks. But right now there *are* special problems, and while these result from a broad social phenomenon, you must deal with them as an individual.

Like Persistence, you may think that in order to achieve success, you will have to change lots of things about yourself. Well, you *can* change some things for the better, but it's a good bet that you really can't (and shouldn't) change all that many. You may wish that you were older (you will be eventually), or had a deeper voice, or had five years' more work experience. You may need more education, or more patience. Any change here will be gradual. The trick is to take action *now*. Work with what you have and take it from there.

If you follow the advice presented in this book, you will take the time to carefully assess both your strengths and weaknesses. If long-term changes are needed, such as an advanced degree, start planning. Research several programs, talk to people who have already completed the programs—but don't use this period of reflection and exploration as an excuse for not seizing control of your immediate situation. Right now, today, begin to use yourself and your skills to best advantage. No matter how awful or dead-end a job may seem, you can always turn it to some use in your own personal development.

Hard work is impressive *if* it is highly visible. Image is important—sometimes, anyway—and having your head in the right place helps a lot. But the real key is action. You have to do something practical—that is the one sure way to control your situation so that you can, indeed, walk down the road to success.

# Bibliography

## Continuing Education

Blaze, Wayne, and John Nero. *College Degrees for Adults.* Boston: Beacon Press, 1979.

Bricker, George W., and Samuel A. Pond. *Bricker's International Directory of University Sponsored Executive Development Programs.* Chatham, Mass.: Bricker Publications, 1980.

*Continuing Education: A Guide to Career Development Programs.* Syracuse, N.Y.: Gaylord Professional Publications, 1977.

Cross, Wilbur. *Weekend Education Source Book.* New York: Harper's Magazine Press, 1976.

Eppen, G. D., et al. *The MBA Degree.* Chicago: Chicago Review Press, 1979.

Gross, Ronald. *The Life Long Learner.* New York: Simon & Schuster, 1977.

Harrington, Fred Harvey. *The Future of Adult Education.* San Francisco: Jossey-Bass, 1977.

Hawes, Gene R. *Getting College Course Credits by Examination to Save $$$.* New York: McGraw-Hill, 1979.

Lederer, Muriel. *Guide to Career Education.* New York: Quadrangle Books, 1976.

Mendelsohn, Pamela. *Happier by Degrees: A College Reentry Guide for Women.* New York: E. P. Dutton, 1980.

Nyquist, Ewald B., Jack N. Arbolino, and Gene R. Hawes. *College Learning Anytime, Anywhere.* New York: Harcourt Brace Jovanovich, 1977.

## Financial Aid

*College Blue Book: Scholarships, Fellowships, Grants and Loans.* New York: Macmillan Information, 1977.

*Educational Financial Aid Sources for Women.* New York: Clairol, Inc., Loving Care Scholarship Program, 1978.

Feingold, S. Norman, and Marie Feingold. *Scholarships, Fellowships and Loans.* Arlington, Mass.: Bellman, 1977.

*Guide to Graduate and Professional Study, 1977–1979.* Moravia, N.Y.: Chronicle Guidance Publications, 1977.

*The Harvard Guide to Grants.* Cambridge, Mass.: Harvard University, Office of Career Services and Off-Campus Learning, 1980.

Jawin, Ann J. *A Woman's Guide to Career Preparation: Scholarships, Grants and Loans.* New York: Anchor Press/Doubleday, 1979.

Keeslar, Oreon. *Financial Aids for Higher Education: 1978–1979 Catalogue.* Dubuque, Iowa: William C. Brown, 1977.

Schlacter, Gail Ann. *The Directory of Financial Aids for Women.* Los Angeles: Reference Press Service, 1978.

## Job Discrimination and Women's Rights

Abramson, Joan. *Old Boys–New Women: The Politics of Discrimination.* New York: Praeger, 1979.

Babcok, Barbara A., et al. *Sex Discrimination and the Law: Causes and Remedies.* Boston: Little, Brown, 1975.

Blau, Francine D. *Equal Pay in the Office.* Lexington, Mass.: Lexington Books, 1977.

Eisler, Diane T. *The Equal Rights Handbook.* New York: Avon Books, 1978.

Farley, Lin. *Sexual Shakedown: The Sexual Harassment of Women on the Job.* New York: McGraw-Hill, 1978.

Lynch, Jane Shay, and Sara Lyn Smith. *The Women's Guide to Legal Rights.* Chicago: Contemporary Books, 1979.

MacKinnon, Catharine A. *Sexual Harassment of Working Women: A Case of Sex Discrimination.* New York: McGraw-Hill, 1978.

Madden, Janice F. *The Economics of Sex Discrimination.* Lexington, Mass.: Lexington Books, 1973.

Pendergrass, Virginia, ed. *Women Winning: A Handbook for Action Against Sex Discrimination.* Chicago: Nelson-Hall, 1979.

Pomroy, Martha. *What Every Woman Needs to Know About the Law.* New York: Doubleday, 1980.

*The Rights of Women: The Basic ACLU Guide to a Woman's Rights.* New York: Sunrise Books, 1973.

Shaeffer, Ruth G., and Edith F. Lynton. *Corporate Experiences in Improving Women's Job Opportunities.* Report Series #755. New York: The Conference Board, 1979.


## Luck

Carr, A. H. Z. *How to Attract Good Luck.* New York: Simon & Schuster, 1952.

Gibson, John E. "What It Takes to Be Lucky: A Self-Generated Syndrome," in *How to Size Up People.* St. Paul: Carillon Books, 1977.

Gunther, Max. *The Luck Factor.* New York: Macmillan, 1977.


## Negotiating

Chastain, Sherry. *Winning the Salary Game.* New York: John Wiley & Sons, 1980.

Coffin, Royce A. *The Negotiator: A Manual for Winners.* New York: Everyday Handbook Series, 1976.

Ilich, John, and Barbara S. Jones. *Successful Negotiating Skills for Women.* Reading, Mass.: Addison-Wesley, 1981.

Nierenberg, Gerard I. *Fundamentals of Negotiating.* New York: Hawthorn Books, 1977.

Tarrant, John J. *How to Negotiate a Raise.* New York: Van Nostrand Reinhold, 1976.

Warshaw, Tessa Albert. *Winning by Negotiation.* New York: McGraw-Hill, 1980.

Zartman, William, ed. *The Negotiation Process.* Beverly Hills, Ca.: Sage Publications, 1978.


## Networking

Kleiman, Carol. *Women's Networks: The Complete Guide to Getting a Better Job, Advancing Your Career, and Feeling Great as a Woman Through Networking.* New York: Lippincott & Crowell, 1980.

Stern, Barbara. *Is Networking for You?* Englewood Cliffs, N.J.: Prentice-Hall, 1980.

Welch, Mary Scott. *Networking: The Great New Way for Women to Get Ahead.* New York: Harcourt Brace Jovanovich, 1980.


## Personal Publicity

Doyle, Thomas F., Jr. *How to Write a Book About Your Specialty.*

Hunter, J. B. *Your Personal Column Will Help You Win Recognition, Enhance Your Status and Influence in the Community and Your Profession.*

Marshall, Sol H. *Establish Yourself as an Authority.*

(All three available for $3.45 each from Creative Book Co., Box 21–4998, Sacramento, Ca. 95821.)

Appelbaum, Judith, and Nancy Evans. *How to Get Happily Published: A Complete and Candid Guide.* New York: Harper & Row, 1978.

Berman, Steve. *How to Create Your Own Publicity for Names, Products or Services and Get It for Free!* New York: Frederick Fell, 1977.

Harris, Morgan, and Patti Karp. *How to Make News and Influence People.* Blue Ridge Summit, Pa.: Tab Books, 1976.

Lewis, H. Gordon. *How to Handle Your Own Public Relations.* Chicago: Nelson-Hall, 1976.

O'Brien, Richard. *Publicity: How to Get It.* New York: Harper & Row, 1977.

Sackheim, Maxwell. *How to Advertise Yourself.* New York: Macmillan, 1978.


## Political Acumen

Archer, Dane, Ph.D. *How to Expand Your S.I.Q. (Social Intelligence Quotient).* New York: M. Evans, 1980.

Bird, Caroline. *Everything a Woman Needs to Know to Get Paid What She's Worth.* New York: David McKay, 1973.

Brothers, Dr. Joyce. *How to Get Everything You Want Out of Life.* New York: Simon & Schuster, 1978.

Catalyst. *Making the Most of Your First Job.* New York: G. P. Putnam's Sons, 1981.

————. *Marketing Yourself: The Catalyst Women's Guide to Successful Resumes and Interviews.* New York: G. P. Putnam's Sons, 1980.

————. *What to Do with the Rest of Your Life.* New York: Simon & Schuster, 1980.

————. *When Can You Start? The Complete Job Search Guide for Women.* New York: Macmillan, 1982.

Djeddah, Eli. *Moving Up.* Berkeley, Ca.: Ten Speed Press, 1978.

Drucker, Peter. *Management: Tasks, Responsibilities, Practices.* New York: Harper & Row, 1974.

Elphick, Art. *Winning: How to Make Yourself More Likeable.* St. Paul: Carillon Books, 1978.

Foxworth, Jo. *Boss Lady: An Executive Woman Talks About Making It.* New York: T. Y. Crowell, 1978.

————. *Wising Up: The Mistakes Women Make in Business and How to Avoid Them.* New York: Delacorte, 1980.

Haldane, Bernard. *Career Satisfaction and Success.* New York: AMACOM, 1974.

Harragan, Betty Lehan. *Games Mother Never Taught You: Corporate Gamesmanship for Women.* New York: Rawson, Wade, 1977.

Hart, Lois Borland. *Moving Up!* New York: AMACOM, 1980.

Hennig, Dr. Margaret, and Dr. Anne Jardim. *The Managerial Woman.* New York: Anchor Press/Doubleday, 1977.

Janeway, Elizabeth. *Powers of the Weak.* New York: Knopf, 1980.

Josefowitz, Natasha. *Paths to Power: A Woman's Guide from First Job to Top Executive.* Reading, Mass.: Addison-Wesley, 1980.

Kanter, Rosabeth Moss. *Men and Women of the Corporation.* New York: Basic Books, 1979.

Kennedy, Marilyn Moats. *Office Politics: Seizing Power, Wielding Clout.* Chicago: Follett, 1980.

Korda, Michael. *Power: How to Get It, How to Use It.* New York: Random House, 1975.

———. *Success! How Every Man and Woman Can Achieve It.* New York: Random House, 1977.

Lathrop, Richard. *Who's Hiring Who.* Berkeley, Ca.: Ten Speed Press, 1977.

Maccoby, Michael. *The Gamesman.* New York: Simon & Schuster, 1977.

Moore, Charles G. *The Career Game: A Step-by-Step Guide Up the Ladder of Success.* New York: Ballantine, 1976.

Pogrebin, Letty C. *Getting Yours: How to Make the System Work for the Working Woman.* New York: David McKay, 1975.

Redford, S. R. *Jobmanship: How to Get Ahead by "Psyching Out" Your Boss and Co-Workers.* New York: Macmillan, 1978.

Steele, Addison. *Upward Nobility: How to Win the Rat Race Without Becoming a Rat.* New York: Times Books, 1978.

Stewart, Nathaniel. *The Effective Woman Manager.* New York: John Wiley & Sons, 1978.

Trahey, Jane. *Jane Trahey on Women and Power: Who's Got It, How to Get It.* New York: Rawson, Wade, 1977.

Uris, Auren and Jack Tarrant. *Getting to the Top Fast.* Chicago: Henry Regnery Company, 1976.

Westin, Alan. *Whistle Blowing! Loyalty and Dissent in the Corporation.* New York: McGraw-Hill, 1980.

Winter, David G. *The Power Motive.* New York: The Free Press, 1973.

Whyte, William H., Jr. *The Organization Man.* New York: Simon & Schuster, 1972.


## Skills Development

Flesch, Rudolph. *Rudolph Flesch on Business Communication: How to Say What You Mean in Plain English.* New York: Barnes & Noble, 1972.

Goldfein, Donna. *Everywoman's Guide to Time Management.* Millbrae, Ca.: Les Femmes, 1977.

LeBoeuf, Michael. *Working Smart: How to Accomplish More in Half the Time.* New York: Warner Books, 1980.

Linver, Sandy. *Speakeasy.* New York: Summit Books, 1978.

Morris, James A., Jr. *The Art of Conversation: Magic Key to Personal and Social Popularity.* West Nyack, N.Y.: Parker, 1976.

Mullins, Carolyn J. *The Complete Writing Guide to Preparing Reports, Memos, Etc.* Englewood Cliffs, N.J.: Prentice-Hall, 1980.

Rudin, Marvin. *Practical Time Management.* Mountain View, Ca.: Autel Corporation, n.d.

Stone, Janet, and Jane Bachner. *Speaking Up.* New York: McGraw-Hill, 1977.

Walters, Barbara. *How to Talk with Practically Anybody About Practically Anything.* New York: Dell, 1971.

Wassmer, Arthur C. *Making Contact: A Guide to Overcoming Shyness, Making New Relationships and Keeping Those You Already Have.* New York: Dial Press, 1978.

Zimbardo, Philip G., and Shirley Radl. *The Shyness Workbook.* New York: A & W, 1979.

# Index

*Self-Directed Search Program, The* (Holland), 82
Self-discovery exercise, 216
Self-esteem, 14, 61, 80, 244
Self-evaluation of likes and dislikes, 2–9
Self-fulfillment, xv
*Self* magazine, xxviii
Seliger, Susan, 262
Seminars, 168–71
Service industries, 39, 67
Service jobs, 95
Sexual discrimination, xxvi, 75
  dealing with, xxv–xxvi, 132
  dirty tricks, 73–74
  forms of, defined by law, 94–95, 96
  information sources on, 102–104
  legal action against, xxvi, 71, 74, 93–101
  class actions, 93, 94, 97, 100–101
  effects on your career, 99–101
  legal fees, 94
  steps to take before bringing, 96–98
Sexual harassment, 74, 94–95
Shainess, Dr. Natalie, 217
Short-term planning, 112
  *see also* Career planning
"Significant others" in your life, 29–35, 267
  career planning and, 112
  quiz, 30–33
  tips for dealing with subverters, 33–35
"$64,000 Question, The," 159
Size, 39, 40, 41, 231
Skalka, Dena, 238
Skeptics, 219
Skills, 69, 113–45, 223, 232
  business etiquette, 133–38
  checklist to evaluate, 147–55
  communication, 122–26, 128, 129, 134–35, 151–52
    *see also* Speech; Written communication
  decision-making, 116, 148–49
  do-it-yourself plan for attaining, 156–62
  formal training for attaining, 163–80
  job suitability and, xxii
  management, 127–32, 152–55, 168

planning and organizing, 117–20, 128, 149–50, 168
problem-solving, 113–16, 147–48
salary negotiation, 138–45
time-management, 80, 120–21, 150–51, 168
Small talk, 136–37
Smoking, 135–36
Snyder, Elayne, 125
Social clubs, 74, 100, 203
Socializing outside the office, 48–49
Social occasions, etiquette for, 136–38
Societal attitudes, xxiii, 230
Solar-energy-equipment manufacturing, 39
Solar energy technician, 70
Speech, 75, 105, 107, 108, 123, 185, 215, 247
  speech-making, 125–26, 190–91
Staff positions, 67, 80
  vs. line positions, 91–93, 174, 259
Stanford University business school, 40
State governments, working for, 86n, 88
State laws, 73
Stationery, 134, 138
Status, 85–86, 234–42
Steel industry, 39
Stereotyping, 263–64
Stewart, Nathaniel, 127–28
Stiehm, Dr. Judith, 203–204
Stock options, 89, 90
Stokes, Geoffrey, 100
Stress, 79, 80, 85, 90
Subverters, 33–35
Success, xxii–xxiii, 85
Sullivan, Barbara Boyle, xxi–xxii, 110, 257
Support, xxii, 29–35
Supreme Court, xvi

Tarrant, Jack, 260–61
Task-orientation, 109
Teachers, 86, 258
Teamwork, 36, 39, 246
Technology, 39, 65, 71–72
Telephone etiquette, 134–35
Temperament, job suitability and, xxii
Terzian, Carl, 190
Thank you notes, 137–38